Skilled Dialogue

Skilled Dialogue

Strategies for Responding to Cultural Diversity in Early Childhood

by

Isaura Barrera, Ph.D.
University of New Mexico, Albuquerque

and

Robert M. Corso, Ph.D.
University of Illinois at Urbana-Champaign

with **Dianne Macpherson, M.S.W., C.I.S.W., C.A.S.**

·P A U L·H·
BROOKES
PUBLISHING Cᵒ®

Baltimore • London • Sydney

Paul H. Brookes Publishing Co.
Post Office Box 10624
Baltimore, Maryland 21285-0624

www.brookespublishing.com

Typeset by Barton Matheson Willse & Worthington, Baltimore, Maryland.
Manufactured in the United States of America by
Versa Press, Inc., East Peoria, Illinois.

Permission to reprint the following is gratefully acknowledged:

Excerpts from MY GRANDFATHER'S BLESSINGS by Rachel Naomi Remen, M.D.,
copyright © 2000 by Rachel Naomi Remen, M.D. Used by permission of Riverhead
Books, an imprint of Penguin Putnam Inc.

Poem "Warrior Child" (appearing on pages 207–209 of Appendix A)
by Nanci Presley-Holley from *Children of Trauma* by Jane Middleton-Moz,
copyright © 1989. Published by arrangement with Health Communications Inc.

Unless otherwise specified, the stories in this book are based on the authors'
experiences. In some cases, permission has been granted to use actual names and
details. In other cases, individuals' names and identifying details have been changed
to protect their identities. Still other vignettes are composite accounts that do not
represent the lives or experiences of specific individuals, and no implications should
be inferred.

Library of Congress Cataloging-in-Publication Data

Barrera, Isaura.
   Skilled dialogue : strategies for responding to cultural diversity in early childhood /
by Isaura Barrera and Robert M. Corso with Dianne Macpherson.
       p. cm.
   Includes bibliographical references and index.
   ISBN 1-55766-637-7
   1. Multicultural education.   2. Early childhood education   I. Corso, Robert M.
II. Macpherson, Dianne.   III. Title.

LC1099 .B39 2003
372.12—dc21

                                                          2002038264

British Library Cataloguing in Publication data are available from the British Library.

Contents

About the Authors vii
Foreword   *Susan A. Fowler* ix
Preface xiii
Acknowledgments. xvii
Introduction xix

**Section I   The Challenge of Dialogues Across
              Differences**

Chapter 1   Cultural Diversity: The Challenge   3

Chapter 2   Culture: The Underlying Reality   23

Chapter 3   Cultural Competency: The Response   33

**Section II   From Difficult Dialogues to Skilled
              Dialogues**

Chapter 4   Skilled Dialogue: Foundational Concepts   41

Chapter 5   Anchored Understanding of Diversity:
             The First Skill.   53

Chapter 6   3rd Space: The Second Skill   75

**Section III The Practice of Skilled Dialogue in
              Early Childhood Environments**

Chapter 7   Crafting Specific Responses to Concrete
             Situations.   91

Chapter 8   Respectful, Reciprocal, and Responsive
             Assessment.   121

Chapter 9   Respectful, Reciprocal, and Responsive
             Intervention and Instruction.   153

Afterword   *Isaura Barrera*.   187

References.   191

Appendix A   Trauma from a Cultural Perspective
             Dianne Macpherson 199

Appendix B   Looking Closer 221

Appendix C   Photocopiable Materials. 223

Appendix D   Guidelines for Using an Interpreter/Translator
             During Test Administration 245

Index 249

About the Authors

Isaura Barrera, Ph.D., Associate Professor, Special Education Department, College of Education, University of New Mexico, Lomas Boulevard, Hokona Hall 290/Special Education, Albuquerque, New Mexico 87131. Dr. Barrera is a native of South Texas whose interest in cultural diversity was stimulated at an early age, as she realized that the colorful autumn leaves that she cut out in first grade had no correspondence to any leaves she had actually seen. She has worked for more than 25 years in early childhood special education programs in San Antonio, Texas, and western New York State, as well as in New Mexico. Dr. Barrera holds a bachelor's degree in major communication sciences and a master's degree in speech pathology from Our Lady of the Lake University in San Antonio, Texas. She holds a doctoral degree in education research and evaluation, with concentrations in early childhood and bilingual special education, from the State University of New York at Buffalo. As an associate professor in the Special Education Department at the University of New Mexico in Albuquerque, Dr. Barrera coordinates the Early Childhood Special Education concentration within the graduate special education program. She continues to work nationally as a consultant. Her research focus is the Skilled Dialogue approach and its related materials, including a preschool language screening protocol for linguistically diverse preschoolers.

Robert M. Corso, Ph.D., Evaluation Coordinator, Early Childhood Research Institute, University of Illinois at Urbana-Champaign, 61 Children's Resource Center, MC-672, 51 Gerty Drive #105, Champaign, Illinois 61820. Dr. Corso received his doctoral degree in early childhood special education from the University of Illinois at Urbana-Champaign (UIUC). He is a visiting assistant professor in the Department of Special Education at UIUC, where he coordinates several large-scale training and technical assistance projects. Each program shares a common goal and belief that all children and families—regardless of their cultural or linguistic background or their ability level—should experience an inclusive and welcoming community. He has published several works on supporting practitioners in delivering culturally and linguistically appropriate early childhood/early intervention services.

Dianne Macpherson, M.S.W., C.I.S.W., C.A.S., is a clinical social worker in private practice in Arizona. She has 25 years of clinical experience in school, mental health, chemical dependency, and clinical practice settings. Her positions have included working as a bilingual education elementary school teacher and acting as a guest lecturer/consultant, teaching undergraduate and graduate special education students to identify and intervene for mental health issues in the classroom. Ms. Macpherson has clinical practice experience in agency settings for forensic mental health, hospital-based chemical dependency programs, and managed behavioral health care. Her private practice work has focused on the psychiatric evaluation and treatment of children, adolescents, and adults with a wide range of mental health and addiction disorders—primarily those individuals with impaired functioning as a result of trauma, abuse, and extreme stress. Ms. Macpherson also has served as a professional trainer/workshop facilitator at local, state, and national conferences related to the sequelae of trauma and abuse. Ms. Macpherson's web site (http://www.specialkidsconsulting.com) provides information to families as well as to school and mental health professionals on topics related to addressing difficult and complex learning and behavior problems in children and adolescents. The site also provides access to expert consultants in related fields.

Foreword

Skilled Dialogue: Strategies for Responding to Cultural Diversity in Early Childhood is a perceptive book that is essential reading for all who wish to understand issues of cultural diversity and the role of culture within an early intervention framework. Through the introduction of two critical concepts, Anchored Understanding of Diversity and 3rd Space, the authors establish a new framework for fostering cross-cultural interactions. The authors foreshadow this framework by establishing in Chapter 1 the fundamental issue that "diversity is both relative and inclusive"—it requires comparison. "Diversity is a dynamic and relational quality, sometimes present and sometimes not, depending on context" (p. 6). They astutely present the issue that those who name a child or family as culturally diverse automatically name themselves as diverse as well. If the namers fail to perceive their own diversity, then they set only one context as normative against which all others are compared. Whoever names what is normative also establishes a hierarchy of power. The imbalance that results can undermine future efforts between interventionists and families in communicating in a respectful, nonjudgmental way; in fact, it can prevent any future relationship.

In Chapter 1, the authors continue to make the very salient point that identity and diversity are related but not equivalent. That is, although one's identity may be static, the degree to which that identity differs from others is dynamic. Again, the emphasis is on the relational nature of interactions. The authors state, "Cultural diversity must be recognized as a characteristic that resides in interactions and comparisons *between* persons rather than as a characteristic possessed by individual persons themselves" (p. 8). Having established the relational nature of diversity, the authors present compelling examples of culture bumps that can challenge the development of mutually respectful and constructive relationships.

In Chapter 2, the authors provide one of the clearest discussions of culture that I have encountered in the early childhood literature. They contrast surface culture (observable manifestations of customs, traditions, and beliefs) with a "deeper, less visible reality" that contains a community's unique worldviews born of shared experiences and extending across generations (p. 25). This deeply nuanced and layered view of culture takes the reader beyond a simple "you are not like me" view. The authors lead the reader to look at the function of behaviors viewed as different or diverse in order to recognize and honor that behavior and underlying system of beliefs as a coherent strategy that functions well within the community of origin. They provide the example of using direct questions in conversation, an effective form of information seeking in EuroAmerican Normative Culture (ENC) but a sign of disrespect in other cultures. Failure to recognize different patterns of conversation (in this case, forms of information seeking) creates a culture bump that may prevent efforts to engage in a respectful and fruitful discussion among individuals who share a common concern for the welfare of a child with disabilities.

The concepts of cultural competency and Skilled Dialogue are introduced in Chapter 3. The critical concepts of respect, reciprocity, and responsiveness are discussed as the very foundation of Skilled Dialogue and prerequisites for Anchored Understanding of Diversity and development of 3rd Space—skills that can contribute to cultural competency. As stated by other contemporary researchers and writers, this book's authors stress that cultural competency is an ongoing process and not an accumulation of knowledge. Although the authors acknowledge that objective knowledge about cultural groups is useful, they caution readers against clustering characteristics about groups into either-or choices that oversimplify and limit the rich complexity of human behavior.

Section II introduces the framework for developing Skilled Dialogue, a tool to navigate cultural differences and misinterpretations. This section of the book creates a new paradigm for conceptualizing the role of an interventionist. It clearly moves the perspective of the reader from "expert" or even "partner" to "explorer" and "learner" in navigating within a cultural context that is divergent from one's own. The authors do this first in Chapter 4 by defining three qualities of Skilled Dialogue: respect, reciprocity, and responsivity. These are essential human values that enable the exchange of perspectives and experiences on an equal footing. Respect acknowledges and accepts boundaries that exist between persons and suspends the need to make differing boundaries or perceptions match. Reciprocity recognizes that each person in an interaction "has experience and perceptions of equal value" and that one point of view should not dominate or restrict interactions (p. 45). The concept of mystery is introduced to responsiveness, which the authors define as "being willing to give up certainty, to not know exactly what to do or what to say" (p. 47). As they clearly point out, responsiveness is not responding; rather, it is allowing space for the unexpected and new.

Having defined the essence of Skilled Dialogue, the authors then introduce the two key concepts that comprise Skilled Dialogue—Anchored Understanding of Diversity and 3rd Space. These complex skills are the focus of Chapters 5 and 6. Simply stated, Anchored Understanding of Diversity combines one's general knowledge of culture with a compassionate and concrete context that can come only through personal interactions and the capacity to recognize the uniqueness of individuals within their community and culture. Essential to this skill is the notion of openness plus curiosity about the other's point of view and a belief that the other's behavior makes sense within his or her cultural or personal perspective. The authors provide tools to assist interventionists in moving beyond simple questions to a deeper understanding, for instance, of a child and family's home language usage.

The concept of 3rd Space may require a significant cognitive shift for many readers. The authors define it as "creatively reframing contradictions into paradoxes" and describe it as a mindset as well as a skill (p. 75). Readers are urged to develop a new mindset—one that does not require a forced choice between, for example, parent involvement and noninvolvement. Rather, readers are encouraged to live with the apparent tension between choices and generate third, fourth, or fifth choices that take into account diverse perspectives. The concept of 3rd Space is to create, in effect, a new common space, one in which decisions are not made nor problems solved. Instead, the 3rd Space focuses on creation of respectful, reciprocal, and responsive interactions, which in turn increases the probability that all participants will identify an optimal response. This may include the identification of differences and contradictions and acknowledging respect for such differences, as well as exploring how differences or contradictions can be complementary. The authors do not present these approaches as easy or quickly acquired but liken them to seeing pictures hidden in 3-D pictures that require "breakthrough thinking." This is a complex chapter that deserves multiple readings.

At the start of Section III, Chapter 7 introduces a number of process tools that the reader can use in determining diversity of culture and in setting the stage for Anchored Understanding of Diversity. I found the examples of the Cultural Consonance Profile (Figure 19) and the Critical Incident Analysis Sheet (Figure 21) to be particularly thought provoking, enabling the reader to reframe differences in approaches taken by families and interventionists. To assist the reader in practicing the two process skills of Anchored Understanding of Diversity and 3rd Space, the authors provide an extended vignette in Chapter 7 and four vignettes that recur in the different contexts of assessment and intervention in Chapters 8 and 9. These chapters are rich with information and recommendations for assessing and intervening within a shared cultural perspective.

In summary, *Skilled Dialogue* is remarkable in its ability to convey the real difficulties and challenges in crossing from one culture to another. The rewards provided are well worth the effort and study. In essence, this book is centered on improving and enhancing human relations so that all parties concerned with a child's development form a coherent team to support the child's growth within a cultural context that makes sense to the child and his or her family. Only such interventions are sustainable over time.

The authors bring their experiences and understanding of crossing cultures to bear in *Skilled Dialogue*. In the Afterword, Isaura Barrera shares her own journey and motivation in forming the team to write this book. It is a must read for all who work with children and families.

Susan A. Fowler, Ph.D.
Dean, College of Education
Professor, Special Education
University of Illinois at Urbana-Champaign

Preface

Creating a world without walls for respectful communication and collaboration is critical in both the world at large and in the field of early childhood special education. There is a growing need in both worlds for bringing compassionate creativity to interactions among people. These two elements—compassion and creativity—are essential if we are to be truly competent in the face of the complex challenges posed by cultural diversity and eliminate the walls that separate and divide communities and persons.

Although this book addresses early childhood special education practice, it cannot do so without reference to the broader contexts that this practice reflects. Educational responses to cultural diversity are embedded in moral and political contexts as well as educational ones. The following *Hymn of Peace* conveys the larger vision that underlies the authors' approach to the challenges of cultural and linguistic diversity in early childhood special education environments:

> *When our creeds lead us to judgment and our beliefs have veiled your truth,*
> *be the vision that will help us see your gifts in those we judge.*
> *Then we shall break the bread of understanding,*
> *Open wide our hearts with love*
> *As your unending gifts renew us,*
> *Our uplifted arms send forth the dove.*
>
> *When our fears close in around us and build walls that lead to war,*
> *be compassion that will rule us and heal our wounded world of fear.*
> *Then we shall break the bread of understanding,*
> *Open wide our hearts with love*
> *As your unending gifts renew us,*
> *Our uplifted arms send forth the dove.*
>
> *When we raise accusing fingers, let your truth deflect their course.*
> *As your silence dawns within us, break us open to your light.*
> *(Schoepko & Wham, 1995)*

It is important to attend to the moral, political, and educational dimensions of cultural diversity for the sake of all children, both those judged as being "diverse" and those not so judged, and of the world within which they are raised. Skilled Dialogue is an approach to cultural competency developed by the first author in response to this need. The approach has been piloted and field-tested since the mid-1990s in a variety of environments. Its primary purpose is to facilitate respectful, reciprocal, and responsive interactions across diverse cultural parameters. Given this purpose, Skilled Dialogue shifts the fulcrum of discussions about cultural diversity from knowledge to relationship. Yankelovich made a strong case for the "magic of dialogue": "The methods of science and professional expertise are excellent for generating factually based knowledge; the methods of dialogue are excellent for dealing with this knowledge wisely" (1999, p. 191). For the sake of the children and the practitioners, it is important to learn to interact with each other not only wisely but also compassionately.

CONTRIBUTING DATA SOURCES

Three data sources contributed unique perspectives to the authors' understanding of culture and diversity, as well as to the development of the Skilled Dialogue process. Literature from a variety of disciplines was a primary source of information.

The theoretical underpinnings of Skilled Dialogue draw on ideas and concepts from literature both within and outside the early childhood special education discipline. Researchers in cross-cultural anthropology, for example, were among the first to address culture and cultural diversity in relation to development and learning (e.g., Price-Williams & Gallimore, 1980; Super & Harkness, 1981). Scholars in bilingual education (e.g., Baca & Cervantes, 1984) and multicultural education (e.g., Banks, 1988; Banks & Banks, 1993) have addressed these topics for several decades. The interface between bilingual/multicultural education and special education came to the fore in the early 1980s as Baca and Cervantes (1984) and Cummins (1984, 1989) published their works. This book's discussion of culture and cultural diversity builds on perspectives from all these sources as well as from more recent sources within the early childhood special education discipline (e.g., Lynch & Hanson, 1998). Finally, sources outside of education (e.g., Childs, 1998; Fletcher & Olwyer, 1997; Wheatley, 1992) contributed to the concept of cultural differences as both paradoxical and complementary, a central idea of the Skilled Dialogue approach.

In addition to these published sources, the development of Skilled Dialogue was significantly informed by unpublished pilot research on intercultural communication as it is understood and addressed by respected practitioners in the field. The authors wish to acknowledge Colleen Alivado and Elaine Costello for their contributions to this study. The work of these two highly competent practitioners was detailed by Kramer (1997), an early collaborator in the development of Skilled Dialogue professional development materials.

Finally, the authors' own professional and personal experiences across a variety of cultures have provided a rich source of information. All three authors have lived and studied issues of cultural diversity and cultural competency from unique perspectives. Isaura Barrera grew up in Texas just a few blocks from the Texas–Mexico border. She spoke only Spanish until the age of 5, when she started school. She was one of only two English-fluent students entering first grade. Similarities and differences in language and culture were frequently discussed with family at home and with relatives from both sides of the border. Professionally, Dr. Barrera has lived, worked, and studied in both the Southwest and the Northeast regions of the United States.

Robert M. Corso grew up outside of the Chicago area as part of an Irish Italian family. He vividly remembers witnessing, as a 9-year-old going from door to door collecting newspaper money, a neighbor's scathing comments about an African American family who had just moved to the neighborhood. That was his first encounter with cultural intolerance. As an adult with a degree in early childhood education, he worked with families from diverse cultural backgrounds in the Midwest. Several years later, he moved to New Mexico, where he administered a variety of nonprofit health and human service programs that primarily served Navajo families. He currently lives in Illinois and works as part of a research institute examining culturally and linguistically appropriate early childhood practices.

Dianne Macpherson is, as she frequently states, a "resident alien." Born and raised in Canada, she moved to the United States as an adult after spending time teaching bilingual children. This background gives her a unique international perspective on how U.S. culture contrasts with British-Canadian culture. She lives in Phoenix, where she works as a clinical social worker with children and families from a variety of cultures. It was conversations between Dr. Barrera and Ms. Macpherson that first sparked the idea of Skilled Dialogue as a process to bridge diverse cultures and mindsets, particularly their own!

Acknowledgments

This book is dedicated to J., E., and S., whose sustained willingness to engage with me respectfully, reciprocally, and responsively enriches me beyond measure. I also gratefully acknowledge all of the graduate students and other practitioners who shared their insights and their stories with me. I especially acknowledge Lucinda Kramer, who worked with me during the early development of this material.—IB

In writing this book, it has been my hope that I can play a role in parting the invisible curtains and shadows that exist between people, which act as veils of indifference to each other's wonder. I thank my wife, Laurie Beth, for supporting me in this life endeavor and dedicate this work to my children, Indigo and Angelo, and to all of my relations in hope that we may all experience a world with fewer curtains, shadows, and walls.—RMC

Introduction

The challenges of conducting skillful dialogue across differences become especially compelling for early childhood special education practitioners as they meet and interact with children and families from diverse cultural backgrounds. In addition to the evident challenge of language differences, differences in values, beliefs, and practices also pose significant challenges for communication and collaboration. Questions such as the following reflect these challenges:

- How can I communicate with Sally's family and ensure that they understand what I am saying?

- How can I respect Mr. and Mrs. Quentin's cultural beliefs and practices about carrying Alred when I feel that these beliefs and practices are not in the best interests of Alred's learning to walk?

- This family doesn't seem to understand the importance of working with me when I am in their home. How can I increase their engagement during my sessions with their child?

- This is my third appointment with Mrs. Brown. We've already had to reschedule twice. The first time she said she forgot. The second time she had to go to her sister's to help her with something and didn't call me to let me know she'd be gone. How can I communicate the importance of keeping appointments?

- Ahmed apparently does not want to work independently. He constantly requests my presence and won't start his activities until I approach him. How can I teach him to be more independent?

Equally challenging questions emerge from families themselves as they meet diversity in early childhood environments. Examples of these questions include

- How can we communicate with the people who come into our home to help us and ensure that they understand us?

- When we disagree with what practitioners tell us is in the best interests of our child, how can we respect them yet also stay true to our beliefs?

- The therapists who work with our child don't seem to understand the importance of teaching our child to respect her elders in ways that we value. How can we get them to support this need for our child?

- We have had several appointments with our child's teacher. Each time, a family issue has prevented us from getting there in time. We know that the teacher doesn't like this, but how can we tell him that we cannot simply interrupt our family members and tell them we have to leave?

- Our child is caring and likes to be with us. We like to do things for him. How can we communicate that the autonomy that practitioners value so much is not so important to us? We believe that persons should do for each other and be close to each other.

Giving equal value and voice to both sets of questions can be complex, especially when the questions seem contradictory. Skilled Dialogue provides one approach to identifying and responding to such questions respectfully, reciprocally, and responsively.

KEY TERMS

Cultural competence in relation to young children with special needs is a comparatively new area of interest and research in early childhood special education. As a result, associated definitions and content have yet to achieve the same level of consistency as other more established areas of early childhood special education interest and research. In many ways, this lack of consistency is a strength, leaving the door open for new and multiple ways of addressing the topic. In other ways, however, such instability is a limitation. Common understanding of terms and concepts cannot be assumed to the degree that it can be in other areas of the early childhood and early childhood special education fields. Therefore, key terms are briefly defined here and are discussed in detail as they are addressed in subsequent chapters.

- *Cultural competence:* The ability to skillfully address communication and learning across diverse cultural parameters. It is more specifically defined by the authors as the ability to craft respectful, reciprocal, and responsive interactions across diverse cultural and linguistic parameters.

- *Cultural diversity/cultural linguistic diversity:* Behavioral, value, linguistic, and other differences ascribed to people's cultural backgrounds. Note: Cultural diversity almost invariably includes some level of diversity in how language is understood and used. The authors use *cultural diversity* and *cultural linguistic diversity* synonymously.

- *Culture:* "The abstract values, beliefs, and perceptions of the world that lie behind people's behavior, and which are reflected in their behavior" (Haviland, 1993, p. 29).

- *Culture bumps:* The dissonance experienced when differing values, beliefs, perceptions, or behaviors come into contact (Archer, 1986; Barrera & Kramer, 1997). This dissonance can occur when one person behaves in a way that is unanticipated or judged as inappropriate by another (e.g., does not arrive at a scheduled appointment on time, does not ask direct questions).

- *Early intervention/early childhood special education:* Programs and services provided to children with disabilities from birth to age 8 years.

- *Enculturation:* The process of learning the behaviors, language(s), beliefs, and roles common to one's first or home culture(s).

- *EuroAmerican (EA):* Used by the authors in place of terms such as *White* to refer to native speakers of English with Northern European heritage who identify EuroAmerican Normative Culture (ENC) as their primary cultural framework. Although *EA* tends to include persons with English, Scandinavian, and other such backgrounds, it can include persons from, for example, French or Scottish backgrounds to the degree they would identify ENC as their primary cultural framework. An additional reason for using this term in place of *White* is that the latter is not culture-specific and can refer to various groups of people, regardless of their cultural backgrounds (e.g., American Indians refer to all non-Indians as "White").

- *EuroAmerican Normative Culture (ENC):* The institutionalized cultural norms against which cultural linguistic diversity is defined. This term has been chosen by the authors instead of more common terms, such as *White* or *European,* to highlight its reference to institutionalized cultural norms rather than to the personalized cultural frameworks of particular individuals.

- *Guiding beliefs:* Statements of beliefs that underlie and guide the Skilled Dialogue process.

- *Minority:* Persons and/or communities that are accorded less social and political power by the groups considered to be the majority or normative group within a particular country. Loosely related to actual demographic numbers.

- *Privilege:* When used as a verb, refers to the act of attributing more power or higher status to a behavior, value, or attribute than to another, as in "to privilege verbal skills over nonverbal skills."

- *Skilled Dialogue:* The process described in this book for communicating and interacting across diverse cultures or mindsets.

ORGANIZATION OF THIS BOOK'S CONTENT

Figure 1 illustrates the organization of this book's sections and chapters. This organization reflects the primary author's ways of thinking, which are rooted in a culture other than the EuroAmerican Normative Culture (ENC) that is common to academic and special education disciplines (cf. Kalyanpur & Harry, 1999). Professional writing in these disciplines mirrors ENC's preference for linear and deductive organization (Hall, 1977; Stewart & Bennett, 1991). Written material from these disciplines is typically presented sequentially, one step at a time, with initial parts acting as building blocks for subsequent parts. This book, however, is organized in a somewhat less linear and more reiterative fashion, reflecting the influence of other cultures. Several concepts are discussed more than once. Ideas in one chapter are often revisited in subsequent chapters; the whole substance of some ideas may not be clear until all of the material is read. To facilitate links between ideas, material in each chapter is cross-referenced to material in other chapters. Another aspect of the book's organization that reflects the primary author's culturally diverse ways of thinking is the extensive use of direct quotes, both within chapters and, in Sections II and III, as initial thought-provoking introductory notes. Using quotes in this way reflects the cultural value of "distributed knowledge"—the belief that knowledge is embodied rather than abstract and that each person holds only one piece of a multifaceted truth. (See further discussion of distributed knowledge in Chapter 4.) Although some readers may be unfamiliar with this type of organization, its consonance with the Skilled Dialogue model becomes clear as the text progresses. Graphic content maps aid in following this organization.

Three beliefs underlie and guide the Skilled Dialogue approach. These are critical for responding to challenges such as those reflected in the sample questions that appeared at the beginning of the Introduction:

1. Culture must be understood before cultural diversity can be competently addressed.

2. Diversity is a dynamic and relational reality.

3. *Cultural competence* can be best described as the ability to craft respectful, reciprocal, and responsive interactions across diverse cultural and linguistic parameters.

Section I summarizes key information relevant to understanding these ideas. Chapter 1 focuses on culture. Chapter 2 discusses cultural diversity and its nature as a relational reality. Chapter 3 offers a brief overview of cultural competency and introduces Skilled Dialogue.

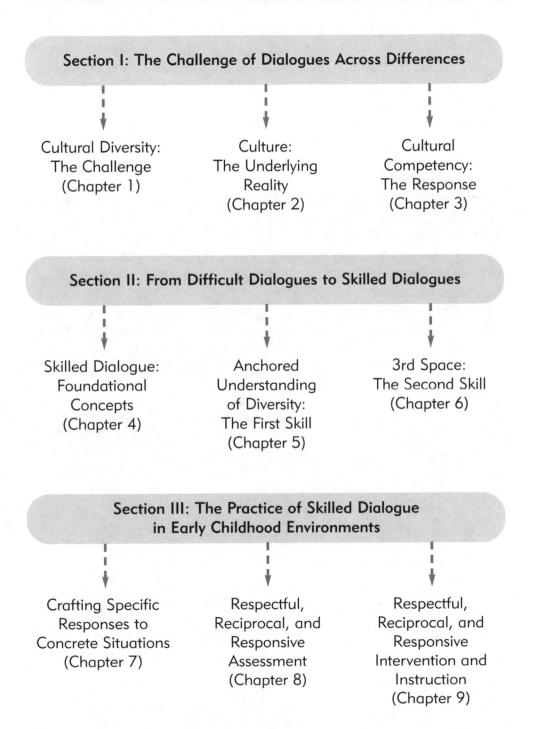

Figure 1

Skilled Dialogue:
Strategies for Responding to Cultural Competency in Early Childhood

Section I: The Challenge of Dialogues Across Differences

Cultural Diversity:
The Challenge
(Chapter 1)

Culture:
The Underlying
Reality
(Chapter 2)

Cultural
Competency:
The Response
(Chapter 3)

Section II: From Difficult Dialogues to Skilled Dialogues

Skilled Dialogue:
Foundational
Concepts
(Chapter 4)

Anchored
Understanding
of Diversity:
The First Skill
(Chapter 5)

3rd Space:
The Second Skill
(Chapter 6)

**Section III: The Practice of Skilled Dialogue
in Early Childhood Environments**

Crafting Specific
Responses to
Concrete Situations
(Chapter 7)

Respectful,
Reciprocal, and
Responsive
Assessment
(Chapter 8)

Respectful,
Reciprocal, and
Responsive
Intervention and
Instruction
(Chapter 9)

Section II describes Skilled Dialogue as a process for developing respectful, reciprocal, and responsive interactions across diverse cultural perspectives. Chapter 4 introduces general concepts and characteristics associated with Skilled Dialogue. Chapters 5 and 6 discuss its two key skills: Anchored Understanding of Diversity and 3rd Space. Examples specific to early childhood settings and interactions illustrate these skills in action.

Section III focuses on the application of Skilled Dialogue to specific early childhood situations involving cultural linguistic diversity. Vignettes drawn from actual experiences are provided to guide the reader through the Skilled Dialogue process. Finally, an afterword summarizes some concluding thoughts about the larger personal and biological context within which rests the need for respectful, reciprocal, and responsive interactions with children and families.

Appendix A addresses trauma in cultural contexts. Issues of trauma cannot, of course, be discussed in any comprehensive manner within this appendix, nor was that the goal in including it. Rather, the purpose is to alert practitioners to issues of trauma. These issues are especially challenging when trauma co-occurs with cultural diversity. The authors particularly want to highlight the potentially traumatizing effects of cultural discontinuity and/or rejection. Appendix B is a reprint of an article exemplifying how new information can reframe one's perception of a situation. Two additional appendices are also included, one containing photocopiable materials for practitioners' use (Appendix C) and another with a brief summary of key guidelines for working with interpreters/translators (Appendix D).

The Challenge of Dialogues Across Differences

Section I examines core concepts related to the challenge of communication and interactions across diverse cultural parameters. As shown in Figure 2, three concepts are fundamental to understanding this challenge. The first concept, cultural diversity, is addressed in Chapter 1. Though used commonly, this concept requires closer examination. Chapter 2 summarizes information about the source of cultural diversity: culture and its dynamics. Finally, Chapter 3 reviews the idea of cultural competency and introduces the need for an approach such as Skilled Dialogue.

Figure 2

The Challenge of Dialogues Across Differences

Cultural Diversity:
The Challenge
(Chapter 1)

Culture:
The Underlying
Reality
(Chapter 2)

Cultural
Competency:
The Response
(Chapter 3)

- What is cultural diversity?
- What are the primary challenges posed by cultural diversity?
- What are the benefits of recognizing and attending to the challenges of diversity in early childhood environments?

- What is culture?
- Why is it important to understand culture before addressing cultural diversity?
- What is culture's relevance to development and learning?

- What is cultural competency?
- How is cultural competency being addressed in early childhood special education?
- How does Skilled Dialogue address cultural competency?

Cultural Diversity

THE CHALLENGE

GUIDING
BELIEF

Cultural diversity is a dynamic and relational reality that exists between persons rather than within any single person. For this reason, its challenge lies not so much in different behaviors as in the diverse meanings attributed to those behaviors.

As Anna breast-feeds her 18-month-old child, she sees other mothers around her following the same practice. Her behavior stems from cultural templates that she learned as a child, as Anna was breast-fed until she was 2 years old. This is a valued practice that is considered the norm in her culture. All credible persons around her advocate this as a desired and valued practice.

Doris also breast-feeds her 18-month-old child. Doris's behavior, however, stems from a more conscious choice. She belongs to La Leche League International. Although other mothers in La Leche League breast-feed their older children, most of Doris's relatives and friends do not advocate this practice. Doris was not herself breast-fed after 6 months of age. Many "experts," including her own relatives, disagree with Doris's choice.

An early childhood practitioner who believes in ceasing breast-feeding to develop children's self-feeding skills would face distinct challenges in working with these mothers. Decreasing or ceasing breast-feeding would carry different meanings for Anna and Doris. Although both mothers might consider cessation negative, Anna would also consider this abnormal or at least contrary to accepted practice. To change her behavior means going against all that she believes and has experienced since childhood. It also means risking almost certain censure from her family and community. Doris, however, has a framework for understanding the argument behind cessation. She might even have access to specific literature supporting an early shift to bottle-feeding. In addi-

tion, Doris probably knows other mothers who do not breast-feed their older children. Discontinuing breast-feeding certainly goes against Doris's beliefs, but it would not challenge her worldview and would carry a small risk of censure from her family and community.

This vignette illustrates how primary differences between two persons from different cultures lie not simply in different behaviors, but also, and perhaps more significantly, in the meaning given to those behaviors and in the risk associated with changing them (Landrine, 1995). The challenge for early childhood practitioners lies in understanding that meaning and risk—assuming that a valid reason exists for encouraging a behavior change in the first place.

Another challenge posed by cultural diversity is believing and trusting that unfamiliar ways of supporting the children's development and learning can be as effective as familiar ones. Assuming that there is only one way to support development and learning frequently leads to unnecessary miscommunication between practitioners and families. It may even end up inhibiting desired development and learning.

When early childhood practitioners believe that parents must change their behaviors, it is critical to ask whether that assumption is rooted in an ethnocentric perspective (i.e., one valued only within one culture) or in more general developmental concerns that are valid across cultures. Sometimes, for example, a practitioner may strongly believe that parents should stop carrying their 2-year-old child so that the child will be motivated to learn to walk. It is important to examine whether that belief reflects the ethnocentric (and non–research based) assumption that carrying children past a certain age inhibits their motivation to walk. In a cultural context in which most children are carried until they become too heavy and still learn to walk, such an assumption invalidates not only families' individual perspectives but also their larger cultural perspective. Sometimes, it may indeed be necessary to invite family members to encourage a child's walking. Yet, except in rare cases, such encouragement should not implicitly or explicitly state that the family's current culturally sanctioned practices are developmentally inappropriate (see Appendix A at the end of this book). Telling families, "This practice is inappropriate," is quite distinct from saying, "I'm wondering what you think about encouraging Rosie to walk a bit more," or "I'm wondering whether perhaps more time walking independently would help Rosie. What are your thoughts about that?" The first can communicate disrespect and may trigger shame in a family. It also can all too easily be heard as a judgment of incompetence. The second opens dialogue in a respectful fashion.

There are, of course, situations in which culturally sanctioned practices may indeed be identified as inappropriate (e.g., corporal punishment that involves physical harm). Even in these cases, however, practitioners can acknowledge the community or cultural value placed on the practice while sharing information about alternatives. When state law judges a practice abusive, the legal implications of continuing that practice can be discussed. Appendix A discusses these types of situations in more detail.

WHAT IS CULTURAL DIVERSITY?

Differences between persons may be perceived and explained through a variety of lenses, such as personality, trauma experiences, gender, and personal history. Culture is only one lens that can be used in seeking to explain behavior. This book's focus on culture should not be interpreted as discounting or devaluing other sources of diversity; rather, this focus is simply the result of time and space constraints for the book.

Many people use the term *cultural diversity*[1] to identify differences that are perceived to stem from culture. In general, this definition focuses on differences in racial or ethnic heritage or identity without examining or controlling for actual differences in behaviors, languages, values, and beliefs (Barrera & Corso, 2000). For example, a presenter at a national conference reported data for African American families based on the clustering of families that had immigrated from Africa and the Caribbean, as well as families born and raised in the United States.

At first glance, a definition of cultural diversity based solely on stated ethnic or racial identity seems adequate. It is easy to take one's understanding of cultural diversity for granted and move on to the more urgent issue of dealing with the challenges that such diversity poses for practitioners. Doing that, however, risks perpetuating assumptions that inhibit optimal responses to cultural diversity in early childhood environments:

1. Cultural diversity is a static quality inherent in individuals—an assumption that leads to labeling and stereotyping

2. Cultural diversity can be reliably determined by ethnicity—an assumption that ignores the nature of culture as a universal social process

3. Cultural diversity is the "problem," a risk factor that must somehow be lessened or reduced—an assumption that limits practitioners' abil-

---

[1]As noted in the Introduction's "Key Terms" section, the authors use *cultural diversity* and *cultural linguistic diversity* synonymously.

ity to respect diverse practices and gain access to their potential as a positive resource

Responding optimally to cultural diversity in early childhood environments involves questioning these assumptions. The following subsections address aspects that the authors have found to be critical to understanding cultural diversity in a more responsive fashion.

Diversity Is a Relational Reality that Depends on Those Involved

Diversity is both relative and inclusive. It is a property of two or more things or persons being compared one to the other. The question, "Can this family be identified as culturally diverse?" cannot be answered without adding, "As compared with whom? This practitioner? That practitioner? The culture reflected in early childhood practices and curricula? The family's neighbors?" The most accurate answers to the initial question, therefore, can only be "Probably, in relation to these people or that environment" or "Probably not, in relation to these other people and that other environment." All of us are in fact diverse in relation to some people and some environments; all of us also are not diverse in relation to other people and other environments. Diversity is a dynamic and relational quality, sometimes present and sometimes not, depending on context.

All too often, however, diversity is addressed as a static characteristic that is true of only certain persons. The characteristics of these persons are then defined as being diverse independent of their context. A simple example illustrates the shortcomings of such a perspective.

A practitioner is introduced to an East Indian family and asked, "Would you identify this family as culturally diverse?" The practitioner might say yes because this family's beliefs and behaviors differ significantly from those of other families with whom he or she works. However, the practitioner cannot truly answer until the family is placed next to another family or in a particular environment. If that second family or environment also conforms to East Indian culture, then the answer would be "No, it's probable that the two families are culturally similar" (i.e., neither can be judged to be culturally diverse from the other). If the second family or environment conforms to Chinese American culture, however, the practitioner could answer, "Yes, in all probability, each family can be considered culturally diverse from the other."

This example illustrates a key aspect of diversity: its relativity. No single person can be said to be diverse, culturally or otherwise, except in reference to other persons or environments. Diversity, unlike other characteristics (e.g., hair color, height), cannot exist independently of its context. Recognizing this point is essential to responding respectfully to cultural diversity and honoring those who are diverse from us.

When a person names particular children and families as being culturally diverse, that individual must simultaneously name himself or herself as being diverse from them. Calling "them" diverse without also calling oneself culturally diverse fails to recognize the relational aspect of diversity. It implicitly assumes a hierarchy of power within which only the namer has the privilege of setting the norm and naming the other(s) in reference to that norm. The imbalance of power inherent in such an assumption can undermine cultural competency as effectively as explicit racism. When families and children detect that a practitioner perceives only one context as normative, a firm foundation of trust cannot be established. Respectful communication is weakened or cannot occur at all.

Ethnic Identity and Differences Are Only Indicators of Cultural Diversity

Ethnic identity is personally, socially, and politically important. Educationally, however, it is specific behavioral and linguistic characteristics, rather than ethnic identity, that must be recognized and addressed. Ethnicity is only one indicator of the possible presence or absence of particular behavioral and linguistic characteristics. Although cultural diversity is not an individually possessed characteristic, its relative nature means that it also is not a group-defined characteristic. That is, it cannot be defined solely by membership in a particular ethnic group or community.

For example, a university professor who identifies himself as Navajo yet follows no traditional Navajo practices may not be similar to other parents who identify themselves as Navajo but live on a reservation and follow traditional Navajo practices. The fact that this father is ethnically Navajo has important implications. Yet, can he be accurately judged as culturally diverse? In comparison to whom? Under what circumstances? The same question could be asked of a non–American Indian parent who does not identify as Navajo but has lived on a Navajo reservation from childhood and participates extensively in traditional Navajo practices. Would this person be considered culturally diverse? As compared to whom? Under what circumstances? These are not simple questions. They represent a complex reality, as explained by Seelye and Wasilewski:

> You are stretched between cultures when you have been raised in a multicultural household or when you have lived for years in a second (or third) culture where you are dependent on doing things the local way if you are to survive. (1996, p. 6)

It is important, therefore, to look beyond ethnicity to a family's values, beliefs, and behaviors, which may or may not be consonant with that ethnicity.

Identity and Diversity Are Related but Not Equivalent   The cultural or ethnic identity that an individual holds for him- or herself is relatively static. How much that identity differs from others, however, is more fluid. It is this comparison that determines the degree of cultural diversity that an individual or a group experiences or that is attributed to that individual or group.

A person can be ethnically diverse and yet not be culturally diverse in the neighborhood school. An example would be a Hispanic child who was adopted from Latin American parents at birth and is now being raised by monolingual English-speaking parents who identify themselves as Scandinavian. Another person might believe that he or she is highly culturally diverse although others may not perceive him or her as significantly culturally diverse (e.g., an English-fluent child raised within a strong traditional Jewish culture). The combination of possibilities is endless and ever changing.

To be reliably determined, therefore, cultural diversity must be recognized as a characteristic that resides in interactions and comparisons *between* persons rather than as a characteristic possessed by individual persons themselves. From this perspective, cultural diversity is present only when there is "the probability that, in interaction with a particular child or family, the [practitioner] might attribute different meanings or values to behaviors or events than would the family and someone from that family's environment" (Barrera, 1996, p. 71).

What ultimately determines the degree of cultural diversity is not so much who a person is as who surrounds that person. Omitting this critical interactive dimension from one's understanding of cultural diversity increases the probability that responses to children and families identified as diverse will be inflexible and perhaps even stereotypical.

Cultural Diversity Is Never the "Problem" to Be Addressed

Cultural diversity is never problematic in and of itself. It is the response of individuals and institutions to diversity that can be problematic. For example, having little or no proficiency in English in an environment where only English is spoken is not a problem, in and of itself. Limited proficiency in English only becomes problematic when no accommodations are made (e.g., not offering to translate or to seek a translator, not teaching English or learning the other language, not seeking alternative means of communication).

Within a social environment where individuals—no matter how different or similar to others—are truly respected and validated, diversity's true nature as a strength and resource eclipses perceptions of it as a problem or risk factor. It is essential to perceive diversity as the rich source of multiple options that it is. Biologists have begun to understand the essential nature of what they term *biodiversity*. Nabhan (1997) noted the necessity of appreciating and maintaining diversity in nature, culture, and story. He quoted D.M.J.S. Bowman: "So what is biodiversity? My belief is that the variety of life on the planet is like an extra-ordinarily complex, unfinished, and incomplete manuscript with a hugely varied alphabet, an ever-expanding lexicon, and a poorly understood grammar" (p. 20). Losing that manuscript, Nabhan affirmed, shortchanges all of us as well as the planet on which we live. His plea to appreciate and sustain biodiversity speaks eloquently to appreciating and sustaining cultural diversity. In the magazine *Cultural Survival,* MacIntosh made a similar, striking comment: "There are nine different words in Maya for the color blue in the comprehensive Porrua Spanish-Maya Dictionary but just three Spanish translations, leaving six butterflies . . . [whose true color] can only be seen by the Maya" (2001, p. 4).

Seelye and Wasilewski noted correlations between genetic diversity and cultural diversity. In both cases, unexpected resources can be found when templates that lie outside the norm are explored:

> *Cultural diversity enriches our ability to survive. Just as "irrelevant" genetic mutations may be on call within our DNA, individuals with different cultural viewpoints may be on call within our societies to aid the group in adjusting to life's changing conditions. Diverse, multiple perspectives—even unpopular ones—offer humans an important mechanism for survival. (1996, p. 16)*

WHAT ARE THE PRIMARY CHALLENGES POSED BY CULTURAL DIVERSITY?

Cultural diversity, like all diversity, requires that practitioners exercise their abilities to appreciate variety and respond to a wide range of behaviors and beliefs respectfully and reciprocally, whether in teaching and learning situations or in social ones. This global challenge can be further broken down into more specific challenges such as communicating across different languages or needing to differentiate a behavior indicative of disability from one that reflects unimpaired ability. For easier understanding, these specific challenges can be clustered into three common types. *Challenges of information* are posed by insufficient information about the cultural dimensions in which persons are most likely to encounter differences. *Challenges of judgment and interpretation* emerge as individuals strive to understand and interpret the meanings associated with particular behaviors. *Challenges of relationship,* which are acknowledged less frequently than the other two types, are generated when persons remain unaware of or fail to acknowledge the dynamics of power and social positioning that influence every interaction. The following subsections detail each of these challenges.

Challenges of Information

Dissonance and discomfort often result when insufficient or different information exists about another's behavior. Archer introduced the concept of a *culture bump*, which "occurs when an individual from one culture finds himself or herself in a different, strange, or uncomfortable situation when interacting with persons of a different culture" (1986, pp. 170–171). Barrera and Kramer (1997) applied this idea to cultural diversity in early childhood special education environments, defining *culture bump* as the cognitive and emotional dissonance experienced between persons when differing values, beliefs, and worldviews come into contact.

Culture bumps signal unfamiliar territory. This may be exciting and stimulating; it may also be confusing, irritating, or even frightening. Because culture bumps mark the boundaries of understanding and/or tolerance, they tend to have both visceral and cognitive dimensions. A practitioner may, for example, have a strong negative emotional reaction to a parent who asks questions that seem too personal (e.g., "How many children do you have?") or to a parent who is repeatedly late for sessions. An analysis of common experiences across cultures indicates that most culture bumps result from dissonance across one or more of three cultural dimensions that underlie how cultures frame reality: funds of knowledge (Moll & Greenberg, 1990; Velez-Ibañez & Greenberg, 1992), sense of self, and perceptions of power. Cultures selectively support particular beliefs, values, languages, and behavioral expectations. Moll and Greenberg used *funds of knowledge* to refer to "specific knowledge of strategic importance" to members of a community or culture (p. 323). Analogous to "cultural capital" (Lubeck, 1994), this concept refers to the depth and breadth of knowledge to which one has access.

Persons learn who they are and how to act (i.e., acquire a sense of self) within the funds of knowledge valued in their culture(s). For instance, is being independent a highly valued skill? Or is learning how to interact well with others and live in harmony a more important skill? Equally influenced by culture are perceptions of power. Does being highly verbal confer power? Or does it place one's credibility at risk? Directly or indirectly, cultures shape assumptions, biases, and stereotypes about what is important and valuable within each of these dimensions.

Table 1 illustrates the content of each dimension in relation to three areas common to early childhood curricula: communicative-linguistic, personal-social, sensory-cognitive. Questions are provided for use in exploring each dimension in relation to self and others. Table 2 presents specific examples of culture bumps within the three dimensions, which are organized around the same three curricular areas. Chapter 5 provides additional information on culture bumps, while Chapters 7, 8, and 9 give suggestions for identifying and responding to culture bumps.

Table 1. Cultural dimensions underlying common culture bumps related to developmental/curricular areas

Developmental/ curricular area	Cultural dimensions		
	Sense of self	Funds of knowledge	Perceptions of power
Communicative-linguistic	What do I consider the relationship of language to identity?	What language(s) do I speak?	How do I express/ maintain power through language?
	How does my language and communication maintain my sense of self?	What do I consider the roles and rules for use of language and communication?	What status is given to the language(s) I speak?
	What are values and rules for the use of personal and family names?	How do I define the relative value of verbal and nonverbal communication?	What has been my experience as a speaker of this language (or these languages)?
		How is literacy perceived? To what degree is oral literacy valued? Written literacy?	
Personal-social	How does my sense of self play out in social interactions and settings?	What is my understanding of social roles and rules?	What has been my experience of power in relation to the larger society? Peers? Authorities? Others?
	Who do I believe I am (individual identity)?	What do I consider appropriate behavior?	In what situations do I feel competent/powerful? In what situations do I feel unskilled/powerless?
	How do others see me (attributed identity)?	What degree of importance do I give to the individual? To the community?	
Sensory-cognitive	What does *identity* mean to me?	What are my values/ beliefs concerning	How do I define *power*? How do I believe that it is acquired and exercised?
	What characteristics do I believe are essential to sense of self?	• Ways to best teach/ learn	What do I believe confers power on a person?
	What is the relationship of self to the larger environment (i.e., one's place in the world)?	• How the world works	To what degree am I conscious of my own power?
		• Ways to best solve problems and make decisions	
		What is my worldview?	

Table 2.   Common culture bumps in relation to developmental/curricular areas

Developmental/ curricular area	Common culture bumps
Communicative-linguistic	The language used by practitioners and/or reflected in early childhood environments (e.g., tapes, posters) may be different from that used in the child's home, so the family may have difficulty communicating with providers and supporting desired activities and interactions. Also, the family may feel unwelcome or shamed.
	The child may have limited or no proficiency in the language used by practitioners and/or reflected in early childhood environments (typically English). He or she may be unable or limited in ability to understand and respond to verbal interactions and directions. This affects self-esteem and sense of competence as well as communication.
	The rules and strategies for using language that child and family have mastered may differ from those assumed by the practitioner, resulting in miscommunication and confusion. For example, a child or family member may fail to "speak up" because he or she is waiting for pauses that are, according to their values and experiences, long enough.
	The roles and rules for sending and receiving nonverbal messages may differ between the family and the practitioner. One common example is corrections: In some cultures, corrections between adults are always nonverbal, if at all possible. Another example are signals for entering a group conversation. In some cultures, one must wait for a silent pause of several seconds; other cultures teach listeners to listen to intonation rather than silence as a signal that it is okay to speak.
	The family's/child's culture may value nonverbal communication over verbal communication. For example, family members may send silent behavioral messages that they are confused or wish to stop interaction rather than say so in words.
	The language spoken in the child's primary caregiving environment may be perceived to have a lower status than English. Sending this message—whether intentionally or unintentionally, explicitly or implicitly—can have a negative impact on learning and intergenerational interactions.
	The definition of *family* differs across cultures. Who is in a family? What is the function of family? What roles are essential to family? All of these answers and more describe how the concept of family is structured and defined within a particular culture. Even when the same word is used in the same language, miscommunication can occur. Bumps may occur when similar concept structures and definitions are assumed. This may be particularly troublesome when translating concepts (e.g., *education* and *educación* are not equivalent words).
Personal-social	The family/child may be unfamiliar with, may not value, or may not understand behaviors and beliefs that are common to EuroAmerican Normative Culture (ENC).
	The family/child may be unfamiliar with, may not value, or may not understand professional early childhood cultures and may not exhibit expected behaviors such as arriving on time.
	The family/child may have a different understanding of what "self" is and how "self" functions. Many common early childhood concepts, such as autonomy, presume a particular sense of self. A child may, for example, appear to have trouble "detaching" from his or her mother because such detachment is not part of the child's or family's cultural repertoire related to "self" and how "self" should function.
	Identity and competence are defined differently from culture to culture. Families may have different perceptions from practitioners and, thus,

Table 2.   *(continued)*

Developmental/ curricular area	Common culture bumps
	may appear to have difficulty understanding or accepting intervention goals.
	Developmental goals and expectations can differ significantly across cultures, as can norms for "good" parenting. Differences in beliefs and experiences in this area can trigger major difficulties between families and caregivers.
	Families/children from culturally diverse groups that have been identified as social and political minorities may have had negative or shaming experiences that influence their interactions with practitioners. Practitioners may discount the power of their own position, and, consequently, misunderstand interactions with families and children.
	The sources of assistance and support that persons seek may be different across cultures. Reliance on extended families is one example. Families have skills for gaining access to resources within their cultural contexts—for instance, they may be quite skilled at approaching family members but have fewer skills for "interviewing" professionals to determine which one best suits their needs.
Sensory-cognitive	The areas and kinds of knowledge that are valued can differ across cultures. ENC, for example, tends to value early verbal proficiency; other cultures (e.g., Mexican American) value early social skills. Families may, for example, not value the early verbal labeling of colors or shapes found in many early childhood curricula.
	Family/child may value, and promote, certain learning strategies over others. Some cultures value and promote modeling over direct questioning strategies, for example. Family/child may be unfamiliar with, may not value, or may not understand strategies used by early childhood practitioners.
	Family/child may value certain strategies for problem solving and decision making (e.g., going to the family elder, imitating a peer) that are not common to early childhood settings and interactions and that may seem, consequently, "wrong," ineffective, or inefficient.
	Family/child and practitioners may have strikingly different conceptions of how the world works. Beliefs about health are one example. Are diseases caused by germs or by displeasing a Higher Power? Worldviews are seldom explicit; they are composed of what individuals take for granted as "the way it is."

Challenges of Judgment and Interpretation

Beyond the challenges posed by insufficient or conflicting information are challenges posed by the diverse meanings and values attached to specific beliefs and behaviors. Everyone depends on predictable patterns and familiar scripts for interactions with others (e.g., a script for greeting a person one has not seen for a long time). The culture bumps generated by cultural diversity result from disruptions of these patterns and scripts. The unfamiliar or unexpected behaviors that persons "bump" into can both confuse and confound them. They can easily misinterpret, distrust, or misjudge those behaviors. For example, initiating a task-specific conversation without first talking more generally and establishing rapport can be misinterpreted as an indication of insensitivity. The converse—spending time in general conversation before addressing a specific task—can be misinterpreted as wasting time. While serving as director of an early intervention program in South Texas during the 1970s, the first author experienced an example of this dissonance. The social worker for the on-site program was from South America, and many of the families with whom she worked were Mexican American. Several parents had little or no formal schooling, and several were recent immigrants from rural areas of Mexico. For these parents, the early childhood intervention environment was unfamiliar and significantly different from environments that they knew how to negotiate. To get them involved and exchange critical information about their children, the program's social worker started a morning crochet class, which was an immediate success. She established a strong rapport with these parents, and in easy conversation while crocheting, both obtained and shared needed information. After a few classes, however, the principal asked the social worker why she was wasting time on crocheting during school hours! The program director then had to explain that the classes were a highly efficient way for the social worker to accomplish the goals for which she had been hired.

A second challenge posed by cultural diversity, therefore, is eliminating or at least minimizing incorrect behavioral interpretations, negative judgments, and miscommunications. Stated positively, cultural diversity challenges us to interpret unfamiliar behaviors correctly and honor those who exhibit them. Understanding and anticipating culture bumps is relatively easy. Compassionately responding to them, however, can be very difficult, especially when differences challenge strongly held values or beliefs. For example, if a speech-language pathologist encountered a family that valued nonverbal communication over verbal communication, how would he or she respond to the needs of their child, who demonstrates a significant language delay according to both the practitioner's and the parents' assessments? As another example, how might a practitioner react to a mother who continued to dress and feed her 3-year-old child in many situations? Section III offers strategies for responding to these and similar situations.

Challenges of Relationship

Challenges of relationship are rooted in the issues of power and social positioning that accompany all interactions, especially those within the human services professions. These issues have received less attention within early childhood special education than within other related disciplines, such as bilingual special education and multicultural education (Cushner & Brislin, 1996; Delpit, 1995; Gollnick & Chinn, 1990). Yet, it is ultimately the challenge of recognizing these issues and becoming responsive to them that determines whether one can apply specific knowledge and interpretations successfully to particular situations. Darder said that "in order to understand the relationship between culture and power we must also comprehend the dynamics that exist between what is considered truth (or knowledge) and power" (1991, p. 27).

All cultures judge certain behaviors, values, and beliefs as more powerful or more desirable than others. These are consequently associated with higher social status than other behaviors, values, and beliefs. Some cultures, for example, value being highly articulate over being a quiet observer. In other words, these cultures "privilege" verbal skills over observational ones (e.g., would consider a highly articulate person more competent than a quiet one as a potential employee).

Beliefs and behaviors are always value laden. For that reason, one cannot competently respond to cultural diversity without also examining issues of power and social positioning. One example that reflects these issues is the use of the term *minority*. A notion (and reality) of privilege underlies the classification of certain populations as minorities,[2] even when this is not the case numerically. Populations identified as culturally and linguistically diverse are typically those considered to hold minority status. This is not a coincidence. When compared with the culture that sets institutionalized norms, these populations typically experience reduced voice and participation (Darder, 1991; Delpit, 1995; Gollnick & Chinn, 1990). This is most often attributed to lack of familiarity with those norms. An even stronger reason, however, is the privileging of certain behaviors and attributes over others and the consequent status and power accorded to only those who exhibit these behaviors and attributes. Authors such as Skutnabb-Kangas and Cummins (1988) and Wildman (1996) eloquently addressed this issue.

It is important to recognize the degree to which cultural diversity challenges early childhood special education practitioners to examine the role that privileging certain behaviors plays in their perceptions of and interactions with the children and families they serve. How do practitioners perceive families' behaviors as being different from their own? How do practitioners respond to them when children or families exhibit behaviors that they personally do not consider desirable or that are not considered desirable within EuroAmerican Normative Culture (ENC)? Do early childhood special education practitioners realize the power that they hold?

---

[2] As noted in the Introduction's "Key Terms" section, the term *minority* is used throughout this book to denote social and political realities, which may remain in place even when groups attain majority status numerically.

When offering an assessment of families' behaviors, do practitioners, for example, communicate that certain behaviors differ from what they consider most effective? Or do practitioners communicate that families' behaviors are wrong without questioning the validity of such judgments?

It is equally important to recognize the degree to which families' and children's past experiences with power and privilege influence their perceptions of and responses to practitioners' behaviors. The dynamics of power and social positioning are instrumental in shaping the experiences of cultural uprooting, disruption, and shaming, which are unfortunately familiar to many families and children from "minority" populations. Igoa spoke to this in relation to immigrant children:

> *When one engages in a thorough investigation of the child's environment, intellectual and emotional failures often are found to be a result of undercurrents between the child and adult and/or institution wherein the child feels unloved . . . , unchallenged, and disempowered. (1995, p. 8)*

Skutnabb-Kangas and Cummins (1988) addressed this reality even more explicitly. One of their book's chapters contains a poignant poem that captures aspects of both cultural disruption and the consequent shaming that can occur. The words are spoken by a Finnish mother who has recently immigrated to Sweden and is now finding that she cannot communicate with her 3-year-old child in Swedish, the language that has become the privileged language for that child.

> *"It goes sometimes*
> *. . . until I can't*
> *say the word*
> *you want to learn*
> *. . . until I can't*
caress you
in Swedish
> *. . . until I see you*
> *slowly walk*
> *away from me*
> *toward others*
> *who can . . .*

(From Jalava, A. [1988]. Mother tongue and identity. In T. Skutnabb-Kangas & J. Cummins [Eds.], *Minority education: From shame to struggle* [pp. 168–169]. Philadelphia: Multilingual Matters; reprinted by permission.)

Practitioners who are more English fluent than many of the parents with whom they interact must be careful not to reenact this scenario. The challenge posed by issues of power and social positioning is sobering. Nevertheless, it cannot be neatly split from the other challenges posed by cultural diversity.

WHAT ARE THE BENEFITS OF RECOGNIZING AND ATTENDING TO THE CHALLENGES OF CULTURAL DIVERSITY IN EARLY CHILDHOOD ENVIRONMENTS?

It is important to examine why there is a need to recognize and attend to the challenges posed by cultural diversity in early childhood environments. Is such recognition and response necessary only when significant numbers of certain cultural groups are present? Is it important for all children or only for some? Three reasons for recognizing and responding to cultural diversity are discussed next.

Responding to Shifting Demographics

The most common reason given for recognizing and attending to the challenges posed by cultural diversity is demographic. Increasing numbers of culturally and linguistically diverse children and families are present in all communities (Garcia, 2001). It was once possible to live out one's life in a community where everyone spoke the same language, held similar values and beliefs, and followed similar practices. That scenario is rapidly changing in almost every area of the United States. In the 21st century, children from groups currently considered "culturally diverse" constitute a significant presence in U.S. schools (Brice, 2002). There are, or so it is believed,[3] a greater number of children and families in early childhood environments with limited English proficiency and/or limited familiarity with the values, expectations, and behavioral norms common to institutionalized aspects of these settings. As a consequence, there is an ever-increasing probability that early childhood practitioners will serve children and families whose language(s) and culture(s) differ from their own. The practitioners' familiar ways of communicating and interacting will no longer be sufficient to respond competently to these children and families.

There can, however, be an implicit (and sometimes explicit) "We are doing it to meet *their* needs" dimension to this reason for attending to cul-

---

[3]Current numbers tend to be compared to statistics without reference to data from the late 1800s and early 1900s, when it was common to find significant percentages of families that spoke languages other than English in many parts of the United States (Takaki, 1993).

tural diversity. Certainly, the ability to respond to shifting demographics more appropriately and competently is one of the benefits of recognizing and responding to cultural diversity. Nevertheless, recognizing and attending to cultural diversity in early childhood environments is important mainly because doing so is critical to meeting the needs of all children, not just those identified as being culturally linguistically diverse.

As stated previously, the number of children and families with language(s) and worldviews diverse from those found in early childhood environments should not be primary in determining the need for cultural competence. It is as critical to respond appropriately to one child or family as it is to 20 or 30 or 300. Supporting children's developmental needs and implementing appropriate and responsive curricula are equally if not more compelling reasons for attending to the challenges of cultural diversity. Diversity is, after all, only the inverse of uniqueness.

Supporting Children's Developmental Needs

Cole stated,

> The earliest essential condition for continued development following birth is that the child and those who care for him or her must become coordinated in such a manner that the adults are able to accumulate enough resources to accommodate the newcomer. (1998, p. 17)

The key phrase in this quote is "become coordinated." Becoming coordinated with an infant's rhythms of moving and talking, for example, requires a common fund of knowledge about those rhythms. An example of culture's role in such coordination comes from an early intervention practitioner working with a Korean infant. This practitioner described her frustration in trying to soothe the infant when he became fussy. She would hold him and rock him, but the infant would only become more agitated. One such time, the infant's aunt observed the interaction. She quickly reached for the child and began to jiggle him up and down rapidly. He quickly quieted. The aunt explained that rocking a child gently from side to side was done only prior to nursing or feeding from a bottle. The practitioner had unknowingly added to the infant's frustration by signaling that food was forthcoming when it was not. She could not "coordinate" her movements with the infant's needs.

One of the core needs of all children is to have their behaviors and beliefs mirrored and valued by adults around them. As Brazelton and Cramer noted, "Mirroring is a fundamental dimension of . . . the development and maintenance of a healthy self-image" (1990, p. 12). Such mirroring and valuing is essential to the development of a sense of identity as well as to optimum cognitive and emotional development. Josselson (1994) referred to "eye to eye validation," the heart of which is being known and recognized for who one truly is. The recognition of cultural parameters (e.g., language, values) is a key component of such validation. Children's needs and strengths can only be appropriately identified relative to cultural and social experiences (Kendall, 1996).

When children do not find a sufficient degree of culturally responsive mirroring and validation, confusion and shame may result, often with concomitant delays or disruptions in learning and development (Donovan & McIntyre, 1990). Family members are, of course, the main source of such mirroring and validation. They are the most important caregivers and role models in the eyes of their children. Even so, external institutions and communities also play a critical role in supporting or inhibiting mirroring and validation. The presence and modeling of practitioners in the home and in other environments can significantly support or inhibit culturally responsive mirroring and validation for both children and their families. This is especially so with children and families from minority populations whose language, values, beliefs, and behaviors may have already been invalidated or mirrored negatively.

Having one's identity and experiences acknowledged, mirrored, and validated in environments outside of the home is being increasingly recognized (Bredekamp & Copple, 1997; Koplow, 1996). Brazelton and Greenspan (2000), for example, identified the importance of such cultural continuity and made three critical points, which summarize this discussion. First, they stated, "Communities and cultures provide the context or framework for the other irreducible needs that we have discussed" (p. 159). They then pointed out that "the reference points for subtle emotional meanings are always stronger in one's basic language" (p. 161), thus encouraging the use of home language in interactions with young children. Finally, they concluded that programs "succeed or fail to the degree to which they are sensitive to cultural needs and the degree to which people who are a part of the culture shape them" (p. 171).

Developing Appropriate and Responsive Curriculum

Bowman and Stott remarked, "Cultural differences can lead teachers to misunderstand children, to misassess [sic] their developmental competence, and to plan incorrectly for their educational achievement" (1994, p. 121). It is clear that a sound and developmentally appropriate curriculum cannot be developed without attending to children's unique characteristics as well as to the funds of knowledge that they bring with them to educational interactions. A key pedagogical principle advocates "beginning where the child is." Only through understanding developmental expectations and experiences associated with specific cultures can one truly determine a child's status in relation to particular goals and interventions. For example, when an Inuit child does not demonstrate age-appropriate understanding of the rules of participating in small group activities (from an ENC perspective), what is the best curricular response? Developing activities to teach small group participation? Developing activities that expand the child's existing knowledge to include rules for this setting? It depends on the degree to which the practitioner acknowledges and understands cultural diversity.

Other pedagogical principles espouse attention to varying teaching and learning formats according to variations in children's learning and development (Edwards, Gandini, & Forman, 1995). This can be done most competently with sensitivity to the range of teaching formats and learning styles valued in various cultures. On the one hand, a Hispanic child whose attention regularly wanders during reading circle may, in fact, have attention problems. On the other hand, the practitioner may not be physically close enough to the child, unaware that in Hispanic culture interpersonal distance signals when it is or is not acceptable to pay attention.

All pedagogical principles reflect the cultural context in which they were formulated (Bowers & Flinders, 1990). Understanding and adjusting to this reality clarifies the relevance of these principles for all children, not just those identified as culturally diverse. Familiarity with the range and complexity of cultural diversity is an invaluable aid to competently answering questions such as the following:

1. What books should I include in my early childhood library?

2. To what degree should I use one-to-one activities as compared with small group activities?

3. To what degree should I support reliance on following a mother's lead as compared with promoting independent problem-solving?

4. Should I organize my activities around relatively formal schedules?

5. To what degree should I rely on verbal response formats in activities?

Rothstein-Fisch (1998) gave several cogent illustrations of how understanding cultural diversity affects curriculum and pedagogy. One involves two children who perceived a discussion about eggs from two very different perspectives. One child shared "the teacher's value orientation," which dictated that eggs be described as isolated physical entities (e.g., white, oval, breakable). The second child, from a different culture, assumed that the teacher "was interested in the object as a mediator of social relationships," as would be true in her home culture. This child wanted to "talk about how she cooked eggs with her grandmother" (p. 30). Without recognizing and attending to the cultural diversity that generated such distinct perceptions, it would be easy to simply label one response as right and the other as wrong. Doing so, however, would prevent the expansion of existing skills and perceptions not only for the child from the dissimilar culture, but also for the child who shared the teacher's culture.

Of course, there are risks both to making cultural diversity the primary lens for assigning meaning to behaviors and events and to discounting culture and cultural diversity as variables that significantly influence behaviors and events. The former perspective tends to result in stereotyping; the latter results in cultural "melting," which also obliterates individuals' identities. Persons cannot be defined solely by their cultural identities, yet neither can they be adequately defined without some degree of reference to these identities. To maintain the balance between these two realities, it is helpful to understand culture in its own right.

Culture

THE UNDERLYING REALITY

GUIDING BELIEF   *Cultural diversity cannot be adequately addressed if culture itself is not first understood.*

At preschool, an Euro-American boy was playing with blocks. Nearby, Jasmine, the daughter of immigrant Latino parents, took one of the blocks that the boy was not using, and began to play with it. The boy's response was to hit Jasmine, whereupon she began to cry. The teacher reprimanded the injured, crying Jasmine, admonishing her not to take the other children's toys.

It just happened that Jasmine's mother had been looking through a one-way window and observed the entire incident. She became terribly upset that the teacher not only failed to reprimand the boy for his act of aggression, but instead scolded Jasmine for something perceived as completely normal in her household: sharing objects. (Greenfield, Raeff, & Quiroz, 1996, quoted in Rothstein-Fisch, 1998, p. 28)

The study of culture is an extensive area in itself. Early researchers of culture listed more than 100 definitions of culture (Haviland, 1993). Malina's definition of culture summarizes key points:

Culture is a system of symbols relating to and embracing people, things, and events that are socially symboled. Symboling means filling people, things, and events with meaning and value (feeling), making them meaningful in such a way that all the members of a given group mutually share, appreciate, and live out of that meaning and value in some way. *(2001, p. 11, emphasis added)*

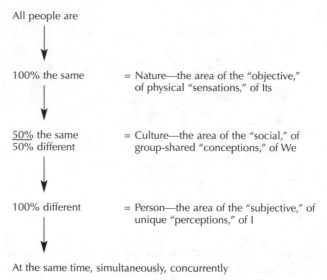

All people are

↓

100% the same   = Nature—the area of the "objective,"
                         of physical "sensations," of Its

↓

50% the same   = Culture—the area of the "social," of
50% different   group-shared "conceptions," of We

↓

100% different   = Person—the area of the "subjective," of
                         unique "perceptions," of I

↓

At the same time, simultaneously, concurrently

Figure 3.   Similarities and differences spectrum. (Reproduced from *The New Testament World,* Third Edition, revised and expanded by Bruce J. Malina. © 2001 Bruce J. Malina. Used by permission of Westminster John Knox Press.)

WHAT IS CULTURE?

A detailed discussion of *culture* is outside the purpose and scope of this book. The seven ideas that follow are intended to introduce the understanding of culture that is key to Skilled Dialogue. For additional information on culture, readers are referred to other sources cited in the references.

1. "All human beings are entirely the same, entirely different, and somewhat the same and somewhat different at the same time" (Malina, 2001, p. 7).

Culture is one of three simultaneous realities within which persons live. On one hand, the first reality—human nature—makes everyone the same, with relatively little room for diversity. The generic heart portrayed in a medical textbook reflects this limited diversity. On the other hand, the third reality—personhood—makes everyone unique, with little room for commonality. No two people's fingerprints are the same. Culture resides in the second reality—in the interface between almost total uniqueness and almost total similarity. People are neither so unique that they have nothing in common, nor so "human" that they have only commonalities. Figure 3 illustrates this point. As Malina noted,

> *To understand your story adequately, I need to know not only the who, what, when, where, and how of your . . . human nature and unique personhood, but*

also the whys and wherefores of our commonly shared cultural story that . . . gives mutually appreciable meaning and value to both" [sic]. (2001, p. 9)

It is important to recognize simultaneously both uniqueness and similarity to avoid stereotyping and maintain connections.

2. There is a distinction between *culture* and *cultures*, just as there is a distinction between *language* and *languages*.

One may talk about language in general (e.g., all languages name things), or one may speak about specific languages (e.g., English uses nouns to name things). In the same way, one may talk about *culture* as a universal process (e.g., all cultures differentiate roles), or one may talk about specific cultures (e.g., culture X differentiates between the roles of parent and family decision maker in this fashion). Understanding both aspects of cultures is important. The first (i.e., culture in a universal sense) emphasizes that *all* persons are cultural beings. Everyone has a culture, whether he or she can name that culture. Everyone participates in a single human reality but chooses to act within it in different ways. The second aspect (i.e., culture in the particular sense) encourages honoring the rich gifts that diversity offers to everyone. Chapter 6 introduces 3rd Space, a skill that focuses on the importance of "holding two ideas in one's mind at the same time," as a component skill of Skilled Dialogue. This skill is relevant to understanding the relationship between culture and cultures as well as the relationship between uniqueness and similarity. Focusing on only individual uniqueness distorts the true meaning of culture, which is a shared reality. In the same manner, focusing on similarities erases the very concept of cultural diversity.

3. Cultures are mental models or paradigms developed by communities over time to make sense of their physical, emotional, and social environments and to determine how best to operate within them.

There are multiple and equally valid models or cultures, just as there are multiple and equally valid languages. Just as a language is more than just the sounds and words produced, a culture is more than just observable beliefs, behaviors, or values. Each culture includes a deeper, less visible reality: unique worldviews or paradigms that structure and sanction communities' ways of perceiving, believing, and evaluating reality. Some cultures, for example, support a worldview in which human beings are superior to all other creatures; others support a worldview in which human beings are servants of creation. These worldviews are not directly visible but can be inferred from more visible behaviors.

The aspects of culture that are most easily perceived (e.g., foods, behaviors) are, thus, only surface manifestations of deeper, less visible aspects. For instance, respect for elders—a valued aspect of interpersonal behavior in some cultures—is a manifestation of a deeper worldview that understands personal experience, rather than written text, as a source of knowledge and wisdom. Figure 4 outlines the layers of culture, showing that beneath surface manifestations lie particular funds of knowledge, including those related to perceptions of self and power. In turn, these funds are shaped by worldviews born of a community's shared experiences across families and across generations.

Although these aspects can be discussed separately, they are inextricably linked. Any change at one level affects all other levels. A request to

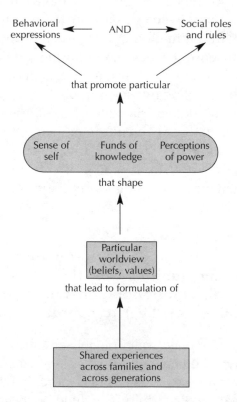

Figure 4.   The layers of culture.

change a behavior, for example, touches on the deeper realities that deter-mine the value and meaning of that behavior (see vignette in Chapter 1).

4. Persons learn and internalize "sets of cultural cues that lead [them] to perceive, feel, act, believe, admire, and strive in ways that make sense to [them] as well as to others" who share these cues (Malina, 2001, p. 16).

Persons are enculturated into particular ways of being; that is, they learn particular cultural cues from their caregivers. For example, they learn to perceive particular behaviors as appropriate and others as inappropriate; they learn to admire certain characteristics and to value certain behaviors over others. When persons move out of the environments in which they are raised, they may learn a different set of cues. It is difficult to overesti-mate the degree to which ways of perceiving, feeling, acting, believing, admiring, and striving are based on the cues designated as important by culture(s). Just as persons learn the language(s) they speak from others al-most unconsciously, they also learn the culture(s) that they "speak."

5. There are both levels of culture and levels of participation in cultures.

Cultural identity, however, is not a simple "this-or-that" phenomenon. Everyone participates in one or more cultures to a greater or lesser degree. In fact, "many millions of people have their roots in two or more distinct cultures" (Seelye & Wasilewski, 1996, p. xvii). Ethnic labels identify some but not all of these cultures. Many may have no clear labels. Kalyanpur and Harry referred to Banks in saying that *culture* may be

> *Described [as] a complex picture of micro and macro levels . . . whereby the macrocultural framework is an overarching national frame that includes many microcultural groups, each of which participates to varying extents in the macro culture, while simultaneously retaining varying amounts of its original cultural traditions. (1999, p. 4)*

The term *Hispanic culture,* for example, refers to an overarching cluster of beliefs, values, practices, and language. Individuals participate in this culture to varying degrees depending on a variety of factors (e.g., family history, personal experience). Compounding this participation is a simulta-neous participation in one or more additional cultures (e.g., American Indian, ENC). Individuals and communities reflect but do not ever completely define a macro culture, which in a sense exists only at an ideal level.

6. Culture functions to connect groups as well as to distinguish them.

One function of culture is to maintain the coherence of groups, with survival as a guiding goal. Cultures thus set parameters that connect people. These very same parameters also unavoidably distinguish one community from another. Speaking Spanish, for example, distinguishes persons who participate in Hispanic culture from those who do not. It also serves to connect persons who speak Spanish with each other. This dual aspect of culture makes sense when it is placed on the previously discussed similarities and differences spectrum (Figure 3). Like a combined centripetal and centrifugal force, culture acts to keep the necessary balance between connection and separation.

7. Personal and group histories simultaneously enhance and limit the degree to which children and families gain access to and express cultural values.

Culture is by definition a general concept similar to *man, woman,* or *society.* No single man, for example, reflects the entirety of that concept. Personal and group experiences shape how culture is made manifest in particular contexts and lives. These experiences can enhance or limit one's access to specific ways of perceiving, believing, evaluating, and behaving. For example, if these experiences include grandparents who share rich stories about family and tradition and patiently teach the ways and words of their culture, then one's access to that culture is enhanced. Conversely, if one has experienced trauma, collectively or individually, then his or her access to such experience may be reduced—possibly by choice. Individuals as well as whole cultural communities experience trauma in a variety of ways, sometimes from other communities, sometimes from the elements. The interface between culture and trauma, however, has not been addressed in any extensive fashion.

DeVries discusses culture in this context as a "double-edged sword": "The power of culture as a protector, integrator, and security system is evident in studies [on] cultural assimilation" (1996, p. 400). Yet, he also goes on to say,

> *When the cultural defense mechanisms [e.g., mourning rituals] are lost, individuals are left on their own to achieve emotional control. Traumas that occur in the*

context of social upheavals, such as revolutions, create a profound discontinuity in the order and predictability that culture has brought to daily life and social situations. (p. 400)

All cultural discontinuity, whether personal or collective, affects the ability to gain access to and express cultural values—beliefs and behaviors that serve as protectors, integrators, and security systems. This loss of full access can also happen when shame or trauma becomes associated with cultural membership (e.g., when one is ridiculed for not speaking English). Appendix A contains more information on the impact of personal and collective trauma on cultural identity and participation.

WHY IS IT IMPORTANT TO UNDERSTAND CULTURE BEFORE ADDRESSING CULTURAL DIVERSITY?

Discussions of cultural diversity in early childhood special education literature tend to make diversity itself the primary focus. Readers' understanding of culture and its dynamics are assumed. In leading early childhood special education journals, culture is seldom explicitly defined or addressed in any substantive manner (Barrera & Corso, 2000). Focusing primarily on diversity (i.e., differences between groups) without also acknowledging the more general, shared dynamics of culture ironically risks the divisive responses that recognizing diversity is designed to eliminate. A sole focus on diversity holds one population as constant or normative (e.g., ENC) and assesses others against it. It emphasizes how "you are not like me" without also recognizing that "you are like me." This perspective, although informative, literally takes differences out of context and places them center stage—limiting communication at best, polarizing diverse perspectives at worst.

Responding appropriately to cultural diversity requires that one first understands the meaning of culture and how it functions. Then, varied human behaviors and beliefs can be better understood in their own right, as well as in comparison with particular cultures. This understanding consequently promotes diverse skills and knowledge as valued and deeply rooted expressions of self and community. Only when culture is perceived in this fashion can differences be respected without sacrificing connections.

Take the behavior of not asking direct questions. Examined as an isolated "diverse" behavior, it may be judged as less effective than the valued ENC behavior of asking direct questions. Yet, when understood as one of an interconnected cluster of behaviors reflective of a community's culture, the behavior can be valued in its own right. It can be honored as a strategy that functions as effectively within a given cultural context as any alternative developed by another community.

Changing individual behaviors without attention to their context jeopardizes the coherence of related behaviors and the individual's sense of self and power. An example is the implicit (sometimes explicit) pressure on families to speak only English with their young children. This pressure ignores the cultural understanding that changing one's language changes many other things as well. It can diminish the ability to tell one's children traditional stories, to sing them familiar lullabies, and to pass on wisdom from one's parents. These limitations, in turn, diminish the emotional richness of such interactions with children, which can disconnect them from their own identity, and so on.

Placed within its proper context, cultural diversity can be appreciated for what it is: the reflection of human creativity and wisdom. Its gifts emerge as persons understand its source and its function.

WHAT IS CULTURE'S RELEVANCE TO DEVELOPMENT AND LEARNING?

As discussed previously, culture is a pervasive dynamic that influences every aspect of one's perceptions and interactions with others. Culture shapes and patterns our child rearing and our teaching practices. All cultures, by their very natures, channel values and social mores from one generation to another (Phillips, 1994; Polk, 1994). Cross-cultural literature provides many examples of the critical connection among culture, development, and learning.

Greenfield and Cocking noted, "The key fact about human culture is its intergenerational transmission through the socialization process" (1994, p. 3). Through the process of enculturation, all children are socialized into particular languages, roles, and rules to prepare them for successful participation in their communities (Damen, 1987; Phillips, 1994). Values, perceptions, and beliefs are passed from one generation to another, implicitly through modeling, as well as explicitly through messages such as, "This works; it's good" or "That doesn't work; it's not good."

A family's template for promoting development and learning is rooted in its cultural funds of knowledge (Moll & Greenberg, 1990; Velez-Ibañez & Greenberg, 1992). In particular, Moll and Greenberg compared funds of knowledge to an "operations manual of essential information and strategies households need to maintain their well-being" (p. 323). These "operations manuals" are contained within and transmitted through a community's culture (Landrine & Klonoff, 1996). Some might even say that culture is a set of these manuals.

Knowing how to greet adults who are not family members, for example, comprises a specific fund of knowledge. The content of this fund differs across cultures. In some homes, children are taught (i.e., enculturated) to remain silent as a sign of respect. In other homes, children are expected to step up, say hello, and shake hands when introduced.

Acculturation refers to acquiring additional funds of knowledge for functioning outside of one's home culture. According to Damen, acculturation "involves the process of pulling out of the world view or ethos of the first culture, learning new ways of meeting old problems, and shedding ethnocentric evaluations" (1987, p. 140).

The difference between enculturation and acculturation resembles the difference between learning a first and learning a second language. Encultration generally is not stressful. Within one's home culture, learning is relatively easy because it is supported by modeling and by children's identification with significant caregivers. Acculturation, conversely, can be accompanied by varying levels of stress (e.g., Igoa, 1995; Landrine & Klonoff, 1996). Asking young children to acquire funds of knowledge that are unfamiliar or not valued at home can challenge their emotional and cognitive resources. This is especially so when the fact that children are still mastering their home culture is not adequately recognized. Although acculturation is certainly necessary in today's multicultural world, its impact can be positive or negative, depending on one's degree of understanding about its cognitive and emotional demands. When children feel torn between two worlds, for example, or when unfamiliar expectations are not explicitly explained, energy that would ordinarily be available for learning must be shifted into coping mechanisms.

Cultural Competency

THE RESPONSE

GUIDING BELIEF — *Cultural competency is a process that is best determined by one's ability to craft respectful, reciprocal, and responsive relationships with others.*

Mrs. Tahiti went to her daughter Rachel's early childhood program to meet with Ms. Clemson, the program's speech-language pathologist. With the assistance of an interpreter, Mrs. Tahiti told Ms. Clemson that she had a question about advice she had received the previous year. "I was told to speak to Rachel in English more often at home. That's very hard for me because I am not as comfortable using English as in Tagalog, my own language. Should I stop using Tagalog? How can I best help my daughter develop strong communication skills?"

WHAT IS CULTURAL COMPETENCY?

The ability to recognize and attend to the challenges of cultural diversity is commonly referred to as *cultural competence* or *cultural competency*. These terms are used interchangeably to describe knowledge, skills, and practices necessary for optimum communication and interaction across cultures. Lynch and Hanson identified five aspects of cultural competence:

1) An awareness of one's own cultural limitations; 2) openness, appreciation, and respect for cultural differences; 3) a view of intercultural interactions as learning opportunities; 4) the ability to use cultural resources in interventions; and 5) an acknowledgment of the integrity and value of all cultures. (1992, p. 356)

The term *cultural competency,* however, is not always positively received in that it de-emphasizes the fact that such competency is a process to be learned rather than a fixed set of skills to be mastered. The authors use it in this book to refer to practitioners' ability to respond respectfully, reciprocally, and responsively to children and families in ways that acknowledge the richness and the limitations of families' and practitioners' sociocultural contexts (Barrera & Kramer, 1997).

HOW IS CULTURAL COMPETENCY BEING ADDRESSED IN EARLY CHILDHOOD SPECIAL EDUCATION?

Early childhood special education's approach to cultural competency has much to offer and has been effective in many ways. In large part, it reflects the approach of other disciplines, such as family therapy (McGoldrick, 1998). This approach offers significant insights and supports the development of what Nakkula and Ravitch termed *forestructure:* "what one has already learned and internalized in life, and the manner in which the learning has been organized in preparation for the future assimilation of anything new" (1998, p. 5).

In working with practitioners, however, the authors have found that two views of cultural competency can be problematic. The first perceives factual information as the key aspect of cultural competency. This understanding seems to stem from the format of much of the literature on cultural competency. For example, various texts have individual chapters dedicated to particular cultures (e.g., Lynch & Hanson, 1997; McGoldrick, 1998). This information is invaluable in developing necessary forestructures. Yet, when it is viewed as the key aspect of cultural competency, it can inhibit that competency. Yankelovich noted that when left unexamined, a view that considers knowledge the most important component of cultural competency subtly privileges the ENC perspective that "knowledge and understanding of issues [are gained] primarily through factual information" (1999, p. 24). Such a view places persons at risk for "interpose[ing] a vast social distance" between themselves and those with whom they interact (1999, p. 151). In turn, this distance can limit the ability to establish respectful relationships with families, especially when they have different cultural perspectives on gaining knowledge and understanding. It is possible to learn all about others and not really know them in all their complexity and individuality.

Objective knowledge about cultural groups can only approximate the more subjective and dynamic knowledge gained from interacting with individual members of those cultures. In addition, conveying the message, however implicitly, that practitioners need to learn cultural parameters for all of the families with whom they interact is overwhelming, especially given the increasingly multifaceted nature of cultural identity (Seelye & Wasilewski, 1996). In addition to freezing what is naturally a dynamic reality, static knowledge can lead to remedial or stereotypical responses to diversity. Even armed with such knowledge, practitioners often remain unable to respond to the question "What do we do now, in this specific and concrete situation with this particular family/child?"

A second view that can be problematic is one that clusters cultural characteristics into either-or choices. Such polarization is supported by literature on cultural diversity that contrasts diverse cultural characteristics in two-column tables. Inadvertently and unintentionally, these privilege a polarized either-or perspective. The implicit message is that, for example, a culture values individualism *or* it values collectivism. The idea of a culture that values both or values something else entirely is rarely communicated.

Two aspects of polarization are troublesome for developing cultural competency. The first is the exclusivity implicit in either-or dichotomies— that is, moving toward one pole is viewed as distancing from the other pole. For instance, the closer one is to being "right" (however defined), the more distant one is from being "wrong." This aspect of dichotomies is detailed in Chapter 6.

The second problematic aspect is that polarized listings seem to present two perspectives but actually describe behavior only from a single perspective. Behaviors are typically polarized from the perspective of the observing culture. For example, a culture may value and exhibit a behavior that is considered "dependent" if it does not fit into ENC's concept of "independent" (e.g., not making decisions without consulting with an elder). Yet from the perspective of the observed culture, such behavior might be more accurately described as "interdependent" or "socially conscious." See Chapter 5 for additional discussion of this understanding of diversity.

The tendency toward exclusive polarization reflects ENC as a whole (e.g., Stewart & Bennett, 1991). Polarization's exclusivity is sometimes so strong that the term *exclusive polarization* seems redundant. Apparently, human beings are genetically wired to perceive reality in binary pairs (Newberg, D'Aquili, & Rause, 2001). The tendency to perceive these pairs as exclusive opposites, however, is strongly influenced by culture (Stewart & Bennett, 1991). Some Asian cultures, for example, tend to perceive pairs as complementary aspects of a single paradoxical reality, as reflected in the familiar symbol for yin and yang (see Figure 5).

The ability to achieve cultural competency can be limited by the tendencies to rely on objective knowledge and to polarize perspectives. Relying too strongly on objective knowledge distances one from the rich complexity of cultures and, consequently, reduces one's ability to understand

Figure 5. Yin and yang symbol.

and respect families as both individually unique and culturally similar. Exclusive polarization obscures the complementary nature of diverse behaviors and the rich resources that they can generate both singly and jointly.

HOW DOES SKILLED DIALOGUE ADDRESS CULTURAL COMPETENCY?

Skilled Dialogue is designed to complement current approaches to cultural competency while counterbalancing the tendencies to privilege objective knowledge and polarize dichotomies. Skilled Dialogue is rooted in the following concepts, which are highlighted as Guiding Beliefs identified at the beginning of Chapters 1 and 2:

• Cultural diversity is a dynamic and relational reality that exists *between* persons rather than within any single person. For this reason, cultural diversity is challenging not so much in different behaviors as in the diverse meanings attributed to those behaviors.

• Cultural diversity cannot be adequately addressed if culture itself is not first understood.

These beliefs support the understanding that cultural diversity is primarily based in relationship and communication issues (i.e., related to the challenges of dialogues across particular kinds of differences) rather than in cognitive issues (i.e., fueled by knowledge or lack of it). This understanding leads to a third core belief, which is stated in this chapter's Guiding Belief and forms the foundation for Skilled Dialogue:

• Cultural competency is a *process* that is best determined by one's ability to craft respectful, reciprocal, and responsive relationships with others rather than by the extent of the information that we have regarding particular culture(s).

Skilled Dialogue addresses cultural competency from a grounded relational worldview that acknowledges and honors both individual uniqueness and cultural similarity. Bush and Folger identified the most important value of this worldview as "transformation, the achievement of human conduct that integrates the strength of self and compassion toward others" (1994, p. 242).

Skilled Dialogue does not negate the value of specific knowledge; however, it emphasizes the need to anchor such knowledge in concrete and particular circumstances and relationships with individual children and families. When so anchored, information can offer invaluable support to the development of respectful, reciprocal, and responsive interactions that integrate "contradictory" perspectives to create nonexclusive options. Such options, in turn, honor and mine the richness of diversity. Section II of this book explores the process of Skilled Dialogue in more detail, focusing particularly on its two component skills: Anchored Understanding of Diversity and 3rd Space.

From Difficult Dialogues to Skilled Dialogues

Section II further describes the Skilled Dialogue process that was introduced in Chapter 3. As shown in Figure 6, Chapter 4 examines three major aspects of Skilled Dialogue: its foundational beliefs, characteristic qualities, and component skills. The two component skills are key to developing and sustaining the qualities associated with Skilled Dialogue; therefore, a chapter is dedicated to each. Chapter 5 details Anchored Understanding of Diversity, and Chapter 6 explains 3rd Space. The goal of Section II is to familiarize the reader with Skilled Dialogue prior to presenting its specific applications in Section III.

Figure 6

From Difficult Dialogues to Skilled Dialogues

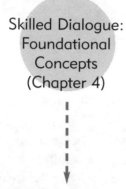

Skilled Dialogue:
Foundational
Concepts
(Chapter 4)

Anchored
Understanding
of Diversity:
The First Skill
(Chapter 5)

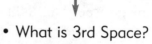

3rd Space:
The Second Skill
(Chapter 6)

- What is Skilled Dialogue?
- What beliefs lay the foundation for Skilled Dialogue?
- What three qualities characterize Skilled Dialogue?
- What are the two component skills of Skilled Dialogue?

- What is Anchored Understanding of Diversity?
- How does one acquire Anchored Understanding of Diversity?
- What are some examples of Anchored Understanding of Diversity in early childhood environments?

- What is 3rd Space?
- What are some examples of 3rd Space in early childhood environments?
- How can 3rd Space options be created?

Skilled Dialogue

FOUNDATIONAL CONCEPTS

In the dialogic process differences are deeply honored. Seemingly paradoxical viewpoints are reconciled as coherence is achieved. Eventually solutions arise that are inclusive of all points of view. The final decision is always greater than the sum of the individual perspectives. (Shelton, 1999, p. 151)

Skilled Dialogue is an approach developed in response to the need to meet the challenges posed by cultural diversity. Yankelovich defined *dialogue* as "the process of successful relationship building" (1999, p. 15). Shelton elaborated that listening is the heart of dialogue. Yet, it is not just any kind of listening. It is a listening in which "one's position is temporarily suspended rather than defended" (1999, p. 151). Skilled Dialogue applies this understanding of dialogue to interactions across diverse cultural and linguistic parameters. In response to these challenges, Skilled Dialogue focuses on compassionately and creatively crafting respectful, reciprocal, and responsive relationships across diverse cultural parameters. Its specific nature is best described by a discussion of its foundational beliefs, characteristic qualities, and component skills.

WHAT BELIEFS LAY THE FOUNDATION FOR SKILLED DIALOGUE?

Three beliefs, which have already been discussed in this book, lay the foundation for Skilled Dialogue. Chapter 1 notes that diversity is a relational reality that exists between rather than within persons. The process of Skilled Dialogue understands diversity as a reality that emerges only as

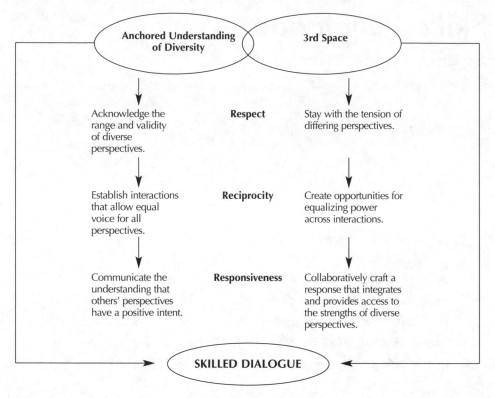

Figure 7.   Characteristic qualities and component skills of Skilled Dialogue.

persons or communities are compared one to the other, not as a characteristic of individuals or communities. Chapter 2 explains that culture must be understood before cultural diversity can be addressed competently. An understanding of culture as a dynamic that shapes the behaviors and beliefs of all persons is essential to truly understanding elements that are considered "diverse." The statement "I have no culture"—uttered by numerous practitioners at various workshops conducted by the authors—points to the pitfalls of not understanding culture. These two beliefs frame the third one, which is introduced in Chapter 3: The degree of cultural competency achieved is based more on the ability to craft respectful, reciprocal, and responsive relationships than on the extent of information possessed about particular cultures. The belief that one must have information about others before one can be culturally competent is itself a cultural artifact. To adhere to it is to privilege some cultures over others and, in so doing, to undermine the very competency that is sought.

Figure 7 illustrates the Skilled Dialogue process, showing its three characteristic qualities, which are discussed more fully in the following section, and its two component skills, which are introduced at the end of the chapter. These two skills are further detailed in Chapters 5 and 6.

WHAT THREE QUALITIES CHARACTERIZE SKILLED DIALOGUE?

In interactions across diverse cultural parameters, three qualities are key to determining whether interactions can be described as skilled or un-skilled: respect, reciprocity, and responsiveness.

Figure 7 shows that each quality is expressed in a slightly different fashion, depending on which skill it supports, Anchored Understanding of Diversity or 3rd Space. While Chapters 5 and 6 address the distinctions in the expression of these qualities across skills, this section discusses the three qualities themselves. The following vignette provides a starting point for the exploration of respect, reciprocity, and responsiveness:

> *Betsy, an early childhood interventionist, poses the following question: "How can I be culturally responsive when I go into the homes of families from cultures that make sharp distinctions between parents and 'experts'? Take Karen, for example. She's a single mother from Puerto Rico whom I visit weekly. When I ask her to tell me what she'd like for her child Maya or when I ask her to work with Maya, she says that I am the expert and that I should tell her what needs to be done. Sometimes she'll even leave me alone with Maya. I know that Karen cares about Maya and is just expressing her respect for me, but how can I get Karen more involved in Maya's activities while I am visiting?"*

Respect

> *Making oneself vulnerable is an act of trust and respect, as is receiving and honoring the vulnerability of another. Such an offering of oneself aligns with Martin Buber's idea that a person who says "You" does not "have" something, but [rather] "stands in relation [to someone]." Dreams, when "offered," do not become the possession of the other. They represent the trust and respect that forges a connection. (Lawrence-Lightfoot, 1999, p. 93)*

Respect is a hallmark of Skilled Dialogue. Used in this context, *respect* refers to an acknowledgment and acceptance of the boundaries that exist between persons. Boundaries are markers that simultaneously connect and distinguish one from others. They identify the parameters of the spaces that one chooses to occupy. Physical boundaries, for example, delineate the physical space around a person. When these boundaries are crossed without permission, that person feels disturbed or even violated. When boundaries are acknowledged and crossed with permission, trust and connection are supported. Similarly, emotional boundaries identify when words and actions convey insult or praise; they define parameters of relatedness. Cognitive boundaries outline what one believes to be true; when these are crossed, misunderstanding, confusion, or anger may result. When these boundaries are validated, one tends to feel a greater sense of confidence and competence. Spiritual boundaries relate to one's connection with the larger aspects of the universe (e.g., God, Spirit, Energy, Self). When these are crossed, one may feel lost or somehow less well defined. In all of these aspects, boundaries reflect basic assumptions about oneself, others, and the surrounding world. These assumptions are the core of the meanings that individuals attach to their actions and words (e.g., Janoff-Bulman, 1992). Both boundaries and their underlying assumptions are shaped and supported by the cultural contexts in which persons are raised and later choose to live.

Acknowledgment and acceptance of boundaries different from one's own becomes problematic when that diversity challenges basic assumptions about what should be (e.g., someone stands "too close" as they speak to us). At times, ENC seems to convey the idea that once distinctions or differences are identified, connections may be unsustainable (Althen, 1988; Stewart & Bennett, 1991). This idea reflects a lack of recognition that it is the meanings attached to distinctions, not the distinctions themselves, that divide or connect. The Rio Grande River may be thought of as dividing two countries, Mexico and the United States. Yet, the first author grew up alongside this river and learned to recognize how it also connects these two countries. For people on both sides of the border, the river is a common source of water and recreation; everyone talks of "our" river and "our" bridge. In fact, the Rio Grande, like all boundaries, both joins and distinguishes. Being aware of and acknowledging the boundary that it sets distinguishes one country from the other and simultaneously provides a common point of contact.

Regarding the vignette about Betsy and Karen, how can respect for diverse boundaries be communicated in such situations? Respectful communication first requires accepting that parents like Karen, who perceive practitioners as the "experts," have a right to their perception of reality, even when that perception differs from what practitioners might prefer. Practitioners need to recognize that parents' truths, or boundaries, stand independent of their own. That is, parents' boundaries neither define nor depend on practitioners' boundaries. Karen's perception of Betsy's role as the expert in charge, for example, does not actually define Betsy's role in an absolute sense. Similarly, Betsy's perception of Karen as "passive recipient" does not actually define Karen; it only describes Betsy's perception of her. Neither Betsy's nor Karen's truths define the whole of reality; there are many more aspects to who they each are and to the roles they play in relation to Maya.

Respecting parents like Karen, who leave the practitioner alone with their child, requires 1) acknowledging the boundaries that they set, which may cast practitioners in the "expert" role, and 2) accepting that they have the same right to those boundaries as practitioners have to theirs. This acknowledgment and acceptance establishes the foundation for Skilled Dialogue. It does not, however, mean that practitioners or families have to accept the status quo and abandon seeking further change. It only means that there is a willingness to acknowledge differing perceptions and boundaries as well as to suspend the need to make them match. Chapters 5 and 6 give specific strategies for expressing respect in relation to each of Skilled Dialogue's two component skills.

Reciprocity

Great artists are not first problem solvers; they are first creators, who solve problems secondarily as a necessary and inevitable result of their commitment to producing a remarkable artistic result. (Childs, 1998, p. 34)

Reciprocity builds on respect. It seeks to balance power between persons in dialogue. At its core is the recognition that each person in an interaction is equally capable. To understand reciprocity in this sense is to distinguish the more common understanding of power as expertise or authority from the less common understanding of power as capacity or capability. The Spanish word *poder* reflects this latter understanding. It can be used both as a noun meaning "power" and as a verb meaning "to be able," as in "Yo puedo" (i.e., "I can").

Reciprocity does not, however, require denying that one person has more expertise, knowledge, or authority than another in particular areas (e.g., a social worker who has the authority to remove children from their home). Reciprocity requires acknowledging and trusting that every person involved has experience and perceptions of equal value. Reciprocal interactions provide equal opportunity to contribute and to make choices. The recognition that one point of view should not dominate or exclude diverse points of view, as well as the resulting support of open or free choice over forced either-or choice, are important aspects of reciprocal interactions.

A reciprocal perspective changes how one thinks when encountering differences. Without a reciprocal perspective, one may think, "Oh, here's someone who doesn't have what I have or what I believe they need (and is somehow deficient as a result)." The parenthetical phrase is unspoken yet clear. From a reciprocal perspective, however, one is more likely to think, "Oh, here's someone who may benefit from what I have to offer and from whom I can benefit (because he or she has something new or different that can add to or extend my resources)." The parenthetical phrase in this statement is always clear regardless of whether it is verbalized.

Dunst, Trivette, and Deal noted, "Help is more likely to be favorably received if it can be reciprocated and the possibility of 'repaying' the help giver is sanctioned and approved but not expected" (1988, p. 95). When interactions are reciprocal and differences are acknowledged as potential contributions, no sense of debt is incurred by the persons involved. When one enters interactions only to give—whether knowledge, support, direction, or something else—he or she cannot acknowledge what others have to contribute. This lack of reciprocity inhibits not only what might be received but also the full potential of what is given. In reciprocal relationships, everyone has something to offer. Reciprocity enriches not only the persons involved, but also the outcome of their interactions.

Returning once more to Betsy, who wants more involvement on Karen's part, how might reciprocity be established? Nonjudgmental acknowledgment that diverse perspectives are present is critical. A first step is suspending the need to impose one experience of reality on another (i.e., to push Karen to become engaged in the ways that Betsy values or, conversely, to acquiesce and offer no options for change). A second step is to acknowledge Karen's capacity to contribute in this particular situation and to explore how she is currently participating (e.g., trusting Betsy's expertise, allowing time and space for Betsy's agenda, listening). This acknowledgment might lead to recognizing Karen's participation in other similar interactions with her child and in other environments. Eventually, to establish reciprocity, Betsy must understand that Karen is already equally, if not more, involved with Maya in a variety of ways. This understanding then provides a context for responding to the two women's differing perceptions as well as to the specific needs of Karen and Maya.

Specific strategies for establishing reciprocity in relation to each of Skilled Dialogue's two skills are presented in Chapters 5 and 6. These strategies are further addressed though vignettes in Section III.

Responsiveness

So I no longer have theories about people. I don't diagnose them or decide what their problem is. I simply meet with them and listen. As we sit together, I don't even have an agenda, but I know that something will emerge from our conversation over time that is a part of a larger coherent pattern that neither of us can fully see at the moment. So I sit with them and wait. (Remen, 2000, p. 90)

If respect means recognizing different boundaries and reciprocity means acknowledging that every person has something of value to contribute, then responsiveness means taking the next step. Being responsive "requires a deep respect for [others'] uniqueness, an openness to allowing them to uncover who they are rather than shaping them into who we want or need them to be" (Remen, 2000, p. 281).

First, responsiveness is about turning all assumptions into lightly held hypotheses (e.g., saying "I wonder if" and "Maybe" instead of "I know" and "I'm sure"). To be responsive is to allow oneself to entertain a mystery, to ask, "Who is this other person? I see this or that behavior, and I experience it in a certain way, but who is this person, really?" Forgetting mystery makes it all too easy to place children in the "boxes" of their diagnoses and families in the circles of one's own categories and labels. They are reduced to a singular identity (e.g., the child with attention-deficit/hyperactivity disorder, the resistant mother), and one becomes engaged only with his or her ideas about them. Responsiveness, conversely, requires releasing preconceptions and listening to children and families "with focused attention, patience and curiosity" (Freedman & Combs, 1996, p. 44). Only then can one become responsive to individual families—that is, become attuned to their reality rather than to just one's own ideas about that reality.

In this sense, responsiveness means being willing to give up certainty, to not know exactly what to do or what to say. Remen stated, "Knowing where we are going encourages us to stop seeing and hearing and allows us to fall asleep. . . . [Such knowing allows] a part of [us] to rush ahead to [our destination] the moment [we] see it" (2000, p. 289). Unfortunately, this is an apt description of what often happens when practitioners present families with their diagnostic findings and intervention recommendations. Once a child is assessed, or sometimes even before, it is all too easy to press on to conclusions about what needs to be done.

Responding and responsiveness are not necessarily the same. Responsiveness requires leaving room for the unexpected and the unpredictable. Examples include thoughts such as

- "Maybe this child will be different from all others; maybe he or she *will* be able to do X."

- "Maybe this family will be much more resourceful than I can foresee; maybe they will able to support their child in ways that I can only imagine."

- "Perhaps I have missed truly understanding a particular aspect of this family's concerns and am rushing ahead in a direction unrelated to those concerns."

Being responsive is particularly important in culturally diverse situations because their very diversity challenges us to recognize that people are always more than (and perhaps even radically different from) others' ideas about who they are. Although preconceived ideas and judgments can never be totally eliminated, through mindful attention one can refuse to reduce others' reality to one's limited dimensions. For example, Betsy can refuse to place Karen in a box labeled "inattentive or uninvolved mother." She can listen to Karen "with focused attention, patience and curiosity" (Freedman & Combs, 1996, p. 44) while reminding herself that she knows little of Karen's true capacities. Most important, Betsy can continue to act as if cooperation and collaboration are eminent.

Although they do not use the term *Skilled Dialogue*, Freedman and Combs described its characteristic quality of responsiveness in a way that is particularly relevant to early childhood practitioners:

> *Instead of seeing ourselves as mechanics . . . working to fix a broken machine . . . we experience ourselves as interested people . . . skilled at asking questions to bring forth the knowledge and experience . . . carried in the stories of the people we work with . . . This means turning our backs on "expert" filters:* . . . not comparing the selves they portray in their stories to [what we believe to be] normative standards. *(1996, p. 18, emphasis added)*

Returning once more to Betsy and Karen, in what other ways might Betsy be responsive Karen? Of course, the answer lies in the situation's specifics, so only possibilities can be listed. Betsy might be responsive to Karen through one or more of the following:

- Avoid "freezing" her idea of Karen as a passive parent, unwilling or unable to change.

- Understand that some cultures believe that necessary knowledge is interpersonally distributed; that is, that it need not be personally possessed because it can be obtained though social connections (Moll & Greenberg, 1990). Persons from these cultures consequently feel no need to "duplicate" someone else's expertise and that doing so would be disrespectful.

- Accept that Karen may desperately need respite time and lessened demands for her involvement until Betsy can identify means of helping Karen find that time in ways that support working with Maya during Betsy's sessions.

- Respect Karen's perception of Betsy as an "expert" and explore what this means: Does Karen truly believe that she has nothing to offer (i.e., that only experts' opinions matter)? Or is it that she believes what she has to offer would not be accepted or would not be appropriate? What specific responsibilities is she assigning to Betsy with this perception?

What have Karen's experiences with other 'experts' been like? In what areas does she feel confident of her expertise? Is her withdrawal an expression of fear over doing the "wrong" thing and harming her child? Is Betsy somehow unconsciously communicating her own need to be the expert?

- Invite Karen to share what she has to offer in this situation and structure sessions so that Karen can contribute of her knowledge (e.g., give instructions on cooking Maya's favorite food, which can be used in planned activities to elicit specific language).

- Include in the sessions materials and routines that are familiar to Karen rather than use unfamiliar ones.

These possibilities and other similar ones may not necessarily solve the problem. They will, however, gradually redefine it and change the tenor of interactions between Betsy and Karen, thereby increasing the possibility of arriving at more satisfactory and competent interactions between them. Table 3 compares behaviors that only communicate feeling responsible with behaviors that communicate responsiveness. Following

Table 3. Behaviors that communicate feeling responsible compared with behaviors that communicate responsiveness

When I confuse being responsible FOR others without being responsive to them	When I am responsible for myself and responsive TO others
I tend to	*I tend to*
rescue	support while maintaining boundaries
control	be open minded
carry others' feelings	be sensitive and self-aware
tune others out	listen
feel tired	stay relaxed
feel anxious	feel free
be fearful	be trusting
feel liable, defended, or defenseless	be centered, undefended
I focus on	*I focus on*
the solution	the dialogue
answers	choices
the individual as I judge him or her to be	the individual as a unique person
right and wrong	multiple perspectives
details, performance	the process
I believe in	*I believe in*
controlling	trusting the process
the absolute correctness of my individual perspective	the concept that reality is always bigger than my individual perspective
either-or choices	paradoxes

From McGinn, L.R. (1999). *Dancing in the storm: Hope in the midst of chaos* (pp. 115–116). Grand Rapids, MI: Fleming H. Revell (a division of Baker Book House Company); adapted by permission.

an overview of Skilled Dialogue's component skills in this chapter and more extensive discussions in Chapters 5 and 6, Section III gives further examples and strategies for promoting respectful, reciprocal, and responsive interactions.

WHAT ARE THE TWO COMPONENT SKILLS OF SKILLED DIALOGUE?

As mentioned previously, the qualities of respect, responsiveness, and reciprocity are promoted and sustained through two specific skills: Anchored Understanding of Diversity and 3rd Space. These skills address two needs common to interactions across diverse cultural parameters:

1. The need to place general cultural knowledge into concrete and compassionate contexts

2. The need to focus on the complementary nature of differences and develop creative and inclusive choices that honor the persons exhibiting those differences

Anchored Understanding of Diversity and 3rd Space reflect the importance of authentic relationships rooted in compassionate knowledge and creative choices. These two skills emerged as key as the authors observed, discussed, and studied competent interactions across a range of cultural backgrounds and experiences (Barrera & Kramer, 1997).

Anchored Understanding of Diversity

These observed interactions made clear the contrast between simply knowing about something or someone (i.e., having information) and knowing on a compassionate, deeper, and more experiential level (i.e., Anchored Understanding). Deeper knowing occurs when persons from diverse backgrounds interact on a personal, face-to-face basis and learn each others' stories. Talking generally about American Indians, for example, is entirely different from having that same discussion over time with individual American Indians. In such extended face-to-face interactions, previously held knowledge becomes personal. Its boundaries are tested and stretched. The following statements by practitioners at a workshop reflect how previously held categories and assumptions are both challenged and deepened: "I thought that religion was only a one-day-a-week thing for whites" and "Oh, so that's what it means that Navajos have differing perceptions of time." As Clandinin and Connelly stated, "When [persons] are known intimately as people, not merely as categorical representatives, categories tend to fragment" (2000, p. 141). Categories can only serve a useful purpose when they are held loosely, like puzzle pieces withheld from a single, absolute picture.

Experiential knowing helps us better navigate the tension between categories and individuality. On the one hand, identities are not crafted single-handedly by individuals or even by individual families. Identities are drawn from and embedded in the communities and cultures in which persons participate and within which they grew up. Methods of negotiating development as individuals and skill repertoires are significantly influenced in both process and content by the cultural templates into which persons are acculturated within their families. On the other hand, everyone is unique. No one person reflects a single culture 100% (see Figure 3 in Chapter 2).

This tension between recognizing individuals' participation in common cultural frameworks while acknowledging their unique individuality underlies Anchored Understanding of Diversity, the first skill of Skilled Dialogue. Chapter 5 continues this discussion.

3rd Space

The authors found that the second skill key to competent interactions was people's ability to address the tension generated by contradictions in behaviors and perceptions. Skilled Dialogue's second skill—3rd Space— addresses this tension.

Stewart and Bennett (1991) noted a tendency within ENC to polarize reality into exclusive either-or dichotomies with one positive pole and one negative pole. They also identified a tendency to judge disagreement as the negative pole on an agree-disagree dichotomy. Given these tendencies, it is easy to see why differences can generate substantial discomfort. At workshops conducted by the authors, practitioners and family members commonly express significant discomfort in the presence dichotomous cultural perspectives, and they act to dissolve or remove that discomfort. Comments such as "We'll just agree to disagree," "Let's find a compromise," and "Why can't we all be alike?" are indicative of this discomfort.

Such discomfort brings to the fore the need to hold diverse perspectives in one's mind without excluding one in order to accept the other; 3rd Space addresses this need. The first author developed the term *3rd Space* to describe the larger perspectives that can simultaneously encompass two or more apparently dichotomous perspectives and mine their strengths and resources.[4] See Chapter 6 for more detailed discussion of 3rd Space.

---

[4]Other authors have used the term *third space* in rare cases. Its meaning is distinct in relation to Skilled Dialogue, especially in regard to its emphasis on paradox and integration.

Anchored Understanding of Diversity

THE FIRST SKILL

When we do not agree, perhaps it is because none of us see far enough. People living on opposite sides of a mountain rarely see the land the same way until they meet at the top. (Navajo saying quoted in Shem & Surrey, 1998, p. 11)

Anchored Understanding of Diversity refers to an understanding of differences that is "anchored" both experientially and cognitively. The experiential anchor is the knowing that stems from personal interactions and hands-on experiences. The cognitive anchor is the belief that others' behaviors make as much sense as one's own. This latter belief anchors the understanding of differences as just that—differences—and allows one to suspend or release judgment. Wilson gave an excellent example of these two anchors in practice, describing an encounter that differed significantly from the expected (see Appendix B). His conclusion is particularly relevant to the current discussion of Anchored Understanding:

And as I think about how easy it is, even for those of intelligence and heart, to preconceive and presuppose based on the apparent rather than the true, I want to cry out to all of us—but mostly to myself—to slow down; to look more closely and listen more carefully. For those of us in search of real possibilities in our encounters, we'll surely find them when we ditch our assumptions and listen with our hearts. (2001, p. 64)

"Knowing about" diversity (i.e., unanchored understanding) is important but not sufficient for cultural competency, no matter how detailed or thorough the information. "Knowing about" is based on external information, or public knowledge, to which anyone can gain access. One can, for example, know much about skiing without ever having set foot on snow. From books, videotapes, interviews, and other materials, one can garner this information in a fairly comprehensive fashion. Certainly this type of knowing makes significant contributions to cultural competency. One typically learns about diverse cultures using strategies similar to those just cited. Simply knowing about something, however, tends to leave one detached, standing outside (Yankelovich, 1999), with a relatively general and perhaps even stereotypical picture.

Anchored Understanding of Diversity, conversely, is intentionally particular and reciprocal. It is designed to generate knowledge that "arises not from standing back in order to look at, but by active and intentional engagement in lived experience" (Groome, 1980, p. 141). Such knowledge is personal and idiosyncratic. It accounts for characteristics and experiences that are specific to individuals rather than remain at the level of general descriptions of whole populations.

Anchored Understanding of Diversity is akin to Lave and Wenger's concept *situated learning:* "In contrast to learning as internalization, learning as increasing participation in communities of practice concerns the whole person acting in the world" (1999, p. 49). Similarly, Anchored Understanding of Diversity emphasizes the centrality of direct experiential knowing—knowing that is anchored in shared or relational experiences with individual children and families (e.g., having skied as compared with just knowing about skiing). Such knowing is not public information; it can be obtained only through personal and particular relationships. This relational aspect of knowing, with all its particularity and subjectivity, keeps in check generalizations that stem from knowing about something in a more abstract fashion.

Remen (2000) illustrated in a striking manner the distinction between experientially anchored knowing and unanchored knowing. For more than 2 years, a young physician provided medical care for an older Navajo woman. During this time, the woman's daughter did all of the talking during the clinic visits. The physician had treated the elderly woman for a variety of diseases:

> She gave antibiotics for an infection of the urine, managed the old woman's diabetes and brought her blood sugar into the normal range, digitalized her and reversed her incipient heart failure, revised her diet in keeping with the limitations of a liver that was barely functioning. She ordered many lab tests. She also mobilized social services to help the daughter in caring for her mother and enabled her to find financial support from a government grant. (p. 68)

After the Navajo woman died at the age of 96, the physician received a call from a researcher who was writing a book about American Indian medicine traditions. When he contacted the family of a great medicine woman, the researcher was told that this physician had given their mother medical attention on many occasions and would be able to provide the needed answers because "she knew their mother well" (p. 69). Remen recounted the physician's reflections on this experience many years later:

> *"I think of her sitting there all those months, watching me shuffling my papers and tracking my lab data and knowing what she knew. I wonder what was going through her mind. I had been so busy with my numbers and my tests. What I would give for even one hour with her now, to ask her any of my unanswered questions, to have her perspective on suffering or loss or illness or death. Or simply to ask for her blessing." (2000, p. 69)*

This story reveals that the truth of someone's reality, no matter how similar to or diverse from one's own, lies in the delicate balance between the particular and the general. Although this story does not reference an early childhood special education situation, its application to such a scenario is not a difficult leap. Practitioners are both recipients and generators of a large volume of information *about* the young children and families with whom they work. Similarly to the physician in Remen's (2000) story, practitioners can name the particular type of delay or syndrome that a child exhibits, describe family dynamics and developmental concerns, and possibly even describe the values associated with the family's culture. Yet, when asked to describe a particular child or family, would answers from practitioners and the family match? Could they talk about the family's hopes and dreams? Could they tell someone about a particular child without referencing developmental status or disabilities? Could they define what *success* or *family* means to that particular child and family? The ability to answer these questions reflects the degree to which Anchored Understanding of Diversity is present in relation to any family.

Remen's (2000) story also illustrates the need to anchor one's understanding of diversity cognitively. Believing that only his or her behaviors have a positive intent makes a person less curious about diverse behaviors and certainly less able to respond to them respectfully. How can he or she respect someone whose behavior is believed to have no positive intent (e.g., sitting quietly and asking no questions)? How can curiosity about that person's point of view even exist?

Anchored understanding of others does not require admiring their behaviors but, rather, believing that their behaviors make as much sense from their cultural or personal perspective as do behaviors valued in other cultures. Not doing so risks missing what they have to contribute. For example, a practitioner may not admire the behavior of a mother who sets no firm bedtime for her 4-year-old child. Yet, cognitively anchoring his or her understanding of that behavior requires the practitioner to ask why the mother's behavior makes sense to her. What is her intent? Why does she think that this particular option is more appropriate than the option the practitioner values (e.g., a consistent bedtime)? What does the mother believe would happen if she changed her behavior?

Facts about diversity can be learned relatively easily. Anchoring these facts in experiential contexts, however, is more difficult. Translating them in response to concrete situations is an even more complex process. One can read, for instance, about child-rearing practices common in Italian families and yet not be able to answer questions such as "How does the particular Italian family with whom I work incorporate into their daily lives the practices that I read about?" and "What do these practices look like in this particular Italian family, which has a high degree of acculturation into ENC?" Only an open mind and extended relationships with particular families can yield answers to those questions. Anchoring understanding can change the tone of one's interactions with parents and open the door to collaborative rather than polarized interactions.

Certain culturally sanctioned behaviors may be perceived as abusive or neglectful; in fact, sometimes they may be so. Cultures, like individuals, are not always fully healthy. What happens then? There are no easy or simple answers. Nevertheless, anchoring one's understanding of families' behaviors in these as in all situations entails understanding the positive intent underlying particular behaviors (e.g., to heal a child, to eliminate behaviors believed to be harmful) while also taking necessary action to protect children's well-being. Respect requires an honest communication of boundaries, and reciprocity requires believing that everyone can grow. Behaviors that are responsive only to adult family members and not to children are neither respectful nor competent. Behaviors that are responsive only to children and not to their families likewise diminish respect and competence. Being responsive to parents who, for example, feel compelled to follow practices that harm children simultaneously necessitates being responsive to the emotional and physical safety needs of those children. Although the scope of this book does not permit an extensive discussion of these situations, additional discussion is provided in Appendix A at the end of the book.

HOW DOES ONE ACQUIRE ANCHORED UNDERSTANDING OF DIVERSITY?

Initial attempts to understand diversity typically define differences by contrasting them with that which is familiar. For example, for many years, the first author's understanding of *nuclear family* was mostly defined by what it was not. She explained,

> *Being Hispanic, my experiences were rooted in extended family. I had "aunts" who were not biological kin; I knew my second and even fifth cousins; relatives routinely moved in and lived with us—and even had something to say about how we were raised! An answer to the question "Who are you?" could involve a one-to-two generation genealogy. I did, of course, know that others (e.g., Dick and Jane) lived differently in what were called "nuclear" families. I could even define the term: families limited only to parents and children. I understood that a nuclear family was different from us—that is, it was what we were not. Yet, I had little personal experience with nuclear families to anchor my under- standing. I could not truly say that I knew what it was like to live in a nuclear family. That anchored level of understanding came only as I established close friendships with others raised in such families or currently living within them. At that point, my understanding became much richer. I realized that nuclear families were rooted in an overall cultural perspective that addressed far more than just how many people lived in a house. Only then did my understanding become anchored; only then could I begin to understand nuclear families for what they are, not simply for what they are not.*

Developing anchored understanding takes time and a curious, albeit respectful, mind. It requires establishing ongoing relationships with per- sons from different cultures and then asking many questions. Although this can and should be done with the families with whom practitioners work, their efforts should not be limited to those families. Practitioners should always remain mindful of the imbalance of power that can exist in such "helping" relationships and its influence on overall interactions (see the "Challenges of Relationship" section in Chapter 1).

The authors developed two tools to support Anchored Understanding of Diversity: 1) the Guide to Identifying Cultural Data Related to Potential Culture Bumps and 2) Strategies for Anchoring Understanding of Diver- sity. The tools are explained in the following subsections.

Tool 1: The Guide to Identifying Cultural Data Related to Potential Culture Bumps

The Guide to Identifying Cultural Data Related to Potential Culture Bumps, hereafter called the Guide to Identifying Cultural Data, contains specific questions organized around the cultural areas and culture bumps discussed in Chapter 1 (see particularly Table 2). The questions within each area are further organized into common factors such as degree of acculturation and child's relative language proficiency. Both the questions and the factors were generated from systematic observation and analysis of common situations in early childhood environments. Figure 8 is a sample version of the Guide to Identifying Cultural Data; a photocopiable version of this form appears in Appendix C at the end of the book.

Examining detailed questions such as those shown in Figure 8 can promote respectful interactions by increasing practitioners' awareness of others' boundaries and by helping practitioners identify needed information and ameliorate or eliminate culture bumps. The ensuing discussions of the developmental/curricular areas provide examples and strategies for using this tool (see also Section III).

Communicative-Linguistic   The Guide to Identifying Cultural Data breaks down the communicative-linguistic developmental/curricular area into five factors based on certain cultural dimensions identified in Table 1 (Chapter 1). The first factor—the language(s) of the child's caregiving environment(s)—is practically self-explanatory. Language differences represent one of the more obvious aspect of diversity as well as one of its best-recognized challenges. The Guide for Identifying Cultural Data presents two questions associated with this factor that prompt surpassing the simplistic question "What language is spoken in the home?" and examining the complexity of bilingual and multilingual environments. Table 4 is a sample listing of various home language environments; more are possible. Depending on the adults living with and/or caring for children at home (e.g., grandparents, nannies), additional cultures and languages may be represented.

A Home Language Profile may be useful for documenting data related to this issue. The one provided in Appendix C was adapted by Barrera (1993) and field-tested in several Head Start programs in an urban area in the U.S. Northeast. However home language data is documented, it is important to recognize that the common question "What language is spoken at home?" is woefully inadequate in a significant number of cases. In some homes, each parent may speak a different language with English as a third language. In others, two languages may be used simultaneously. Table 4 illustrates some of the many possible combinations.

The second factor—the child's relative language proficiency—focuses the child's specific language skills. It prompts going beyond the idea of language "dominance." This idea commonly carries the unrealistic assumption that once dominance is determined, only the dominant language needs to be addressed. In reality, often no language is clearly dominant. Typically, one language may predominate for discussions of certain things (e.g., home activities) and another for discussions of other things (e.g.,

Guide to Identifying Cultural Data Related to Potential Culture Bumps

Child's name: _____ Date: _____ Completed by: _____

Note: The questions in the second column tend to arise frequently. There may be others that are not identified on this form. Feel free to add any other questions that need to be answered. Use this guide prior to completing the Cultural Data Table.

Developmental/curricular area	Questions to answer
Communicative-Linguistic	
Language(s) of the child's primary caregiving environment(s)	1. Which language(s) is spoken in the child's primary caregiving environment(s)? 2. Which caregivers speak which language(s) with the child?
Child's relative language proficiency (degree of proficiency in English and other language[s] used)	1. How proficient is the child in understanding and using the language(s) other than English for communicating? 2. How proficient is the child in understanding and using English for communicating? 3. Would the child be considered monolingual? Partial bilingual (speaks and understands one language, only understands another)? Bilingual, dominant in one language (speaks and understands both languages but is significantly more proficient in one)? "Balanced" bilingual (similar levels of proficiency in both languages—may not be strong in either, or may be equally strong in both)?
Patterns of language usage in the child's primary caregiving environment(s)	1. With what situations and topics does each language tend to be associated? 2. Which varieties of each language are spoken (e.g., if English is spoken, in which ways is it similar to or different from what is considered the "standard" variety of English)? 3. If two or more languages are used, what seems to govern which language is used when?
Relative value placed on verbal and nonverbal communication	1. To what degree is communication in the home verbal? To what degree is it nonverbal? 2. What is the relative value placed on nonverbal communication as compared with verbal communication? Is this true in all situations, or only in some?
Relative status associated with the languages other than English and with bilingualism	1. What is the social status accorded in the community to the language(s) other than English spoken in the child's home (e.g., is the accent associated with it considered a mark of distinction or of low education)? 2. What is the social status accorded in the community to persons who are bilingual? Is being bilingual considered a desirable goal?

(continued)

Figure 8. Sample version of the Guide to Identifying Cultural Data Related to Potential Culture Bumps.

59

Figure 8. *(continued)*

Personal-Social

Degree of acculturation into EuroAmerican Normative Culture (ENC)	1. How familiar is the child/family with ENC? 2. How much experience does the child/family have participating in this culture? 3. How skilled is the child/family at negotiating within this culture (e.g., accomplishing desired activities/goals)?
Degree of acculturation into U.S. early intervention/early childhood special education culture	1. How familiar is the child/family with early intervention/early childhood special education culture (e.g., rules and expectations)? 2. How much experience does the child/family have participating in this culture? 3. How skilled is the child/family at negotiating within this culture (e.g., accomplishing desired activities/goals)?
Sense of self (e.g., relative weight given to independence, dependence, and interdependence)	1. How does the family define autonomy? To what degree is it valued? 2. To what degree is cooperation and group interaction/support valued? 3. What are the characteristics of persons with high credibility in the family's culture? Which characteristics/behaviors seem to be most highly valued?
Perceptions of identity and competence	1. How do family members define themselves; (e.g., by ethnic, professional, or other labels; by personal attributes)? 2. Which characteristics denote competence?
Roles and rules associated with parenting and child rearing	1. How would family members describe "good" parenting? 2. What skills/attributes do they consider desirable in a "well-brought-up" child? 3. What roles do different family members play in child rearing? Who is responsible for what?
Knowledge and experience related to power and social positioning	1. What is the family's experience regarding social and personal power? In what situations, if any, would family members describe themselves as powerless or "at a disadvantage"? 2. Does the family belong to and identify with a group with "minority" status?
Values and beliefs associated with instrumental support (e.g., additional services) and emotional support (e.g., personal support)	1. How does the family obtain support? What sources are valued? 2. When does the family believe that it is acceptable to seek instrumental support? Emotional support?

Sensory-Cognitive

Funds of knowledge (type of knowledge that is valued)	1. Which areas of knowledge are valued and supported by the family? 2. About what are the family members very knowledgeable? 3. Are funds of knowledge primarily personal, communal, or institutionalized? 4. To what degree are funds of knowledge oral? To what degree are they written? 5. What role does the family's cultural identity (or identities) play in its funds of knowledge?
Preferred strategies for learning	1. What are the child's/family's preferred strategies for learning (e.g., modeling, questioning)? 2. To what degree are the strategies explicit and direct? To what degree are they implicit and indirect? 3. To what degree are the strategies oral? To what degree are they nonverbal? 4. How do different family members teach the child something that they consider important? 5. Which of Gardner's (1993) seven intelligences tends to be favored?
Preferred strategies for problem solving and decision making	1. What are the child's/family's preferred strategies for problem solving and decision making? Do these differ according to certain characteristics of the problem or situation? If so, how? 2. To what degree is problem solving or decision making independent? To what degree is problem solving or decision making a cooperative activity? If viewed as cooperative, who gets involved in the process? 3. To what degree are the strategies linear? To what degree are they circular or global? 4. To what degree is problem solving deductive? To what degree is it inductive?
Worldview (i.e., assumptions about how the world works and about what is right and what is wrong)	1. How does the family tend to explain events such as their child's developmental challenges? 2. What assumptions does the family hold about how the world works (e.g., mechanistic, organic-ecological)? 3. What views do family members express about cultural and other differences? Do they favor the view that there is only one "right" way, or do they accept that multiple realities can exist?

Table 4. Sample listing of non-ENC mixed home language environments

Type	Culture(s) represented in the home environment	Language(s) spoken by parents/caregivers	Languages spoken with the child
I	Diverse; not EuroAmerican Normative Culture (non-ENC)	Language other than English; no English	Language other than English; no English
II	Diverse; non-ENC; some ENC acculturation	Bilingual; English as well as other language	English only
III	Bicultural; non-ENC is dominant	Monolingual; parents speak English only; grandparents do not speak English	English only used by parents; grandparents mostly use a language other than English; child understands the other language but does not use it
IV	Multicultural; parents are from different non-ENCs; some ENC also represented	Limited English; each parent is fully fluent in his or her own language and understands some of the other's language	Multilingual; English is used as well as both of parents' languages
V	ENC dominant; some evidence of parents' non-ENC	Bilingual; both speak same language (other than English), mainly use English	Bilingual; both English and parents' other language are used

Source: Harding & Riley (1986).

world politics, conversations with in-laws). Children in bilingual and multilingual environments tend to alternate between languages depending on the content and context of situations and conversations (Harding & Riley, 1986). Children may have similar proficiency in two or more languages. They also may possess critical, albeit small, pockets of knowledge (e.g., food or kinship terms) in the language that would not meet criteria as the dominant language (Miller, 1984).

One way of documenting a child's relative language proficiency is through the use of a Relative Language Proficiency (RLP) Profile (see Appendix C). This profile was field-tested with young children (see Metz, 1991). Using elicited language samples as its primary data source, the RLP Profile identifies three aspects of children's language proficiency. The first is the level of receptive and expressive proficiency in a child's language(s) other than English. A second is the level of receptive and expressive proficiency in English. Finally, these two are compared to determine the relative level of proficiency (i.e., the degree of bilingualism or multilingualism).

The RLP Profile was designed in response to two needs. First was the need to separate receptive from expressive proficiency, as these can diverge widely in children from bilingual environments. Second was the need to distinguish between various levels of bilingualism. With the RLP Profile, a child can be determined to be at one of seven levels of bilingualism, from monolingual in one language with minimal exposure to

English to monolingual in English with minimal exposure to another language. Section III discusses its use and provides sample RLP Profiles (also see Metz, 1991, for further details).

The third factor in the communicative-linguistic area is patterns of language usage in the child's primary caregiving environment (i.e., who uses which language for which purpose in the home). Parents may, for example, use one language for discipline and another for teaching concepts. This factor extends those previously discussed by focusing on the contexts within which particular languages are used. This knowledge has important implications for both assessment and intervention/instruction, as it helps to identify what content is known in which language.

Differences related to the fourth factor—relative value placed on verbal and nonverbal communication—are often the source of significant culture bumps. ENC tends to value verbal skills and verbal communication compared with many other cultures (Bowers & Flinder, 1990; Philips, 1972). This value is reflected in assessment content (e.g., vocabulary carries more weight than social skills in many developmental assessment measures) as well as in intervention/instruction environments and expectations (e.g., "Tell me how you feel," "Ask for what you want").

The fifth factor in the communicative-linguistic area addresses the relative status of languages other than English and of the ability to speak those languages. Subtle and perhaps not-so-subtle messages about this status can limit families' trust in practitioners and services. When parents perceive (incorrectly or correctly) that their home language is not valued as much as English, they may feel reluctant to report how much it is used at home. They may also feel that they themselves are less valued. They can also inhibit children's use of language for much the same reasons. The first author made this observation during interactions with children from predominantly Spanish-speaking homes in English-only early childhood environments. When first meeting these children and speaking to them in Spanish, the children's initial response was often to giggle or look away. This response is especially true in communities where Spanish is not commonly spoken in public settings. One older sibling actually articulated this impression by saying that Spanish was not supposed to be spoken in school, even though that was neither the intent nor the reality of the situation. Children may not be aware of language status in an abstract manner, but they are very sensitive to implicit rules and expectations related to communication and language usage.

The range of communicative-linguistic cultural data that impinges on assessment and intervention/instruction is not exhausted by these factors or the questions associated with them. The factors and questions do, however, represent key aspects of such data.

Personal-Social   Questions within the personal-social area address factors pertinent to anchoring one's understanding of diverse boundaries. The first factor highlights families' and children's degree of acculturation to ENC. To what degree are they experienced with and knowledgeable about ENC's values, beliefs, behaviors, and language? To what degree are they skilled in navigating within that culture (e.g., making appointments, meeting time expectations, requesting assistance from practitioners)? Chapter 7 further discusses ways of determining degree of acculturation.

Similarly, the second factor in the personal-social area examines the degree to which families are familiar with and knowledgeable about the early intervention/early childhood special education subculture: its expectations, beliefs, values, and language (e.g., terms such as *developmentally appropriate, assessment*)? How skilled are they in negotiating within that culture (e.g., the referral process, expectations for turn taking in small groups)? When parents are not very skilled in early childhood special education culture, they may not know how to question procedures, for example. Or they may not understand why their child is determined to have inappropriate social skills.

The personal-social area also considers questions addressing several issues that underlie less obvious culture bumps. One is sense of self. Landrine (1995) and Markus and Kitayama (1991) referred to differences between ENC and other cultures in understanding self. Landrine advocated increased awareness of the "Western cultural definition of the self . . . as well as the radically different way in which the self is understood by many ethnic-cultural minorities" (p. 402). Markus and Kitayama noted that in Japanese, "the word for self, *jibun,* refers to one's share of the shared life space" (p. 228), in contrast with ENC's notion of self as a separate and independent entity.

A particularly evident expression of differences in sense of self is ENC's emphasis on independence as a measure of emotional development and its lack of focus on interdependence and communal decision making. This emphasis is implicitly reflected in valued developmental outcomes as well as in behavioral expectations for participation in early childhood environments. Asking questions such as "How does this family or child understand autonomy?" and "To what degree are cooperation and group support or interaction valued?" helps anchor one's understanding of differences in this area. Examples of these variations include not making decisions before consulting with family elders or feeling uncomfortable traveling alone to medical appointments.

Similar questions are associated with perceptions of identity and competence, a third personal-social factor. Developmentally appropriate curricula reflect certain perceptions of identity and competence that may not agree with those held by family members. Without Anchored Understanding of Diversity, early childhood special education practitioners may find themselves working at cross-purposes with families (e.g., advocating independent problem solving while parents discourage it at home). Gonzalez-Mena, Herzog, and Herzog (2000) discussed some examples of varying values and beliefs in this area.

Roles and rules associated with parenting and child rearing form another personal-social factor that must be examined, as they differ significantly across cultures. Gonzalez-Mena (1993) discussed some common areas of difference. For example, she contrasted approaches to autonomy and discussed attachment patterns. She contrasted patterns that promote lifelong family dependence with those that stress producing individuals who are "separate and unique [and] stand alone" (p. 48). In a similar discussion, she noted variations in patterns related to adult involvement in children's play. Some cultures believe that such involvement is essential; others see it as unnecessary and perhaps even inappropriate. Greenfield and Cocking (1994) and Trumbull, Rothstein-Fisch, Greenfield, and Quiroz (2001) also address the diverse roles and rules associated with parenting and child rearing.

The remaining two personal-social factors are more general. Chapter 1 discusses how knowledge and experience about power and social positioning can affect interactions. Because respect and reciprocity are defining characteristics of Skilled Dialogue, this factor is critical. It can be difficult if not impossible to establish respectful and reciprocal interactions if power and social positioning dynamics are not carefully examined. In some cultures, for instance, it is considered rude to question someone who is perceived to have more skill or power. Taking the agreement of parents from these cultures at face value would be counterproductive to establishing reciprocity. Darder (1991) and Klein (1998) addressed related issues.

The final factor identified in the personal-social area focuses on families' beliefs about and methods for gaining access to support. One type is instrumental support, which refers to external support such as additional services. Do family members believe that such support can only be obtained through informal kinship networks? Or do they believe that it can be obtained through impersonal channels? And do they have the requisite skills to do one or both? Emotional support refers to obtaining resources such as an empathic listener or time alone. This factor is particularly important given that a role of early intervention/early childhood special education services is to provide instrumental *and* emotional support. When such support comes in forms that are not understood or valued by families, however, it may not be perceived as support at all. See Dunst, Trivette, and Deal (1988) for more information on and instruments for obtaining data about support.

Sensory-Cognitive   The third area addressed in the Guide to Identifying Cultural Data is sensory-cognitive. Addressing beliefs, values, and behaviors related to reasoning and understanding, this area is broken down into four factors. First are the funds of knowledge that a family possesses and values (see also discussion in Chapter 1). Is knowing how to greet adult relatives properly in social settings a fund of knowledge that the family values and encourages for its children? Is using language to express oneself a valued fund of knowledge? Data on a family's fund of knowledge are critical for determining the degree of consonance between what is promoted in early intervention/early childhood special education environments and within individual families.

A range of sources discuss general information about the funds of knowledge valued in diverse cultures (e.g., Greenfield & Cocking, 1994; Lynch & Hanson, 1997). No two families incorporate these funds into their daily lives in exactly the same way. It is therefore important to validate and anchor this information by getting specific information from individual families.

Two other factors in the personal-social area address preferred strategies for learning and for problem solving and decision making. Because new learning, problem solving, and decision making are critical skills for both children and families receiving services, knowing preferred strategies in this areas can enhance practitioners' respect and responsiveness. Are families conversant with strategies presented to them by practitioners? Can those strategies be easily integrated into home routines? Answers to these and similar questions determine whether families successfully carry out practitioners' recommendations regarding home activities.

Finally, it is important to obtain information on families' worldviews—on how they believe the world works and what is right or wrong. A person's sense of right and wrong lies at the core of his or her response to others' behaviors as being either acceptable or offensive. For example, if someone's worldview is that human behavior is subservient to divine will, then that person experiences behavior that violates that law as insensitive or arrogant, perhaps even evil. Much of this information cannot be elicited directly, either because doing so might be perceived as rude or simply because families cannot readily articulate these aspects of culture.

The questions presented in Figure 8, a sample version of the Guide to Identifying Cultural Data, are not intended to be exhaustive. Nor are they intended to be asked directly in many cases. Asking a family "What are your assumptions about how the world works?" will not always, if ever, elicit a useful answer. Such directness might even be perceived as offensive. Obtaining these answers may require observing family interactions over time and making cautious inferences. It is important not to expect that all answers be obtained in a single visit or interaction. Examples of how these questions can be used in interactions with specific children and families are provided in Chapter 7.

As Chapter 7 states, it is important to explore these questions not only with the families we serve, but also with friends, co-workers, and colleagues. Answering such questions will tend to have less emotional investment and lower risk levels for the latter than for families, who may feel intimidated or fear offending the practitioners on whom they rely for support and assistance. Discussing these questions with a greater number of people makes it more likely that one will make appropriate inferences and will develop a deeply anchored understanding of diversity.

Tool 2: Strategies for Anchoring Understanding of Diversity

Figure 7 in Chapter 4 illustrates that each of Skilled Dialogue's characteristic qualities is expressed somewhat differently in relation to each of Skilled Dialogue's two skills. Figure 9 provides illustrative questions or statements for practitioners' use with families, thereby presenting helpful strategies associated with the expression of each quality in relation to Anchored Understanding of Diversity.[5] (See Appendix C for a photocopiable version of this list.) Each strategy is further reviewed in the following subsections. These strategies are helpful for anchoring understanding of diversity; however, this component skill develops in a variety of ways, depending on people's abilities, preferences, and experiences. For that reason, its development cannot be prescribed in any precise fashion, and Figure 9 is intended only as a primer.

Respect   In relation to Anchored Understanding of Diversity, respect is expressed as a willingness to acknowledge a variety of perspectives as equally valid to achieving a particular goal. The first strategy associated with the expression of respect focuses on mindful listening, which Shafir explained involves widening "the gap of time between perceiving a message and interpreting its content" (2000, p. 42). As strategy 1.1 of Figure 9

---

[5]These strategies were developed as part of field-testing activities done with Dr. Rosalita Mitchell and graduate student Donna Thompson at the University of New Mexico. Their support and contributions are gratefully acknowledged.

Strategies for Anchoring Understanding of Diversity

Qualities that characterize Skilled Dialogue	Related strategies for developing Anchored Understanding of Diversity
1. Respect: Acknowledge the range and validity of diverse perspectives.	*Strategy 1.1:* Listen mindfully to others' comments/responses. 1. How much time am I allowing between perceiving and interpreting the content of others' messages? *Strategy 1.2:* Get information about others' perspectives. 1. Could you tell me more about X? 2. Could you describe for me what X means to you? 3. How would you describe what you want at this point? Could you give me a specific example? *Strategy 1.3:* Examine your own perspective. 1. What do I believe about persons who act in this fashion? 2. What meaning(s) am I attaching to the behavior(s)? 3. How are my assumptions affecting this interaction/communication?
2. Reciprocity: Establish interactions that allow equal voice for all perspectives (i.e., avoid privileging one perspective over another).	*Strategy 2.1:* Allow yourself to believe that others' contributions are of equal value to yours. *Strategy 2.2:* Clarify others' understanding of your perspective. 1. How do you see my actions? 2. What do you hear me saying/asking? 3. What are your thoughts when you see me do/say X? 4. What does responding to my request mean to you? *Strategy 2.3:* Recognize the value of others' contributions. 1. What resources is X bringing to the interaction? 2. What can I learn from X? 3. What is positive about X's behavior?
3. Responsiveness: Communicate respect and understanding of others' perspectives.	*Strategy 3.1:* Remain mindful of and open to mystery (i.e., not knowing). 1. Am I overly focused on my goals, interpretations, and judgments? 2. What important information or alternative interpretations could I be missing? 3. To what degree am I willing to "trust the process" without knowing exactly what will happen? *Strategy 3.2:* Keep paying attention. 1. Listen and ask questions until you can credibly communicate respect and understanding. 2. Observe how others are responding to your words and behavior. *Strategy 3.3:* Reflect understanding of others' perspectives. 1. Let me see if I understand what you mean. Are you saying that . . . ? 2. Can I use an analogy to see if I really understand what you're saying? 3. Is this what you're talking about?

Figure 9.   Strategies for developing Anchored Understanding of Diversity.

shows, a first step to listening mindfully is to ask questions such as the following:

- "How much time am I allowing between hearing others' messages and interpreting their content?"

- "Do I assume I know what is meant almost before the other has finished speaking? Or do I listen and wait to gather additional information from others and from myself?"

Getting such information is the focus of Strategies 1.2 and 1.3 in the figure, which provides sample questions to ask as part of these strategies.

Exploring these questions helps elucidate the "story" that practitioners and families tell themselves about each other or about the situation in which they find themselves. Once determined, the stories themselves can be gently challenged. Are they, in fact, true (Katie, 2002)? For example, the practitioner needs to ask whether his or her story is something like "Here I am; all I am trying to do is help and they don't seem to recognize, much less appreciate, that" or "Their behavior just doesn't communicate any respect for my time and effort." Or perhaps the practitioner's storyline is more like the following: "I seem to be more interested in working with this child than the parents." The family members are in all probability telling themselves different and equally true stories. They might, for example, be saying, "This teacher seems to know so much about my child; maybe I should just let her work with my child so as not to waste any time" or "I don't understand why this teacher seems so concerned about my child's language; I can understand her and, anyway, that isn't what I'm most concerned about."

Whatever their stories, practitioners must anchor their understanding of both their stories and those of families. They need to identify these and question the assumptions that may underlie them. Katie (2002) presented an interesting framework for challenging stories about oneself and others. She suggested asking ourselves "Is it true?" whenever assumptions are made about others' behaviors and then examining why those assumptions may have been made.

Reciprocity   Reciprocity helps to anchor understanding of diversity when it is expressed concretely as the intent to support equal voice for those with whom one is interacting. Three strategies actualize this intent and in so doing promote Anchored Understanding of Diversity. Strategy 2.1 of Figure 9 is simply to allow oneself to believe that all interactions can be reciprocal. This strategy requires entering into these interactions ready to learn as well as to teach, ready to receive as well as to give.

Strategy 2.2—clarifying others' understanding of one's own perspective—expresses acknowledgement that there is no single story (i.e., no universal meaning for behaviors and actions). Questions like the following are helpful at this point:

- "How do you see my actions?"
- "What do you hear me saying/asking?"
- "What are your thoughts when I do/say X?"
- "What does complying with my request (e.g., to read to your child) mean to you?"

These questions may be asked directly of the families or practitioners with whom one is interacting if sufficient rapport has been established. They may also be asked of persons from similar experiential, cultural, and linguistic backgrounds (e.g., other practitioners, community members).

Strategy 2.3—associated with reciprocity—is actively recognizing the value of others' contributions. It is only through acknowledging that everyone brings something of value to an interaction that interactions truly become reciprocal. Three questions are suggested. The first two questions can be asked in every situation: "What resources does this person bring to our interaction (e.g., daily knowledge of child's behavior; connections with community)?" and "What can I learn from this person (e.g., how to function in unfamiliar environments)?" The third question needs to be asked specifically in situations in which practitioners are seeking behavior changes: "What are the positive aspects of this person's current behavior?" This question addresses both respect and reciprocity. Unless one can acknowledge what is positive about someone else's behavior, one is unlikely to respect that person, much less establish reciprocity with him or her.

The following vignette shows how the third question can be used to establish reciprocity in an early childhood program environment:

Sara's parents, Mr. and Mrs. Flores, identified themselves as Hispanic. Sara had two older sisters, and her entire family spent a lot of time playing with her and attending to her needs. At a team meeting to discuss intervention goals for Sara, several team members expressed concern about Sara's developing motor and verbal skills. Margie, the physical therapist, said, "Her family caters to her needs; she never has to ask for anything verbally, and she is always carried by one family member or another. I've asked them not to carry her so much." Connie, the speech-language therapist, added, "We've asked Mr. and Mrs. Flores to encourage Sara to ask for things verbally before giving them to her."

Rose, the meeting coordinator, first discussed the culturally based values and beliefs that seemed to underlie Mr. and Mrs. Flores' behavior and the need to respect these beliefs. She explained that from a cultural perspective, it was important to Mr. and Mrs. Flores to keep Sara from experiencing any additional discomfort. In their eyes, it was important to communicate to Sara that she was acceptable as she was, that her family's love was not contingent on the presence of particular behaviors. Rose then asked, "What is positive about the family's current behavior? How are they contributing to Sara's development?"

After some thought, Margie answered, "Maybe all of that unconditional and consistent attention to Sara has nurtured her trust in adults. I've noticed how willing she is to follow our directions." That statement opened the door to seeing Mr. and Mrs. Flores as collaborators in supporting Sara's development, rather than as parents unwilling to follow the team's recommendations. Tension between the family and team members dissolved, and energy that had been tied up in trying to change the family was freed to create ways of working collaboratively.

Responsiveness   The previous example illustrates how recognizing the value of others' contributions leads to becoming more responsive, the third quality in Figure 9. In relation to Anchored Understanding of Diversity, this quality addresses one's ability to communicate with empathy understanding of others' perspectives. Such understanding does not necessarily connote agreement. Margie and Connie do not need to agree with Mr. and Mrs. Flores' beliefs and practices. They still may want Sara's parents to extend their repertoire of parental behaviors. Even so, Margie and Connie can be responsive when they no longer feel a need to ask the parents to give up their present behavior.

Figure 9 shows that Strategy 3.1 is remaining mindful of and open to mystery rather than trying to find an answer. Some questions that may help one do this include

- "Am I overly focused on my goals and my interpretations/judgments?"

- "What important information or alternative interpretations might I be missing as a result of this focus?"

- "To what degree am I willing to 'trust the process' (and the families engaged in it with me) without needing to know exactly what will happen?"

Remen (2000) noted that focusing too closely on where one is going makes it easy to miss what is before us along the journey. For example, a person may focus too intently on a child's obvious (to a practitioner) need to learn to feed herself independently. In turn, that person may miss the parents' deeper need to feel that they can take care of their child competently. Or the practitioner may miss the rich trust and emotional connection between the parents and their child.

Remaining open to mystery requires asking the simple question that was introduced previously: "Is it true?" (Katie, 2002). In Sara's case, for example, one might ask, "Is it irrefutably in Sara's best interest to learn to self-feed now?" Practitioners may say that if she does not learn now, then Sara will be delayed in developing other skills—but is that true? How might practitioners interact differently with Sara and her family if they were not so certain that they knew best? This is not to say that practitioners should dismiss their goals, only that they should hold them more loosely, leaving room for what might be "outside the box."

Mindful attention to mystery and uncertainty blends with Strategies 3.2 and 3.3. It is important to keep listening and observing without seeking resolution too quickly. The goal at this point is not to reach a solution but to deepen understanding. Strategy 3.3 reminds practitioners never to make assumptions but, rather, to seek clarification and confirmation of perceptions. Respectively, these two strategies address one's ability to 1) reflect back to others' nonjudgmental acceptance of their actions and 2) keep that understanding fluid until feedback confirms that one indeed knows the meaning(s) of particular actions. Only then can it be said that Anchored Understanding of Diversity truly exists in the interaction.

Obviously, anchoring understanding of diversity is a process that cannot be developed in a brief interaction or perhaps even in several interactions. It requires time for self-reflection and multiple dialogues—both difficult and skilled—with diverse persons. The exchange of stories (my story–your story) through conversations over time assists the anchoring of understanding in a unique way (Sanchez, 1999). This does not mean that nothing can be done until one's understanding is fully anchored. Immediate actions, such as calling in social services or conducting interactive activities with children, can and should occur even as this process is ongoing. Critical Incident Analysis Sheets (discussed in Chapters 7, 8, and 9) were developed for use in these types of situations.

WHAT ARE SOME EXAMPLES OF ANCHORED UNDERSTANDING OF DIVERSITY IN EARLY CHILDHOOD ENVIRONMENTS?

Returning to the Chapter 4 vignette about Betsy and Karen, how could Betsy know whether she achieved Anchored Understanding of Diversity? This type of understanding would be reached when, after spending time with Karen and following some of the suggestions in this book, Betsy could say in all honesty that she might under similar circumstances behave as Karen did. As long as a person says "I'd never do that" or "I can't believe someone would do that," Anchored Understanding of Diversity has not been achieved. These types of statements imply that one person is "better" or more competent and thus preclude respect, reciprocity, and responsiveness.

Anchored Understanding of Diversity is compassionate and maintains boundaries, yet it is neither judgmental nor patronizing. Two things happen when Anchored Understanding of Diversity is achieved:

1. Persons realize that others choose the best options available to them, even when those options are counterproductive or even harmful. (As noted previously and in Appendix A, such realization does not preclude taking necessary action to protect a child's welfare.)

2. Persons refuse to limit their judgment of others' capacities to those aspects of their behavior that are considered troublesome.

For instance, both Betsy and Karen are choosing the best option from their repertoires, even though Betsy believes that mothers should work alongside practitioners and Karen believes otherwise. Each sees the other's choice as less than desirable: Betsy does not want to work alone while Karen considers leaving the room a more desirable option. Unanchored understanding on Betsy's part can result in one of two responses: judgmental or subtly patronizing. Betsy's first response might be to judge Karen's choice as wrong and as needing correction. Her second response might be to give up on introducing alternatives because "Karen is doing the best that she can, and her behavior is culturally appropriate." This second response appears respectful but is ultimately patronizing in its exclusion of reciprocity.

To anchor her initial understanding, Betsy needs to be respectful, acknowledging that Karen's choice is valid given her understanding of existing options. She also needs to establish reciprocity, acknowledging that Karen has a capacity to reflect on her behavior and choose to learn new behaviors if warranted. To do this, Betsy might have to become curious about the story that Karen is telling herself: What meaning is she attaching to the behaviors of staying and leaving that make leaving the more desirable choice? Then, Betsy needs to allow Karen the opportunity and time to tell that story and to express her perspective. Finally, Betsy needs to communicate her understanding of her behavior and of Karen's and to obtain feedback until each can say to the other, "Oh, now I see why you desire that behavior over this one."

Anchoring the understanding of diverse perspectives and behaviors requires bringing differences home—that is, allowing them into one's own frame of reference, refusing to leave them "out there" as something so alien that one cannot resonate with them. Yet, this must be done in ways that do not distort either one's own frame of reference or that of others. A second skill is necessary to accomplish this delicate balancing act: 3rd Space. Neither respect nor reciprocity nor responsiveness can be fully established without this critical skill, which complements Anchored Understanding of Diversity and is discussed in Chapter 6.

3rd Space

THE SECOND SKILL

We split paradoxes so reflexively that we do not understand the price we pay for our habit. The poles of a paradox are like the poles of a battery: hold them together, and they generate the energy of life; pull them apart, and the current stops flowing. When we separate any of the profound paired truths of our lives, both poles become lifeless as well. Dissecting a living paradox has the same impact on our intellectual, emotional, and spiritual well-being as the decision to breathe in without ever breathing out would have on our physical health. (Palmer, 1997, p. 64)

The second key skill associated with Skilled Dialogue, 3rd Space, builds on and grows out of Anchored Understanding of Diversity. Anchored Understanding of Diversity leads to a "both-and" perspective, and sometimes that is enough. Other times, however, this perspective does not go far enough. In the vignette about Betsy and Karen, Betsy is still left wanting one set of behaviors while Karen exhibits a contradictory set. How can both working with Maya and not working with Maya be integrated? It is at this point—when apparently contradictory or irreconcilable perspectives need to be honored simultaneously—that 3rd Space becomes necessary.

WHAT IS 3RD SPACE?

3rd Space focuses on creatively reframing contradictions into paradoxes. As such, it invites practitioners to make a fundamental shift from dualistic, exclusive perceptions of reality and to adopt a mindset that integrates the complementary aspects of diverse values, behaviors, and beliefs into a new whole. 3rd Space helps mine the riches of multiple perspectives while simultaneously promoting respect and reciprocity by not excluding one perspective to privilege another. For example, how can Karen's present behavior (i.e., not staying to work with Maya) complement Betsy's goal (i.e., increasing parent–child interactions)? The answer to that question is explored following the chapter's initial discussion of 3rd Space. As both a skill and a mindset, a 3rd Space perspective capitalizes on the potential of diversity to enrich and expand. The following three characteristics of the perspective give an indication of how this is possible.

1. From a 3rd Space perspective, reality is not dichotomous.

From a 3rd Space perspective, differences between views are better described as a spectrum than a continuum. A continuum is by definition directional and exclusive. Its two ends remain opposed to each other: as one draws nearer to one end, the other grows further away. A spectrum is inclusive; it does not contain a directional perspective. This aspect of 3rd Space introduces the possibility of conceptualizing each person's perspective in nonpolarized ways—that is, not feeling that choosing one perspective necessitates moving away from or excluding the other.

2. From a 3rd Space perspective, there are always at least three (or more) choices.

Because reality is not dichotomous in 3rd Space, there is never a need for a forced choice (i.e., an "either-or" choice). Rather than splitting reality into dualistic sets of exclusive choices (e.g., Karen is involved or uninvolved), 3rd Space perspectives always posit the availability of three or more choices (e.g., Karen is involved and uninvolved simultaneously). This characteristic of 3rd Space involves creatively generating alternatives beyond the obvious ones. For example, Betsy could reframe noninvolvement as a type of engagement. Paradise gave an interesting example of this in an article on Mazahua mothers and children, in which she described a "separate-but-together" interaction: "[Mothers and children] are together while each at the same time is involved in his or her own separate activity" (1994, p. 160). This type of interaction is similar to yet different from parallel play in young children; it is actually a type of cooperative interaction but is different from that with which practitioners are familiar.

Even more radically, Betsy could choose to set the perceived problem aside for a while and "waste time" talking with Karen over a cup of coffee while they both watch Maya play with her toys, thus redefining the level of involvement for both. Who knows what that could lead to?

3. From a 3rd Space perspective, differences are understood to be complementary rather than divisive.

Boundaries serve both as distinctions and as points of contact that, like the poles of a battery (Palmer, 1997), generate constructive tension when connected. Third, fourth, and even fifth choices are generated not only to expand behavioral repertoires, but also to explore connections between apparently polarized perspectives.

The idea that two or more diverse perspectives are complementary (i.e., can be somehow integrated to form a greater whole) is the core of a 3rd Space perspective. A classic example of this "the whole is greater than the sum of the parts" perspective is the story of the men who met an elephant in the dark (Perkins, 2001). All of them believed that they could describe this strange animal. "He is like a tree trunk," said the man who bumped into the elephant's leg; "No, he is like a rope," said the one who touched his trunk—and so on. In this story each person was correct, given his limited scope of experience, and also not correct, given the reality of the elephant. Each man's experience yielded only one part of the total picture. Yet, the full picture was not just the sum of each man's impressions—a bizarre creature that is part tree, part rope, and so forth. The full and truest picture could not be known until all perspectives were integrated. Only then could the whole elephant emerge, something more than the simple sum of their individual impressions.

In a similar fashion, the skill of 3rd Space requires that practitioners explore the "elephant" and not just their individual perspectives. What might the elephant be in Betsy's and Karen's case? (Clue: The three parts are Maya alone with Betsy, Maya alone with Karen, and Maya with both Betsy and Karen. See below for further discussion of 3rd Space options and a possible answer to the question just posed.)

Imagine actual rooms in physical space. This space can be perceived in several ways. From a *singular space perspective*, there is literally only one room: the one that I am in. Within this perspective, I believe that my room (e.g., view, value, belief) is the only one that exists. I can neither see nor imagine anything different—or if I can, I judge those things to be nonexistent or without value. If I am told about them, I do not accept them as "real." Real events and interactions only take place in my room. From a singular space perspective, Betsy would be absolutely certain that only *her* beliefs and values are true. She would have difficulty perceiving that others could hold diverse beliefs and values and even greater difficulty believing them to be equally valid and true.

From a *dualistic space perspective,* I realize that mine is not the only room. I accept other views as real but place them outside of my space (i.e., exclude them from my room). I am, so to speak, in one room and persons different from me are in a different room(s). Events and interactions take place in one room OR the other (e.g., my way or your way, this or that, right or wrong). In dualistic space, there is no common space. I cannot meet you unless one or both of us move: I must leave my room (i.e., comfortable space) OR you must leave yours OR we must both leave our rooms and go to another "neutral" room. If I hold a "both-and" perspective (a variation of a dualistic perspective), we each remain in our separate rooms, side by side yet unable to integrate our respective rooms (i.e., perspectives).

From dualistic space, Betsy would understand that Karen's values and beliefs are different from her own and are perhaps even equally valid. Yet, she would have only two ways of responding. If she felt strongly that the differences needed to be resolved, then she would try to reach agreement. That is, one or the other would concede her beliefs/values or each would compromise those beliefs/values to a certain degree. If Betsy felt less strongly about the need to reach agreement, then she could simply let both sets of beliefs remain side by side, separate but equal.

In contrast to mindsets associated with both singular and dualistic space, a *3rd Space perspective* accepts the possibility that our diverse perspectives could be integrated. It asks the question, "If we are in separate rooms, how can we both end up in the same space without moving?" Through this question, 3rd Space challenges us to realize that it is not our respective positions that keep us from occupying common space. Rather, what challenges us is the wall that we have erected between our positions.

Walls are different from boundaries. Boundaries are markers of space and identity (see discussion in Chapter 4). They may generate diversity "bumps," but they do not obstruct one's "view" and can be permeable. Conversely, walls are opaque and impenetrable. Depending on their size and thickness, walls can exclude and result in diversity clashes or sometimes outright crashes. It is important to recognize that a wall is often a boundary that has fossilized over time, becoming hard and dense in response to repeated assaults. For example, if a person's language is repeatedly perceived to have low status or to be inadequate, he or she is likely to form strong walls around it, perhaps refusing to speak it outside of the home or even refusing to speak it entirely.

With a 3rd Space perspective, lowering or removing the wall between rooms allows persons to be in the same room without having to move (e.g., realizing that both languages are equally valid no matter how others perceive them). In 3rd Space, Betsy would be able to ask herself, "For Maya's best interests, how can I integrate my beliefs and values with Karen's to extract their strengths and diminish their limitations?"

The skill of 3rd Space thus invites practitioners into a conceptual space in which reality is not dichotomous, three or more choices always exist, and differences are complementary. It challenges persons to adopt an inclusive mindset that can integrate two or more diverse perspectives into a whole and mine the strengths of both.

WHAT ARE SOME EXAMPLES OF 3RD SPACE IN EARLY CHILDHOOD ENVIRONMENTS?

It is important to note that the purpose of conceptualizing and creating 3rd Space is not to make decisions. Rather, it is to create a common space within which the probability of making optimum decisions is heightened. Fritz commented on the differences between a problem-solving orientation and a creative one: "When you are solving a problem, you are taking action to have something go away: *the problem.* [How can persons honor a difference if they are trying to make it go away?] When you are creating, you are taking action to have something come into being: *the creation*" (1989, p. 11).

Skilled Dialogue invites persons to use the skill of 3rd Space for the purpose of having "something come into being." In this sense, they become creators "who solve problems secondarily as a necessary and inevitable result of [their] commitment to producing a remarkable artistic result" (Childs, 1998, p. 34). Decisions are made and problems are solved, but only secondarily, as a result of practitioners' commitment to creatively crafting interactions that are respectful, reciprocal, and responsive.

As the mindset of 3rd Space is developed, the options that arise cannot be predetermined. They can emerge only from and through respectful, responsive, and reciprocal interactions between persons holding diverse perspectives. Therefore, the following examples are provided only as illustrations of how 3rd Space options have emerged in particular situations. They may or (more likely) may not be applicable to other particular situations.

A group of Head Start staff was asked to select a situation to which they would like to apply the idea and skill of 3rd Space. They immediately chose their recent experiences with Martha, a mother whose 4-year-old son was exhibiting aggressive and hyperactive behavior (e.g., throwing chairs, hitting students, running around the room). The staff had developed a behavior management program that was somewhat successful on site, but Martha would not agree to use it at home. Her response was, "As long as he doesn't burn the house down, I'm okay with his behavior." They added that Martha was an older single mother who worked two jobs, one of which was during the night shift at a juvenile detention facility.

The first step was for the practitioners to achieve Anchored Understanding of Diversity in this situation. They asked themselves many of the questions shown in Figure 8 (Chapter 5). They especially focused on identifying possible positive intents underlying Martha's behavior. After extended discussion, they decided that they could accept Martha's perspective as valid (although undesirable) if Martha perceived her choices as either ignore her son's behavior or end up hitting him out of frustration and exhaustion. For the first time, the group felt that they could respect this mother's decision. Even though they disagreed with her perceived choices, they could now respect her need to avoid physical violence.

But how could they begin to create 3rd Space? The two existing spaces—the space where the mother was inattentive to her son and the space in which the staff felt compelled to force compliance—had significant drawbacks. The ensuing discussion was prolonged. Although the staff could respect Martha's choice, their negative judgment of her behavior seemed to preclude the possibility of creating inclusive 3rd Space options. When the question "How could you compliment this mom in this situation?" was raised, no one had an immediate answer. Finally, one staff member said, "We could compliment her on how well she has encouraged her son to become self-reliant." The change in staff energy after this statement was palpable. A 3rd Space perspective began to develop, in which Martha's behavior (reframed as supporting self-reliance) could be integrated with the staff's desired behavior (nurturing relational and social skills). The staff could approach Martha as an equal partner who provided one part of the whole. The staff reformulated their interactions as "adding to that part" rather than trying to erase it. As a result, they reported that they no longer felt the need to approach Martha from a "We need to fix this" approach and, instead, could approach her from a sincere "How can we work together?" position. The final outcome remained uncertain, but the staff's shift in perspective promised a more positive outcome than their initial position of "Implement our behavior management program at home or we will no longer be able to serve your child."

A second example of finding 3rd Space options is provided in *Reconciling Differences* (Gonzalez-Mena, Herzog, & Herzog, 2000), a video based on the Skilled Dialogue concept of 3rd Space. In this example, two early childhood practitioners role-play a discussion of children's drawing activities.

Dora, a program administrator, observed Lisa, a teacher, help a child to complete a drawing. Dora expressed both developmental and administrative concerns about this behavior. She told Lisa that early education values support independent exploration of skills over the imposition of patterns deemed desirable by adults. She also expressed concern regarding what might happen if teachers helped children to draw during an accreditation visit. The two practitioners discussed their different perspectives for a while, realizing that a deep disagreement as well as some disapproval existed between them. Their discussion did, however, evidence their respect for each other and their desire to reach a mutual understanding. Finally, Lisa began talking about the meaning she associated with helping a child to draw. She recalled her parents drawing with her and the closeness that she experienced during this activity. Dora acknowledged that she has had similar experiences. Lisa's comment "Then, why can't we have both?" opened the door to the creation of an inclusive 3rd Space option that would integrate their diverse perspectives. Although they did not fully develop this option, the tone of their interaction clearly shifted as they discussed it. Their postures and their voices changed from adversarial to collaborative.

These examples illustrate the function of 3rd Space as both a skill and a mindset. A 3rd Space perspective does not "solve the problem." Rather, it changes the arena within which that problem is addressed by increasing the probability of respectful, responsive, and reciprocal interactions. In so doing, an optimal response to the situation becomes more likely.

HOW CAN 3RD SPACE OPTIONS BE CREATED?

The creation of 3rd Space options is best learned through practice. It is not something easily or clearly understood in the abstract. The first step is to acquire the mindset—that is, to entertain the possibility of a shift from perceiving two (or more) perspectives as contradictory to perceiving them as complementary. Some practitioners have experience with such inclusive mindsets. For them, 3rd Space is easier to reach. Other practitioners may have difficulty shifting out of habitual either-or thinking. For these practitioners, the books, activities, and games referenced within this chapter may be of help in anchoring understanding of 3rd Space.

Exploring 3rd Space with others is critical to its development. As with Figure 9, Figure 10 provides illustrative questions or statements for practitioners' use with families, thereby listing specific strategies that support development of 3rd Space in relation to each of the Skilled Dialogue's characteristic qualities.[6] (See Appendix C for a photocopiable version of this list.)

Respect

The first set of strategies is designed to foster and communicate respect, the premier quality of Skilled Dialogue. The Chapter 5 discussion about developing Anchored Understanding of Diversity focused on respect as a

---

[6]These strategies, like those for Anchored Understanding, were developed in pilot research with Dr. Rosalita Mitchell and graduate student Donna Thompson at the University of New Mexico.

Strategies for Creating 3rd Space Options

Qualities that characterize Skilled Dialogue	Related strategies for creating 3rd Space options
1. Respect: Stay with the tension of differing perspectives.	*Strategy 1.1:* Release the natural inclination to focus on solutions/resolutions. 1. To what degree is my tendency to focus on solutions/resolutions interfering with my ability to express respect for perspectives or behavior diverse from my own? *Strategy 1.2:* Listen/observe without judgment. 1. Share verbal indicators of interest and curiosity (e.g., "I see," "That's interesting"). 2. Share nonverbal indicators of interest or curiosity. *Strategy 1.3:* Identify specific tension points. 1. How are we seeing this situation differently? 2. What aspects of others' behavior/perspective am I finding the most difficult or least agreeable? Why? What would happen if I did not contradict, oppose, or try to change that behavior/perspective? Listen to the answers.
2. Reciprocity: Develop opportunities for equalizing power across interactions.	*Strategy 2.1:* Recognize that there is no need to make one perspective wrong to justify another as right. *Strategy 2.2:* Shift the conversation's focus to "equalize" participation. 1. Share vulnerable statements such as "I'm not sure of where to go next." 2. Use an analogy/metaphor that is familiar to the other person or unfamiliar to both of you. *Strategy 2.3:* Explore how contradictory behaviors/perspectives could be complementary. 1. How is one behavior/perspective balanced by the other? 2. What if both are "right" and there is no need to choose between them?
3. Responsiveness: Create a response that integrates and provides access to the strengths and diverse perspectives.	*Strategy 3.1:* Trust the possibility of options that honor diversity. *Strategy 3.2:* Explore responses that integrate contradictions. 1. Use analogies (e.g., half-full/half-empty glass, musical chords). 2. Reframe the "problem": Tell different stories; use different lenses. 3. Brainstorm 3rd (and 4th and 5th) choices other than those that are immediately obvious. 4. Continue until finding a response that is agreeable to all concerned.

Figure 10.   Strategies for creating 3rd Space options.

willingness to acknowledge diverse perspectives as equally valid. In relation to 3rd Space, respect for differences is established primarily through staying with the tension of differing and sometimes even contradictory perspectives. As Perkins noted, this is difficult: "People have a strong tendency to generate a quick vision of the nature of a solution and set off from there" (2001, p. 150). ENC values and beliefs tend to reinforce moving to resolution or reconciliation before tension is sufficiently experienced (Stewart & Bennett, 1991).

The stage for 3rd Space is set only when practitioners can pause respectfully before trying to change something. The first strategy in Figure 10 addresses this need to reflect on and release the natural inclination to focus on solutions and resolutions. Listening and observing without judgment (or giving advice) is a second strategy associated with the quality of respect. Verbal and nonverbal indicators of interest and curiosity are important if others are to feel safe enough to lower or remove their walls. Both judgment and advice, when given too soon, communicate that a person already knows everything.

Paradoxically, identifying specific tension points (i.e., contradictions) is as important to the creation of 3rd Space as is withholding judgment. When contradictions are identified, awareness of others' boundaries is communicated. Differences cannot be honored if they are not first acknowledged. It is often only after persons are sure that others recognize them in all of their particularity that they are willing to lower their walls.

Identifying contradictions can also help persons to explore and question why they want to change, contradict, or even oppose another's perspective. What is it about that perspective that is threatening? For example, as the previously described Head Start staff worked on becoming more skilled in their interactions with Martha, the first author suggested that they ask what would happen if they stopped trying to change Martha's behavior. After some thought, one of them responded, "If we can't change her behavior, Mikey (her son) will continue to be aggressive and hyperactive and will probably grow up to join a gang, drop out of school, and get involved in real violence." This scenario, which was plausible given the populations with whom they worked, gave an important clue to the staff's underlying beliefs. In some sense, they perceived Martha's behavior as a threat to their definition of themselves as teachers who could prevent such outcomes. The problem with such a scenario was that it presented problems as a motivation for changing Martha's behavior. With such a scenario in mind, it was only natural to communicate a high level of judgment and urgency. Neither quality would help Martha feel safe enough to lower her walls and enter into a truly collaborative relationship with the staff. In all likelihood, these qualities would only trigger counter-scenarios of her own.

The first author asked the staff about children with similar backgrounds who had previously attended the program. What had happened as these children grew up? The answers varied, but many children had not followed the path predicted for Mikey. This recognition allowed the staff to realize that their projected outcome was not inevitable; neither was it solely up to them to "save" Mikey and the others whom he might later harm. This realization allowed the staff to approach Martha from a more mindful perspective, which created a greater potential for Skilled Dialogue.

Taken together, the strategies of identifying contradictions and staying with the tension send a strong message of respect. They say, "I recognize that you believe/behave differently from me AND I do not judge you as wrong or somehow less than me for that reason." It should be noted, however, that this message does not preclude continuing to invite others to change or taking action to protect a child. It does preclude doing so in ways that dishonor or shame families.

Reciprocity

In relation to Anchored Understanding of Diversity, reciprocity addresses the equalizing of power across interactions. Developing the skill of 3rd Space requires creating opportunities for that to happen. The first strategy associated with this aspect of 3rd Space is simply recognizing that it is unnecessary to make one perspective wrong to justify another as right. Power cannot be equalized as long as one perspective must be excluded or "proven" wrong to justify change to another. For example, practitioners do not have to communicate that a family's behavior (e.g., speaking a language other than English with their child) is wrong to communicate that an additional behavior is desirable (e.g., developing English language skills). As Cummins remarked,

> Educators who see their role as adding *a second language and cultural affiliation to students' repertoires are likely to empower students more than those who see their role as replacing or* subtracting *students' primary language and culture in the process of assimilating them to the dominant culture. (1989, p. 113, emphasis added)*

Although these words are not specific to early childhood special education, they can be easily paraphrased: Practitioners who see their role as adding to families' and children's behavioral and linguistic repertoires are likely to empower them more than practitioners who see their role as replacing or subtracting from these repertoires in the process of promoting desired developmental goals.

A second strategy for establishing reciprocity in support of 3rd Space is to shift the focus of conversation. A great example of this strategy comes from a conversation that the first author had with Donna Thompson, a graduate student and practitioner:

> *In the middle of our discussion about 3rd Space, Donna unexpectedly asked, "Is that something like the idea of a common denominator?" stopping me in my tracks. Only when we went back over our conversation did we realize that as she sought to anchor her understanding, she had intuitively succeeded in establishing reciprocity. As long as I continued to talk about 3rd Space, the power between us was implicitly unequal: I remained the "expert," and she was the novice. When she shifted the focus to common denominators, a concept with which she was familiar and I was not, I had to stop and remember what little I know about that mathematical reality. At that point we both became learners on an equal footing. The topic—3rd Space—remained constant, but our conversation shifted its focus to common denominators. This is not an easy strategy, but it is highly effective.*

A third strategy that helps establish reciprocity in relation to 3rd Space is exploring how contradictory behaviors or perspectives can be complementary. This means that both are true at the same time (e.g., involvement can be expressed as both engagement and nonengagement). The complementary nature of contradictory behaviors also can be understood by asking how one behavior or perspective balances the other. Chaos, for example, balances order to produce creativity. Order without some degree of chaos freezes into rigidity and precludes change. Chaos without some degree of order becomes destructive disorder and precludes growth.

How might Karen's behavior (i.e., not participating in Maya's intervention activities) balance Betsy's (i.e., working directly with Maya)? What might be the result of that balance? Betsy might say, "You know, maybe there's a way that your behavior complements mine. When you leave Maya and me, you are supporting her development of independent problem-solving skills. If you stayed, she might look to you to help her out, and I think that she is emotionally and cognitively ready to begin solving simple problems on her own." A statement like this could potentially shift Betsy's and Karen's interactions. Their interactions can move from not supporting each other's goals toward being collaborative. How might both Betsy's and Karen's goals be met without sacrificing either? Perhaps Betsy and Maya could accompany Karen when she leaves the room and consider it a "field trip," during which Maya could learn various concepts, movements, or words. Although each is still in her own "room"—Betsy wants Karen to stay and Karen continues to leave—a door has been opened between their two perspectives. A reciprocal "right-right" rather than a "right-wrong" perspective has been established.

Responsiveness

Responsiveness addresses the creation of 3rd Space options. The strategies described for expressing respect and reciprocity set the stage for these options. Strategies for responsiveness focus on generating a response to a particular situation that integrates diverse perspectives and provides access to their strengths. The first suggested strategy is to accept that even if there seems to be no answer, one can be found. That is, trust the possibility of options that honor diversity by not forcing choice.

The second strategy is key to 3rd Space: Explore responses that integrate contradictions. The question at this point is, "What response incorporates both your perspective and mine?" Two metaphors that may be used to communicate this goal are the metaphor of "half-empty, half-full" and the metaphor of a musical chord.

When we look at a bottle of water that is only partially filled there are two common perceptions: half-full and half-empty. We can try to choose between them or we can observe that the bottle is, in fact, both half-full and half-empty. A 3rd Space perspective, however, asks us to shift our perspective from the boundary where water and air meet to the container that holds them: the bottle. Like the elephant encountered by the men in the dark, the bottle is the greater whole that contains both apparently contradictory perspectives (i.e., empty and full). This is similar to how a musical chord integrates various notes into a greater whole while respecting and retaining the unique nature of each. Practitioners can apply this approach to working with families who do not speak English at home by shifting from a "use English at home" perspective to a collaborative one focused on language development (regardless of which language is used).

A special type of jigsaw puzzle provides a concrete metaphor for 3rd Space. Photomosaics are composed of numerous small pictures, each complete, which are integrated to form a bigger and different picture without being changed (see Figure 11). The type of integration shown in Figure 11 is the aim of 3rd Space. Take two people's stories or perceptions and form a bigger, different story or picture that honors the similarities and differences of the individual pictures and is, in fact, created by their juxtaposition and integration.

Reframing techniques constitute another strategy for exploring the integration of contradictory perspectives. De Bono (1970), Fletcher and Olwyer (1997), and Perkins (2001) provided exercises for using reframing. Although it is not always possible, reframing is nevertheless powerful. It entails changing the point of view from which one defines a problem. Perkins remarked, "If the way you've been coding or representing the situation to yourself is not going anywhere, perhaps the problem is unreasonable—so why not try something different?" (p. 132). Laziness, for example, can be reframed and perceived as efficiency. After all, the goal of both is the same: the conservation of energy. Such reframing would increase the probability of a positive response to the person conserving his or her energy!

Telling oneself different stories and using different lenses are two ways of reframing. The following story illustrates reframing by telling different stories. Imagine that you are in a bank one afternoon. You are tired and ready to get home. The person in front of you, who is carrying a small child, cashes her check and then continues to chat with the bank teller. At one point, the woman even hands over the child for the teller to hold. This goes on for several minutes, with the person giving no indication that she is ready to leave. What story might you tell yourself about this situation? One possible story sounds something like this: "How inconsiderate can this person be? Doesn't she have any awareness of people around her? Does she think that she can just stand there and block the line?" There is, however, a second possibility. Imagine that when you finally get to the teller, she turns to you and says, "I am so sorry. I am a single parent; my husband died suddenly last year, and I had to return to work. That was my baby sitter with my daughter. This is the only time that I get to see her after I leave home, as she is often asleep by the time I return from work." How would your response to the earlier actions change? The additional information reframes your perception of the situation. The article

Figure 11. Sample Photomosaic. (Image from Photomosaic™ by Robert Silvers, http://www.photomosaic.com; used by permission.)

in Appendix B provides another example of how additional information can shift or reframe perceptions.

Using different lenses to perceive situations can be another aid to re-framing. Perkins provided an example in the following puzzle:

> *There's a man with a mask at home. There's a man coming home. What's going on here?*
>
> *This is thin information, so perhaps you would like to hear some questions answered. Is the man with the mask a thief? No. Does the man coming home live there? No. Is the man with the mask going to hurt the man coming home? No. (2001, p. 28)*

Processing this information with a lens that translates "home" into "domicile" makes solving this puzzle unlikely. If you are using a sports lens and thinking about baseball, however, the answer is clear.

There are multiple lenses available in any situation. For example, using a cultural lens to understand a behavior such as not speaking up in class may lead to the perception that such behavior is appropriate, although not as effective in some contexts as in others. Using a developmental lens without reference to culture might lead to a very different answer (Brown & Barrera, 1999)—perhaps that there is a language delay or that self-esteem is compromised and needs strengthening.

Finally, brainstorming techniques can also be used to explore potential 3rd Space options. Even with this technique and those previously described, however, it is not always easy to arrive at responses that truly provide access to and integrate the strengths of diverse perspectives. Translating the mindset of 3rd Space into concrete responses is like learning to see the pictures hidden in 3-D illusion picture books (e.g., N.E. Thing Enterprises, 1993), where one stares at a picture until a "buried" image appears. It takes continued practice and often requires what Perkins termed "breakthrough thinking," a type of thinking that purposely challenges "key assumptions" and seeks to represent "problems in a new way, broadening or shifting the boundaries of the search [for possibilities]" (2001, pp. 9, 55).

Section III of this book provides additional guidelines and materials to support the development of 3rd Space and Anchored Understanding of Diversity. Several vignettes drawn from the authors' experiences in culturally diverse early childhood environments are presented and discussed to illustrate the use of these guidelines and materials.

The Practice of Skilled Dialogue in Early Childhood Environments

Section III extends previous discussions of Skilled Dialogue. As outlined in Figure 12, specific tools and suggestions are provided for using Skilled Dialogue with families and children in early childhood environments. Chapter 7 presents a Skilled Dialogue Self-Assessment for practitioners. The chapter then reviews the Skilled Dialogue process in terms of the early childhood special education assessment and intervention and instruction. Ways to determine the degree and impact of cultural linguistic diversity in individual cases are followed by guidelines for identifying respectful, reciprocal, and responsive ways of assessing and working with children and families from populations identified as culturally linguistically diverse. Chapters 8 and 9 focus on common dilemmas that arise in relation to assessment and intervention and instruction respectively. Each of these chapters presents suggested responses to such dilemmas, using vignettes to illustrate their implementation.

Figure 12

The Practice of Skilled Dialogue in Early Childhood Environments

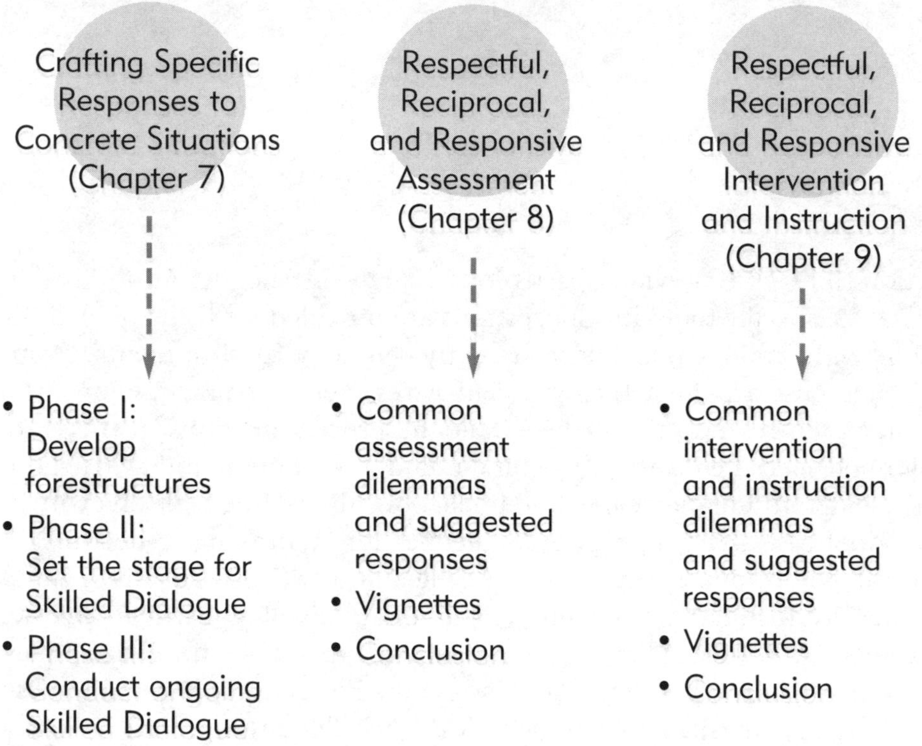

Crafting Specific
Responses to
Concrete Situations
(Chapter 7)

Respectful,
Reciprocal,
and Responsive
Assessment
(Chapter 8)

Respectful,
Reciprocal,
and Responsive
Intervention
and Instruction
(Chapter 9)

- Phase I:
  Develop
  forestructures
- Phase II:
  Set the stage for
  Skilled Dialogue
- Phase III:
  Conduct ongoing
  Skilled Dialogue

- Common
  assessment
  dilemmas
  and suggested
  responses
- Vignettes
- Conclusion

- Common
  intervention
  and instruction
  dilemmas
  and suggested
  responses
- Vignettes
- Conclusion

Crafting Specific Responses to Concrete Situations

We must learn of the simplest [artist] a parable. . . . There is no great art without reverence. The real [artist] has great technical knowledge of materials and tools . . . [and] something much more: he has the feel of the wood; the knowledge of its demands in his fingers; and so the work is smooth and satisfying and lovely because he worked with the reverence that comes of love. (Vann, 1960, p. 19)

Putting skills and strategies into practice is the focus of Section III. More specifically, this chapter's purpose is to describe and illustrate how practitioners can learn and use Skilled Dialogue to craft responses to concrete situations in early childhood environments. Both general guidelines and specific examples are given.

Attempting to trace a process (i.e., capture its flow in words) is a hazardous endeavor. Processes are by definition fluid and dynamic operations that never recur in exactly the same way. For that reason, it is important to note that the materials here and in Chapters 8 and 9 are intended only as a general framework for practice and guidance, not as prescriptive "steps" to be followed. The phases presented next are intended to serve as loose and somewhat arbitrary organizers to support clarity and understanding. Readers should feel free to restructure these phases. Similarly, the forms provided are also intended to serve as a means of further clarifying the information. They are not meant to add one more layer of paperwork to an already extensive documentation process.

The process of learning and practicing Skilled Dialogue is organized around three phases:

- Phase I: Develop forestructures (i.e., acquire general information about culture and its diverse manifestations).

- Phase II: Set the stage for Skilled Dialogue (i.e., obtain specific cultural data about individual families and children to inform assessment and intervention).

- Phase III: Conduct ongoing Skilled Dialogue with children and families (i.e., use Anchored Understanding of Diversity and 3rd Space skills to monitor and enhance the degree of respect, reciprocity, and responsiveness in specific interactions).

Figure 13 depicts these phases and the practices associated with them. Anchored Understanding of Diversity and 3rd Space skills are embedded in each phase. The phases were initially identified by Barrera and Kramer (1997), then further developed by Barrera using a "process tracing" technique in which one "thinks aloud" while moving through a particular

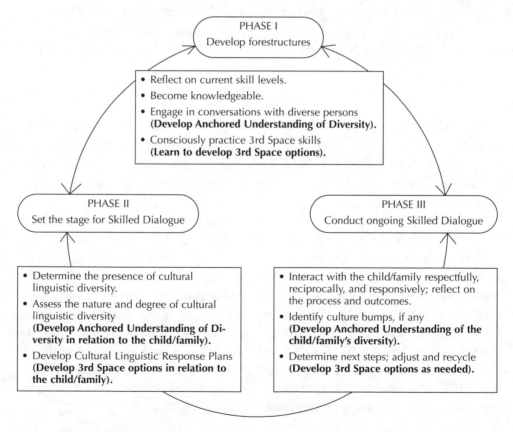

Figure 13.   Phases for learning and practicing Skilled Dialogue.

process (Shavelson & Stern, 1981). No phase is ever considered totally complete, and all phases are ongoing and reiterative. All can occur simultaneously, and their sequence may vary from that given. The value of such uncertainty has already been addressed in previous discussions of responsiveness (see Chapter 4). Langer commented on the value of uncertainty in relation to teaching:

> *Teaching skills and facts in a conditional way sets the stage for doubt and uncertainty and an awareness of how different situations may call for subtle differences in what we bring to them. . . . We can learn a skill by accepting at face value what we are told about how to practice it or* we can come to an understanding over time of what the skill entails. *(1997, pp. 16–17, emphasis added)*

The phases serve as a useful framework for learning and practicing Skilled Dialogue as long as one remembers that their true goal is to support "understanding over time of what the skill entails" (sic). Skilled Dialogue, like language, cannot be truly learned prior to being applied and experienced (i.e., anchored). Therefore, however unskilled they may seem at first, readers are encouraged to implement the various phases. First attempts may seem far from successful, yet each deepens practitioners' understanding and skills. This is especially true for Phases II and III. Initial attempts to complete the forms for these phases may not yield the amount of data given in the examples. Any additional data, however, no matter how slight, enhance practitioners' understanding of and response to specific families and their children. Discussions of how to identify other data also stimulate greater reciprocity between practitioners and families.

PHASE I: DEVELOP FORESTRUCTURES

Developing a meaning base from which to examine cultural diversity and its challenges is a critical first phase to learning Skilled Dialogue. All too frequently, persons find that they are like pilots trying to fix a plane while in flight. They focus on developing cultural competency while in the midst of specific situations, encumbered by constraints of time and immediate needs and without sufficient information. Nakkula and Ravitch (1998) coined the term *forestructure* to explain this meaning base from which persons draw their understanding of subsequent events. They pointed out, "We are projected forward . . . into new activities with prior expectations based on internalized interpretations of our archive of life experiences" (p. 25).

Skilled Dialogue is a proactive process in which success is determined by the quality of the forestructures that practitioners build prior to interactions with specific families and children who are diverse from themselves. Developing these forestructures can and should occur outside of as well as within actual professional interactions with diverse families. Four practices support the development of sound forestructures in relation to Skilled Dialogue:

1. Reflect on current skill levels.

2. Become knowledgeable about foundational concepts and specific cultural expressions.

3. Engage in conversations with culturally diverse friends, colleagues, and others to anchor general information.

4. Practice Anchoring Understanding of Diversity and creating 3rd Space options in everyday situations with friends, colleagues, and strangers.

Reflect on Current Skill Levels

There will always be situations and persons whose diversity challenges even very competent practitioners. Paradoxically, Skilled Dialogue is best practiced with what is, in some worldviews, called a "beginner's mind"— a mind clear of preconceptions and open to the unexpected. Vaill referred to some of the reasons why this is so: life is "full of surprises," "complex systems tend to produce novel problems," and events "do not present themselves in neat packages" (1996, pp. 10–12). These statements are especially relevant to encounters across diverse cultural parameters.

Appendix C contains a self-assessment form that may be used to assess the degree to which Skilled Dialogue has been developed. The ratings are relatively arbitrary and meant only to serve as guides for developing Skilled Dialogue's requisite skills. Though a rating of 5 is identified as the highest level, Skilled Dialogue is a process that is never completely mastered, and one can always continue to refine one's skills as novel cultural perspectives are encountered. The use of this form for a specific case is detailed later in this chapter. In addition, Skilled Dialogue is a process learned through practice, so self-assessment should not be done simply to measure achievement. Rather, it should be done on an ongoing basis not only to monitor skill development, but also to assist with the practice of necessary strategies.

Become Knowledgeable About
Foundational Concepts and Specific Cultural Expressions

It is important to learn as much as possible about the constructs of culture and cultural diversity from as many different perspectives as possible (e.g., anthropological, psychological, educational, political). Chapters 1, 2, and 3 provide basic information on these foundational concepts. It might be useful to revisit this information now that readers are more familiar with the Skilled Dialogue process. A variety of other sources are also referenced in Chapters 4, 5, and 6.

Remember that the goal of acquiring cultural information is not to master this knowledge (i.e., arrive at a "final" answer) but, rather, to develop grounded understanding of the complexity and rich variety of cultural paradigms and their impact on behaviors and interpersonal dynamics. Becoming familiar with a range of diverse worldviews, values, behavioral scripts, social practices, and other cultural expressions is important for more than just learning certain characteristics of particular groups (although this knowledge can be helpful). This practice can soften one's natural ethnocentrism by teaching that there are countless ways of structuring worldviews and behavior, all of which are as valid as or perhaps even superior to one's own. All cultural information, whether specific to the families with whom practitioners work, should be placed into a reservoir of information from which hypotheses can subsequently be generated.

Engage in Conversations with Culturally Diverse Friends, Colleagues, and Others to Anchor General Information

As discussed in Chapter 5, it is not enough to just know about others. It is also critical to anchor cultural knowledge. One great way of doing this is to discuss diverse perceptions, values, behaviors, and beliefs with friends, colleagues, and other willing listeners when not in "practitioner mode." For example, if practitioners have had conversations with persons familiar with Hispanic culture in the Southwest prior to meeting with Hispanic families, they will be better able to anchor their understanding of any diverse behaviors and values encountered. Distinguishing between behaviors that are normative to that culture and behaviors that are atypical will become an easier task. (Readers may want to review Chapter 5.)

Of course, it is also productive for practitioners to discuss cultural dynamics with the families with whom they work. It is important, however, to differentiate between these discussions and those that occur outside of family–practitioner contexts. The distinct power dynamics of these two contexts need to be acknowledged and respected. In most cases, it is easier for a friend or colleague than for a parent or other family member to say, for example, "I'm offended when I hear you say that." Also, some families reported to the authors negative experiences with perceiving themselves as responsible not only for their child's care, but also for the practitioners' education. Other families may find this type of interaction with practitioners to be a positive and rewarding experience. It is important to allow the choice to be voluntary—rather than obligatory because practitioners have failed to identify other resources.

Practice Creating 3rd Space Options in Everyday Situations with Friends, Colleagues, and Strangers

Engaging in conversations about culture with diverse persons in daily environments easily leads to the conscious practice of one of Skilled Dialogue's core skills: 3rd Space. Practitioners must not wait to practice 3rd Space options until they meet diverse children and families in their work! Readers may wish to review Chapters 6, in which this skill is discussed.

Behavioral and value differences are always present. Skilled Dialogue can be useful in crafting respectful, reciprocal, and responsive interactions in any situation that contains differences. When behavioral and value differences generate confusion, frustration, or anger, these feelings can be treated as culture bumps, whether ethnic diversity is present or not. (See the discussion on culture bumps in Chapter 5).

Practitioners can work on identifying what specific differences may underlie dissonant interactions at home or even at the mall. Then, they can determine whether they can anchor their understanding of those differences. Figure 9 in Chapter 5 suggests various strategies for developing such understanding. For example, if a friend is often late for appointments and you value punctuality, can you arrive at anchored understanding of these contradictory approaches to time?

Once anchored understanding becomes easier to achieve, developing 3rd Space options in response to contradictions can be practiced. Figure 10 in Chapter 6 can help generate creative alternatives (i.e., 3rd Space itself).

In the previous example about being late, what solutions might be generated that respect each person's boundaries and do not put the responsibility for change on one person? Is it possible to break out of a dualistic "my way (e.g., on time) or your way (e.g., maybe on time, maybe not)" perspective? Chapter 6 provides some strategies for responding to this question.

Developing 3rd Space options can also be practiced in relation to internal dissonance. For instance, a practitioner may think, "I know that I should be more accepting of this family when they skip appointments. Part of me wants to be accepting, but another part of me doesn't. It just isn't respectful of my time." What 3rd Space options might be developed in response to the internal contradictions reflected in such thinking? Remember that such options may not readily come to mind. Just stay with the question and continue to practice the strategies given in Chapter 6.

Practitioners have reported finding 3rd Space as an "Aha!" experience that seems almost independent of their effort.

PHASE II: SET THE STAGE FOR SKILLED DIALOGUE

This second phase of the Skilled Dialogue process focuses on gathering pertinent cultural and linguistic data relative to specific children and families. This is essential for two reasons. The first is to inform assessment and intervention procedures. The second is to alert practitioners to actual and potential culture bumps that may arise during assessment and intervention so that these can be eliminated or lessened.

Phase II typically starts during initial referral; however, it can occur later when children come from other environments or programs. In either case, Phase II is best completed prior to initiating direct assessment or intervention and instruction services, as its results are designed to inform such services. Three relatively sequential practices occur during Phase II:

1. Determine the presence of cultural linguistic diversity.

2. Assess the nature and degree of cultural linguistic diversity.

3. Identify appropriate strategies for responding to diversity (i.e., strategies for minimizing potential culture bumps and maximizing the family's cultural resources).

The following vignette illustrates each of these practices:

Five-year-old Arturo lives in an urban area in the Southwest. His mother, Tracy, used street drugs during her pregnancy and was incarcerated soon after Arturo was born. Arturo's 55-year-old grandmother, Vidalia, became his guardian at that time, and Arturo continues to live with her and his 8-year-old brother, Jaime, in a two-bedroom apartment. Tracy, now out of jail and on probation, "lives" with them also, although she spends little time at the apartment. Vidalia speaks both Spanish and English to the children. The family has regular contact with Arturo's great-grandmother, Delfina, and great-aunt, Hortensia, who use Spanish almost entirely in their interactions with the children. Tracy does not speak Spanish but understands it fairly well. Neither Arturo nor Tracy has any contact with Arturo's father, although there is irregular contact with Jaime's father.

At 2 years of age, Arturo was referred for early intervention services because of developmental delays in language and cognition. Preparations are underway for Arturo's transition into a school-based kindergarten, and he continues to exhibit significant language and cognitive delays. Assessments indicate developmental ages of 3 years for language and 2–3 years for cognition.

An early childhood special education practitioner, a kindergarten teacher, a psychologist, a social worker, and a speech-language pathologist are reviewing Arturo's file. These team members need to make decisions about placement and any additional assessments that may be necessary. They are somewhat concerned about both Tracy's and Vidalia's level of intervention involvement, which diminished once home-based services were discontinued.

Determine the Presence of Cultural Linguistic Diversity

Sometimes the presence of cultural linguistic diversity is immediately obvious (e.g., the family speaks little or no English); at other times, it may not be obvious. In any case, it is always necessary to examine the possibility of cultural linguistic diversity whenever a family initially contacts an early intervention/early childhood special education program.

As discussed in Chapter 1, determining the presence of cultural linguistic diversity is most reliably determined by asking, "How likely am I to understand and attach meaning to behaviors in the same way as family members and others from similar cultural backgrounds?" The lower the probability of attaching similar meanings to behaviors, the more likely culture bumps will be and, consequently, the greater the need for Skilled Dialogue.

This question also needs to be asked from the larger perspective of program services, procedures, and expectations. It is not enough to establish that practitioners are culturally knowledgeable and competent. It is also critical to examine program services, procedures, and expectations. As with individual practitioners, when program services, procedures, and expectations do not match the family's understanding of behaviors (e.g., being on time), culture bumps are likely and Skilled Dialogue is needed.

There are common indicators of cultural linguistic diversity (i.e., dissimilar understandings between families and the practitioners and programs that serve them). These include differences in ethnic background, usage of a language other than English in the home, extensive residence outside the United States, limited association with persons from ENC, and limited schooling in United States. The *AQS: A Guide to Estimating Level of Acculturation* (Baca & Cervantes, 1998) is a tool that can help in determining degree of diversity. The Family Acculturation Screen, a less formal instrument, is discussed later in this chapter. Yet, it is not always necessary to use a particular instrument. Simple observations and practitioners' own experiences can be equally reliable sources of information, as the purpose at this stage is not to pinpoint exactly how families' and practitioners' understandings differ. Rather, the goal is simply to determine whether diversity is present.

At least some degree of diversity is evident in Arturo's case. Even so, the question, "Am I likely to understand and attach the same meaning to behaviors as the family and/or others from similar cultural backgrounds?" might still elicit different answers depending on the perspective from which the question is asked. From the perspective of the assessment process and curricula typical to early childhood special education services, the answer would probably be "No." Early childhood special education assessment and curricula typically reflect ENC values and beliefs (e.g., emphasis on parental decision making independent of the extended family, focus on early autonomy for the child). Arturo's family, on the other hand, reflects at least some aspects of Hispanic culture, a culture distinct from ENC.

From the perspective of individual practitioners, however, the answer could be "Yes." For example, some Spanish-speaking Puerto Rican practitioners might answer, "Yes, to some degree," although others might answer, "No, I am unfamiliar with Hispanic culture outside of the Caribbean." It is possible that a Hispanic staff member from the same community as Arturo's family would answer, "Yes, without qualification."

The answer probably would be closer to "No" than to "Yes" in this and other similar cases for the program in general as well as for some program staff. Anytime that the answer is "No" for either individual practitioners or for the program in general, the next two practices become critical.

Assess the Nature and Degree of Cultural Linguistic Diversity

Once practitioners determine that at least some degree of cultural linguistic diversity exists between the family and themselves or the program, they need to anchor their understanding of this diversity. Such anchoring requires assessing the nature and degree of the identified diversity in more detail. Figure 14 presents tools for doing this. The two most important tools in the figure are the Cultural Data Table and the Cultural Consonance Profile. Appendix C contains blank versions of these two forms as well as the Home Language Profile, the Family Acculturation Screen, and the RLP Profile (see also Chapter 5), which are used in conjunction with the Cultural Data Table.

A Cultural Data Table summarizes cultural information obtained by answering the questions contained in the Guide to Identifying Cultural Data Related to Potential Culture Bumps (see Figure 8 in Chapter 5 for a sample). These questions are critical to anchoring one's understanding of diverse behaviors, beliefs, values, and languages as well as to predicting potential culture bumps (see Chapter 5). Completing a Cultural Data Table helps organize known information and identify needed additional information. If all of the questions in the Guide to Identifying Cultural Data

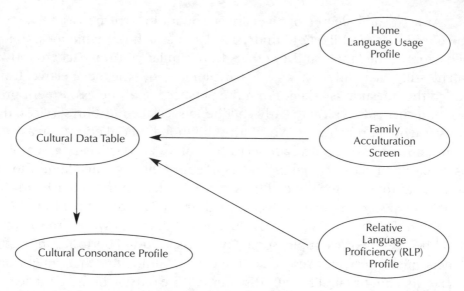

Figure 14.   Tools for assessing the nature and degree of cultural linguistic diversity.

cannot be answered based on the information that is initially available, then home observations and family interviews can be conducted to gather additional information. An RLP Profile (discussed in Chapter 5) may be used to answer questions related to children's language proficiency in more than one language. A Home Language Profile can be similarly helpful in obtaining information on usage patterns at home when more than one language is used. The Family Acculturation Screen can assist in answering questions in the personal-social area. The following discussion illustrates the use of each tool for Arturo.

Figure 15 is a completed Cultural Data Table for Arturo. The next three subsections address the data for Arturo in each of the developmental/ curricular areas. The information that was initially available is shown in typed text. Additional information that was subsequently gathered through family interviews and observations is handwritten.

Communicative-Linguistic   Initial information indicated that Arturo's home environment is sometimes English dominant (e.g., interactions between Tracy and Vidalia) and sometimes Spanish dominant (e.g., interactions between Arturo and Delfina or Hortensia). Additional information gathered through subsequent family observations and interviews revealed that Jaime speaks English in most settings and situations. He was observed to speak Spanish occasionally and appears to retain a basic receptive vocabulary (e.g., responded to requests in Spanish). An RLP Profile was completed for Arturo using an elicited language sample and story-retelling techniques. With Vidalia present, the speech-language pathologist screened

Cultural Data Table

Child's name: _Arturo_   Date completed: _11/6/03_   Completed by: _A. Nielsen and P. Howard_

Directions: Fill in responses to questions from the Guide to Identifying Cultural Data Related to Potential Culture Bumps.

Developmental/curricular area	Comments
Communicative-Linguistic	
Language(s) of child's primary caregiving environment(s)	Grandmother is bilingual (Spanish and English). Great-grandmother and great-aunt are Spanish-dominant. Mother understands Spanish but doesn't speak it. Jaime is 8 years old; he speaks English in most settings and situations and will occasionally use Spanish even though he retains a basic receptive vocabulary.
Child's relative language proficiency (proficiency in English and other language[s] used)	Arturo understands both English and Spanish to some degree. *Proficiency information (see Relative Language Proficiency [RLP] Profile)* *English: receptive (3) expressive (3)* *Spanish: receptive (5) expressive (3)*
Patterns of language usage in child's primary caregiving environment(s)	*Spanish tends to be used predominantly for daily living tasks, and English is used for academically related content (e.g., colors, numbers).* *The variety of Spanish is mostly standard with limited vocabulary and local idioms; the variety of English is standard with limited vocabulary.* *Discussion among adults in the home is mostly in Spanish. Conversations with children are bilingual. Mother and grandmother are the only ones who use English with the children, mostly for school-related topics (e.g., colors, numbers). Only Spanish is spoken when the great-grandmother or great-aunt are present, except on rare occasions (e.g., telephone calls).*
Relative value placed on verbal and nonverbal communication	*Interactions with extended family reflect a strong value on nonverbal communication. Mother and grandmother value verbal communication when in the home without extended family. Family values nonverbal communication; less value is placed on verbal skills.*
Relative status associated with languages other than English and with bilingualism	*Family places instrumental value on English (i.e., use to get things/information); the early intervention/early childhood special education program places instrumental value on Spanish (necessary until English is proficient).* *Within the family is a strong value on bilingualism. The larger community and early intervention/early childhood special education environments place only instrumental value on Spanish (e.g., useful for certain purposes when English is not available) and reflect a stronger value on English.*

(continued)

Figure 15.   Cultural Data Table for Arturo.

Figure 15. *(continued)*

Personal-Social

Degree of acculturation into EuroAmerican Normative Culture (ENC)	Initial information indicates the probability of a low-to-moderate degree of acculturation. Friends and community outside of the family are not mentioned. Jaime's level of acculturation is higher than Arturo's due to age and school experience.
	Great-grandmother and great-aunt have limited familiarity with ENC and tend to interact only within a circle of other Hispanic, Spanish-dominant friends. Grandmother has significant familiarity with ENC. She is a third-grade reading teacher and has many English monolingual friends. Mother, who has a GED, is less familiar with ENC.
Degree of acculturation into U.S. early intervention/early childhood special education culture	Previous contact with early intervention/early childhood special education programs and practitioners indicates at least a moderate degree of acculturation (i.e., expectations, beliefs, practices). Grandmother's and mother's diminished intervention involvement might indicate reduced acculturation into "family as key decision makers" aspect of that culture.
	Great-grandmother and great-aunt have little familiarity with early intervention/early childhood special education culture. Grandmother has moderate familiarity based on Arturo's 2 years in an early intervention program.
	Mother has less familiarity because of her reduced level of participation.
	Jaime has little to no familiarity, while Arturo has significant familiarity.
Sense of self (e.g., relative weight on independence, dependence, and interdependence)	Grandmother's connection with extended family and care of her adult daughter and grandchildren indicate a strong value placed on family and interdependence across generations (i.e., sense of self defined within and by family context).
	Family observations and interview validate initial assumptions: A strong value is placed on interdependence and self-definition within a family context.
Perceptions of identity and competence	Identity seems to be family based, and competence seems to be highly correlated with caregiving and "taking care of one's own" rather than with more externally defined skills and achievements.
Roles and rules associated with parenting and child rearing	Prominent aspects of parenting and child rearing: cross-generational responsibility; child-rearing responsibilities not differentiated across family members.
Knowledge and experience regarding power and social positioning	There may be some issues with authority due to daughter's experiences (e.g., family members may fear authority or feel powerless to interact effectively with them).
	Elders' authority is valued (e.g., grandmother's contact with her mother).
	Family members define themselves as middle-class Americans and do not label themselves as "minorities."
	Great-grandmother and great-aunt belong to an established family that has been active in both social and political arenas for several generations.

Values/beliefs/skills associated with instrumental and emotional support (e.g., gaining access to external resources and getting personal support)	Values seem to be rooted in family and interpersonal networks rather than in more external resources. *Initial assumptions were validated by family observations.*
Sensory-Cognitive Funds of knowledge: what type of knowledge is valued; concept structures and definitions (e.g., how family is defined)	Socioemotional knowledge appears to be valued over cognitive instrumental knowledge (e.g., individual skills like reading a map). *Socioemotional knowledge tends to be valued over cognitive instrumental knowledge. Cultural identities play a significant role. Grandmother values literature and reading. She has a wide range of knowledge. Family history and genealogy are frequent topics of discussion.*
Preferred strategies for acquiring new learning	Forestructure points to the possibility of valuing modeling over explicit verbal instructions and trial and error. *Storytelling, modeling, and questioning are valued over exploration and trial-and-error learning. Teaching strategies tend to be implicit and indirect, both oral (e.g., storytelling) and nonverbal (e.g., modeling).*
Preferred strategies for problem solving and decision making	Turning to family for assistance highlights the possibility of shared decision making. *Great-grandmother is a key decision maker in the family. Problem solving tends to be inductive rather than deductive. The only male involved in family decisions is Jaime's father, who is occasionally consulted.*
Worldview (i.e., assumptions about how the world works and about what is "right" and what is "wrong")	Forestructure predicts a strong possibility of culture bumps with ENC practitioners in this area (e.g., family's belief that it is appropriate for a grandmother to assume responsibility for a grandchild and seemingly let the mother "off the hook"). *Mother's and grandmother's worldviews tend to be bicultural (e.g., they recognize both medical and spiritual reasons for Arturo's delays); great-grandmother's and great-aunt's views tend to be more "traditional."*

Arturo. The practitioner elicited language by showing him pictures of various activities (e.g., a baseball game, a picnic) and asking him to tell her all that he could about the pictures. Then, she told Arturo that she was going to read him a story and asked him to retell it after she was finished. Both procedures were done in Spanish and in English. The resulting RLP Profile (see Figure 16) showed that Arturo understands both Spanish and English. The story retelling activity, however, indicated significantly greater comprehension in Spanish than in English. His expressive skills in English were shown to be similar to his English comprehension skills. When retelling the story in English, Arturo evidenced consistent errors, especially in the use of tense and pronouns. Based on this information, Arturo is considered partially bilingual, with Spanish being his stronger language.

A Home Language Usage Profile (see Figure 17) indicated that discussions among adults in Arturo's home are mostly in Spanish, although conversations with the children are bilingual. Jaime and other neighborhood children around Arturo predominantly use English, sending a powerful message that English is the language of choice outside the home. This message may inadvertently inhibit Arturo's expressive skills in Spanish (see discussion on the impact of language loss in Chapter 8). Tracy and Vidalia are the only adults who use English with Arturo and Jaime in the home, mostly for school-related topics. Spanish is used almost exclusively in the presence of Delfina and Hortensia.

Interactions with the extended family reflect the high value placed on nonverbal communication, although Vidalia and Tracy value verbal communication in other situations (e.g., much discussion about daily experiences was observed). In addition, using both English and Spanish appropriately is valued, as evidenced by Vidalia's modeling and the family's insistence on continuing to use Spanish. Family members reported that speaking and understanding Spanish is important for family interactions and success in the larger community. English was considered important for successful participation in school and the English-speaking community. The implicit message seems to be that English is not as important as Spanish outside of that participation.

Personal-Social   Few questions in this area could be answered using the initially available data. Personal-social data usually are not explicitly gathered, although they may be known if the family has a long association with a particular program. As in Arturo's case, it is often necessary to gather additional information through observations and interviews and the completion of an Family Acculturation Screen (see Figure 18).

Vidalia appears to have been the first family member to acquire significant familiarity with ENC. She was the first family member to speak English fluently and attend U.S. schools. She holds a master's degree and a teaching license, and she has worked as a third-grade reading teacher

Relative Language Proficiency (RLP) Profile

Child's name: _Arturo_   Date: _1/10/03_   Date of birth: _11/15/97_

Chronological age: _5 years, 2 months_   Completed by: _J. Irish_

Site: _Child's home_   Instrument: _Elicited language sample and story retelling_

Proficiency in Language Other than English (Specify language: _Spanish_)

Receptive:	⑤	4	3	2	1
	Good: No significant errors	Mildly limited: Some errors	Moderately limited: Consistent/ significant errors	Severely limited: Frequent and significant errors	Nonverbal and/or unintelligible

Expressive:	5	4	③	2	1

Comments:

Arturo seemed to understand Spanish at an age-appropriate level but had more limited expressive skills. His mean length of utterance (MLU) was below age expectations; he retained a simple noun-verb-object structure.

English Proficiency

Receptive:	5	4	③	2	1
	Good: No significant errors	Mildly limited: Some errors	Moderately limited: Consistent/ significant errors	Severely limited: Frequent and significant errors	Nonverbal and/or unintelligible

Expressive:	5	4	③	2	1

Comments:

Arturo's comprehension seemed limited (e.g., could not answer simple "who"/"what" questions). His expressive skills were similarly limited (MLU below age level; used mainly noun-verb structures).

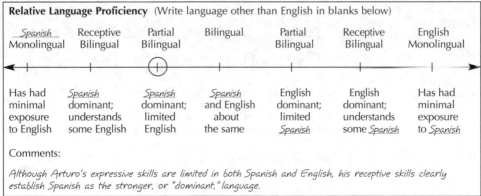

Relative Language Proficiency (Write language other than English in blanks below)						
Spanish Monolingual	Receptive Bilingual	Partial Bilingual	Bilingual	Partial Bilingual	Receptive Bilingual	English Monolingual
Has had minimal exposure to English	_Spanish_ dominant; understands some English	_Spanish_ dominant; limited English	_Spanish_ and English about the same	English dominant; limited _Spanish_	English dominant; understands some _Spanish_	Has had minimal exposure to _Spanish_

Comments:

Although Arturo's expressive skills are limited in both Spanish and English, his receptive skills clearly establish Spanish as the stronger, or "dominant," language.

Figure 16. Relative Language Proficiency (RLP) Profile for Arturo.

for more than 10 years. Tracy did not complete high school but obtained a general equivalency diploma (GED). Jaime's level of acculturation is strong; he has several close friends who are English monolingual and spends time in their homes.

Home Language Usage Profile

Child's name: _Arturo_   Date: _1/10/03_   Completed by: _J. Irish_

Person(s)	Only L$_x$ Specify language other than English used in home: _Spanish_	Mostly L$_x$ _(Spanish)_, some English	L$_x$ _(Spanish)_ and English used equally	Some L$_x$ _(Spanish)_, mostly English	Only English	Other language (specify) ___
Mother				X		
Father					X Jaime's dad	
Siblings				X		
Maternal grandparents						
Paternal grandparents	Not	In	Contact	With	Child	
Caregiver (different from persons listed above)	None	Used	Outside	of	Family	
Neighborhood friends/peers				X		
Teacher(s)				X		
Social peers (e.g., at child care; at preschool)					X	

(*Key:* L$_x$ is the language other than English used in the home.)

Comments:

Based on observations and family interviews, Arturo appears to have little access to Spanish usage outside the home.

Figure 17.   Home Language Usage Profile for Arturo. (*Source:* Williams & DeGaetano, 1985.)

Family Acculturation Screen

Child's name: *Arturo*   Date: *12/30/02*   Completed by: *A. Nielsen and P. Howard*

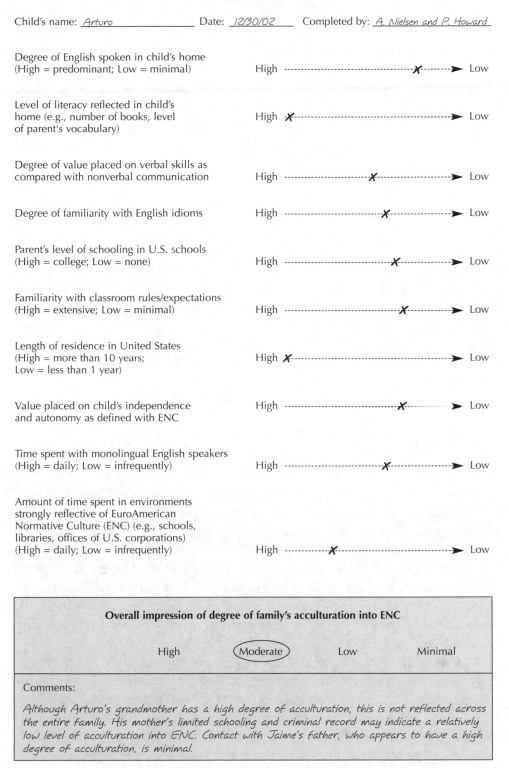

Degree of English spoken in child's home
(High = predominant; Low = minimal)   High ---------------------------------------X-------> Low

Level of literacy reflected in child's
home (e.g., number of books, level   High X--> Low
of parent's vocabulary)

Degree of value placed on verbal skills as
compared with nonverbal communication   High -----------------------------X-----------------> Low

Degree of familiarity with English idioms   High ----------------------------------X----------------> Low

Parent's level of schooling in U.S. schools
(High = college; Low = none)   High --------------------------------------X------------> Low

Familiarity with classroom rules/expectations
(High = extensive; Low = minimal)   High --------------------------------------X------------> Low

Length of residence in United States
(High = more than 10 years;   High X--> Low
Low = less than 1 year)

Value placed on child's independence   High -----------------------------------X------------ > Low
and autonomy as defined with ENC

Time spent with monolingual English speakers
(High = daily; Low = infrequently)   High --------------------------------X----------------> Low

Amount of time spent in environments
strongly reflective of EuroAmerican
Normative Culture (ENC) (e.g., schools,
libraries, offices of U.S. corporations)
(High = daily; Low = infrequently)   High --------------X------------------------------> Low

---

Overall impression of degree of family's acculturation into ENC

High   (Moderate)   Low   Minimal

Comments:

Although Arturo's grandmother has a high degree of acculturation, this is not reflected across the entire family. His mother's limited schooling and criminal record may indicate a relatively low level of acculturation into ENC. Contact with Jaime's father, who appears to have a high degree of acculturation, is minimal.

Figure 18.   Family Acculturation Screen for Arturo.

The family's degree of acculturation in the early intervention/early childhood special education culture is more limited, based on their varying degrees of association with Arturo's early intervention program and practitioners. Family observations and interviews during a 2-week period validated the practitioners' initial assumptions regarding understanding of sense of self, perceptions of identity and competence, and roles/rules associated with parenting and child rearing. These are more reflective of values and beliefs in Hispanic culture than in ENC (see Arturo's Cultural Data Table, Figure 15). Yet, the family members define themselves as middle-class Americans and do not label themselves "minorities." Delfina and Hortensia belong to an established family that has been politically and socially active in the Southwest for almost 100 years.

Sensory-Cognitive   Scant sensory-cognitive data existed in Arturo's case, so much additional information needed to be gathered. This is not uncommon, even though these data are especially relevant to practitioners' understanding of families' funds of knowledge (i.e., the skills and knowledge that they bring to early intervention/early childhood special education environments) and of the teaching/learning strategies valued and modeled in the home.

Arturo's sensory-cognitive data present an interesting bicultural portrait common to many Hispanic families in the Southwest. His family tends to value socioemotional knowledge over the cognitive knowledge and skills typically valued in ENC environments. For instance, they value social skills over years of formal schooling. Even though cognitive knowledge and skills valued in ENC environments are also considered important, they are perceived more as a means to an end than as an end in themselves. Storytelling, modeling, and questioning are the family's preferred strategies for acquiring new knowledge. Discovery and trial-and-error strategies were not observed except when adults helped Jaime with his schoolwork. Vidalia and Delfina used implicit, indirect teaching strategies. Yet, Vidalia was also observed to use the more direct, explicit strategies that she learned from early intervention practitioners who previously worked with Arturo.

Although 89 years old, Delfina remains the family's key decision maker. Her problem-solving strategies, as well as those used by other family members, tend to be inductive rather than deductive. Jaime's father is the only male involved in decision making; he is consulted from time to time when the family perceives a need for male representation (e.g., when needing to purchase a car, obtain insurance, or seek legal help).

The family's worldviews are generationally distinct. Tracy and Vidalia have worldviews that reflect both ENC and traditional Hispanic beliefs.

For example, they recognize medical reasons for Arturo's developmental delays. Yet, they also recognize Delfina's belief that the delays resulted from Tracy's ignoring a dream about having her pregnancy blessed in the local church. They feel no need to choose between these two views. Delfina and Hortensia, conversely, hold to a traditional Hispanic worldview that might be judged as nonscientific ("untrue") within ENC. For them, a pregnancy without a spiritual dimension (i.e., a blessing) leaves both mother and child unprotected against negative influences and actions.

Cultural Consonance Once these forms have been used as necessary to place all available information into a Cultural Data Table, completing a Cultural Consonance Profile is recommended. A Cultural Consonance Profile rates the perceived degree of consonance or match between the home culture and language and the culture and language reflected by early childhood practitioners and in early intervention/early childhood special education environments. A higher consonance rating means less need for significant adaptations to typical early intervention/early childhood special education procedures and processes, although these can never be ruled out completely. The use of a Cultural Consonance Profile is illustrated in the following discussion. Ratings for the degree of consonance are based on the knowledge and perceptions of the practitioners who completed the Profile.

Arturo's Cultural Consonance Profile (Figure 19) shows limited consonance between the program and Arturo and his family in the communicative-linguistic area. The moderate rating in this area was based on the fact that language and communication patterns in the home differed fairly significantly from those found in the kindergarten to which Arturo is being transferred. Spanish is often spoken at home; however, only one practitioner speaks Spanish in the new early childhood special education environment. In addition, this environment reflects ENC values and beliefs regarding other aspects of language usage and patterns (e.g., an emphasis on verbal communication).

Consonance in the personal-social area was rated at the low-to-moderate level, based on available cultural data. The practitioners believed that the family's beliefs, practices, and values in this area reflect Southwest Hispanic culture more than ENC. This is especially true in the areas of sense of self, parenting roles, and values and beliefs related to obtaining support resources.

The sensory-cognitive area was also judged to have a low-to-moderate degree of consonance with early childhood environments and practitioners. Although Vidalia's and Tracy's funds of knowledge and worldviews included aspects of ENC, the funds of knowledge and worldview held by Delfina still wielded great influence in this area. In addition, both Vidalia

Cultural Consonance Profile

Child's name: _Arturo_   Date: _1/08/03_   Completed by: _A. Nielsen_

	Highly similar to early childhood environment(s)/ practitioners' profiles ←→	Highly dissimilar from early childhood environment(s)/ practitioners' profiles

I. Communicative-Linguistic Area

Comments

Language(s) used in child's home	5	4	③	2	1 _____
Child's relative language proficiency	5	4	③	2	1 _____
					Little use of direct question-and-answer
Patterns of language usage	5	4	3	②	1 *routines*
Relative value placed on verbal/ nonverbal communication	5	4	③	2	1 _____
Relative status of language other than English and bilingualism	5	4	3	②	1 _____

II. Personal-Social Area

Family's degree of acculturation	5	4	③	2	1 _____
Sense of self/perception of identity/competence	5	4	3	②	1 _____
Parenting/child-rearing roles and rules	5	4	3	②	1 _____
					Familiarity with social and political power
Knowledge/experience regarding power and positioning	5	④	3	2	1
					Tend to rely on family and personal networks
Values and beliefs regarding support	5	4	3	②	1

III. Sensory-Cognitive Area

Funds of knowledge/concept definition/structures	5	4	③	2	1 _____
Preferred learning strategies	5	4	3	②	1 _____
Preferred problem-solving/ decision-making strategies	5	4	3	②	1 _____
Worldview	5	4	③	2	1 *Bicultural*

Degree of consonance with early childhood environment(s)/practitioners' profiles

Communicative-linguistic area	High	⟨Moderate⟩	Low	Minimal
Personal-social area	High	⟨Moderate	Low⟩	Minimal
Sensory-cognitive area	High	⟨Moderate	Low⟩	Minimal

Comments: *Sensory-cognitive is moderate to low depending on the context and topic*

Figure 19. Cultural Consonance Profile for Arturo.

110

and Tracy were observed to use teaching/learning strategies that reflect Hispanic culture more than ENC.

Arturo's Cultural Consonance Profile shows an overall pattern of low-to-moderate consonance within as well as across areas, which is fairly typical for many children from bilingual and bicultural families. These families retain many beliefs, values, and practices associated with their home cultures while acquiring ENC beliefs, values, and practices that are deemed necessary for successful participation in work and social environments. Some families keep each set of beliefs, values, and practices neatly distinct—just as some bilingual speakers keep their languages distinct. Other families "mix and match" beliefs, values, and practices—just as other bilingual speakers use two languages, rapidly switching them in response to personal and situational variables. In both cases, it is important to recognize which beliefs, values, and practices are operative at which times. Such recognition is critical for developing adaptations and opportunities that maximize the child's learning, family–practitioner collaboration, and adaptations and opportunities that are concrete expressions of respect, reciprocity, and responsiveness. See Chapters 8 and 9 for further discussion of this point.

Cultural consonance ratings are subjective, based on perceived similarities and differences between a child's home environment and the environment where the child will likely be placed. Many variables can affect these ratings (e.g., placement in a different environment, the addition of a Hispanic Spanish-speaking teacher, additional information from the family). The purpose of determining ratings is not to pinpoint a specific variable exactly (i.e., cultural consonance). Rather, it is to stimulate and structure team discussions. Lower ratings would indicate a stronger need to adapt existing procedures and materials to increase the probability of interactions with children and families that are respectful, reciprocal, and responsive.

Develop Cultural Linguistic Response Plans

Once the nature and degree of cultural diversity has been sufficiently assessed, the next step and final practice associated with Phase II is the identification of appropriate strategies for responding to the assessed cultural and linguistic diversity. It is here that the skill of 3rd Space becomes most critical, as practitioners seek to honor diverse values and behaviors while implementing early intervention/early childhood special education procedures and goals.

The recommended approach is to review 3rd Space strategies (see Figure 10 in Chapter 6) and then augment assessment and/or intervention practices by developing Cultural Linguistic Response Plans (see Appendix C for the blank version of these forms). Assessment Cultural Linguistic Response Plans address adaptations specific to assessment. Instructional Cultural Linguistic Response Plans focus on intervention and instruction procedures and activities. These plans are discussed briefly in this chapter; extended discussions with accompanying vignettes are provided in Chapters 8 and 9.

Each Cultural Linguistic Response Plan has two major parts. One reminds the user of the foundation on which each Plan rests: the qualities and skills that define the Skilled Dialogue process. These qualities and skills emphasize that all specific adaptations reflect the Skilled Dialogue process and are not merely put together piecemeal. The second part identifies specific considerations related to either assessment or intervention. The content of this part varies according to the needs of individual children and their families.

Figure 20 is a sample Assessment Cultural Linguistic Response Plan for Arturo and his family that identifies four areas of consideration. These are areas within which assessment dilemmas commonly arise (see Chapter 8 for a more detailed discussion). Five suggestions are given for Arturo's practitioners to consider in this area. The first suggestion responds to the fact that Arturo's language skills are not contained within a single language. The second suggestion recognizes that when items are presented in a child's stronger language first, memory of those items can inflate scores for the weaker language. The remaining three suggestions address recommended practices for bilingual assessments (see Chapter 8 for guidelines on interpreting and reporting assessment data). Considerations related to data gathering procedures focus on two related aspects: 1) integrating family members and their perspectives into the assessment process and 2) integrating familiar strategies common in Arturo's home to control for the effects of unfamiliarity. The third set of considerations addresses the materials to be used in assessing Arturo's development and skills. Using Spanish-language materials that contain funds of knowledge familiar to Arturo will increase the probability of accurate and optimal assessment results. Finally, suggestions are given for reporting assessment results.

Although certainly not exhaustive, these considerations can go a long way toward communicating respect (recognition of Arturo's boundaries and funds of knowledge), establishing reciprocity (promotion of equal voice and privilege for the family's boundaries and funds of knowledge), and promoting responsiveness (creation of inclusive and creative assessment options). More detailed suggestions that practitioners may use in completing their own Assessment Cultural Linguistic Response Plans are given in Chapter 8. A parallel plan addressing intervention and instruction needs to

Assessment Cultural Linguistic Response Plan

Child's name: _Arturo_   Date: _1/13/03_   Completed by: _P. O'Donoghue_

Specific Assessment Considerations

RE: *Language and communication*

1. Use both English and Spanish with slightly more Spanish, especially for directions, explanations, and non–school related content.
2. Test in less-proficient language first to minimize carry-over from one language to the other.
3. Probe all items missed in one language in the other language.
4. Match patterns of language usage in the home as much as possible.
5. Check for the influence of Spanish semantics and syntax on English.

RE: *Data-gathering procedures*

1. Involve family members in assessment; use familiar routines when possible.
2. Use less structured and more dynamic procedures in addition to standardized procedures.
3. Minimize the use of trial-and-error and direct-questioning procedures.
4. Increase the use of modeling and storytelling strategies that are familiar to the child.
5. Use peer-assisted and cooperative formats in addition to independent one-to-one formats.

RE: *Assessment materials*

1. Be aware of funds of knowledge reflected in pictures and objects; tap into familiar funds of knowledge unless explicitly assessing the ability to process unfamiliar material.
2. Include Spanish-language materials.
3. Use materials that are familiar to the child as well as less familiar materials that are common to early intervention/early childhood special education (e.g., a balance beam).

RE: *Reporting assessment results*

1. Identify which items were presented in which language; also note the language(s) used to respond to items.
2. Report adaptations to standard procedures.
3. Detail when results reflect linguistic or cultural variables and when they reflect developmental (delay or disability) variables.

Underlying Process Reminders

	Anchored Understanding of Diversity	3rd Space
RESPECT	Acknowledge the range and validity of diverse perspectives.	Stay with the tension of differing perspectives.
RECIPROCITY	Establish interactions that allow equal voice for all participants.	Develop opportunities for equalizing power across interactions.
RESPONSIVENESS	Communicate respect and understanding of others' perspectives.	Create responses that integrate and provide access to the strengths of diverse perspectives.

Figure 20. Assessment Cultural Linguistic Response Plan for Arturo.

be developed following assessment to ensure that these qualities continue following assessment. See Chapter 9 for detailed discussion of suggestions for completing an Instructional Cultural Linguistic Response Plan.

PHASE III: CONDUCT ONGOING SKILLED DIALOGUE

The need for ongoing Skilled Dialogue arises anytime practitioners interact with children and families from cultural backgrounds that differ from their own or from aspects of ENC reflected in early intervention/early childhood special education programs. Some interactions are structured in a fairly formal manner (e.g., assessment, specific intervention sessions). Other interactions (e.g., gathering additional information on home culture and language, implementing Cultural Linguistic Response Plans) are less formalized or predictable. Phase III of Skilled Dialogue focuses on these less structured interactions.

Critical Incident Analysis Sheets (see Appendix C for a blank version of this form) can be helpful in guiding Skilled Dialogue within these situations. Unlike Cultural Linguistic Response Plans, Critical Incident Analysis Sheets remain the same whether used during interactions related to assessment or to instruction and intervention. These sheets can be used anytime that interactions between practitioners and the child or family are problematic. Figure 21 is a Critical Incident Sheet that was completed before a home visit with Arturo's family (an additional example is provided in Chapter 8). The form shown in Figure 21 was developed from initial information and was intended to serve as a guide for the planned family meeting and observation.

Although it is not always possible to have significant cultural linguistic information prior to visiting a family, it is always important to review the key principles and strategies associated with Anchored Understanding of Diversity and 3rd Space before doing so. The early childhood special education program staff had some initial information on Arturo and his family. Based on this information and their review of the key principles and strategies, the practitioners developed an initial Critical Incident Analysis Sheet (see Figure 21) in preparation for the home visit. They discussed their goals for the meeting and brainstormed possible scenarios as they reviewed key principles and strategies. The practitioners were especially concerned about "getting off on the right foot" with the family because family involvement in Arturo's intervention had diminished.

Figure 21 summarizes the team's discussion about each Key Principle. The principles associated with respect—in relation to Anchored Understanding of Diversity and 3rd Space—emerged as fundamental. The team members wanted to clarify that the visit's purpose was to get to know the

Critical Incident Analysis Sheet

Child's name: _Arturo_   Date: _4/14/03_   Completed by: _C. Kramer_

Incident description: _Early childhood special education practitioners will visit with Arturo's family to obtain additional cultural and linguistic information. Both observation and direct interview techniques will be used. Practitioners will focus on explicit communication of respect, reciprocity, and responsiveness._

Quality	Anchored Understanding of Diversity	3rd Space
Respect	Key Principle: Acknowledge the range and validity of diverse perspectives. • Set a tone of respectful curiosity for conversation. • State the purpose of the visit: to get to know more about Arturo to better serve him and meet the family's needs. • Allow time for informal conversation; be somewhat less direct than usual in presenting questions and eliciting responses.	Key Principle: Stay with the tension of differing perspectives. • Remember to remain nonjudgmental and not to contradict or try to change family beliefs or practices (especially regarding parenting and the mother's role with Arturo). • Remember that the visit's purpose is not to solve problems or to reach an agreement but to get to know each other better. • Notice which aspects of behavior or beliefs are difficult to accept or validate.
Reciprocity	Key Principle: Establish interactions that allow equal voice for all participants. • Give conversational prompts and ask open-ended questions that allow family members to talk. • Ask for their experiences and views; communicate that we are there to learn from them (not just to address differences). • Look for the positive and what the family has to teach or offer in terms of resources.	Key Principle: Develop opportunities for equalizing power across interactions. • Use topics/analogies/metaphors that equalize participation (e.g., talk about common challenges when learning new skills); do not use unfamiliar vocabulary without explanation. • Communicate that family members are also experts and that early intervention/early childhood special education knowledge is not superior to family knowledge.
Responsiveness	Key Principle: Communicate respect and understanding of others' perspectives. • Reflect an understanding of the family's perspective with explicit statements (e.g., "I see how that makes sense") and other cues (e.g., silence, not insisting on our point, accepting disagreement and exploring instead of defending). • Check for understanding by paraphrasing and asking the speaker if that's what was meant.	Key Principle: Create responses that integrate and provide access to the strengths of diverse perspectives. • Explicitly state that we seek to gain access to family strengths and to integrate them with program and practitioner strengths; give examples of how these might complement each other. • Keep asking how the family's perspectives/skills might complement ours (e.g., explore what aspects of the curriculum might be enhanced by the family's emphasis on nonverbal communication).

Figure 21. Critical Incident Analysis Sheet completed prior to home visit with Arturo's family.

115

family better, not merely to obtain agreement for a preset agenda. They wanted to establish interactions within which family perspectives (i.e., boundaries) and practitioner perspectives received equal weight (i.e., voice). The practitioners also wanted to remain nonjudgmental about family practices they considered troublesome (e.g., Tracy's lack of involvement in her son's life) and, thus, to develop opportunities for truly collaborative participation. Informed by this initial exercise, the team members scheduled and conducted a home visit.

Following this visit with the family, the practitioners reflected on both the process and the outcome of their visit. They first used the Skilled Dialogue Self-Assessment to assess their level of skill in this particular instance (see Figure 22). The team members scored themselves fairly high on Anchored Understanding of Diversity. Although they realized that they could still improve in this area, they believed that they communicated respect, established reciprocity, and acted responsively to a significant degree. The team members indicated a lower assessment rating of their ability to achieve 3rd Space. They believed that they had equalized power across their interactions, but they were unsure that they had successfully reframed contradictions. The team was particularly concerned about Tracy's and Vidalia's insistence that their involvement in Arturo's intervention is less critical now that Arturo will be receiving service 5 days a week. They were also concerned about Delfina's apparent dichotomizing of learning: She considered academic learning the school's responsibility and social skills learning (which, in her view, was of greater value) the family's responsibility. The team believed that this dichotomy supported Tracy's and Vidalia's decisions about reduced involvement.

The team members decided to reflect further on this difference between their views and the family's by completing a new Critical Incident Analysis Sheet (see Figure 23). They hoped to identify more specifically why culture bumps were encountered and to examine how they might better respect the family's views while simultaneously communicating the continued need for active support and involvement. The team members first examined the three key principles of Anchored Understanding of Diversity in relation to the differences between their perspective on learning and the family's perspective. They realized that before they could expect greater collaboration, they needed to gain a deeper understanding of the family's perspective. Although they had reviewed the questions used to identify potential culture bumps (see Figure 8 in Chapter 5), they realized that they did not really understand the family's preference for decreased involvement. It was true that Arturo would be receiving services three more times per week, but was there a deeper reason? The team members knew that Vidalia and Tracy wanted the best for Arturo. Why, then, was

Skilled Dialogue Self-Assessment

Child's name: _Arturo_   Date: _1/17/03_

Completed by: _Early childhood team (Brown, Devon, and Blake)_

	Anchored Understanding of Diversity	3rd Space
1 **Basic** **awareness**	☐ I understand and can define basic concepts (e.g., culture, culture bumps, reciprocity, Skilled Dialogue, paradox, funds of knowledge, 3rd Space).	
2 **Beginning** **applications**	☐ I can describe a range of diverse cultural perspectives, behaviors, values, practices, and belief systems (e.g., I can describe child-rearing practices associated with several different cultural groups).	☐ I demonstrate the ability to "stay with the tension" of contradictory perspectives without rushing to solutions/resolutions.
3 **Lower** **intermediate** **applications**	☐ I acknowledge the validity of diverse perspectives by listening mindfully and accurately identifying the meaning associated with both my own and others' perspectives.	☒ I equalize power across interactions by shifting the focus of the conversation and exploring complementary aspects of diverse perspectives.
4 **Upper** **intermediate** **applications**	☒ I identify and explore others' contributions and resources in relation to specific interactions and situations, independently and with fluency.	☐ I understand the process of reframing contradictions into complementary perspectives and can do so independently and with fluency.
5 **Advanced** **applications**	☐ I consistently communicate respect for and understanding of others' perspectives; families report feeling accepted and valued.	☐ I consistently create responses to children/families that integrate and provide access to the strengths of diverse perspectives; families report a sense of free choice rather than forced choice.

Comments:

Anchored Understanding of Diversity: Overall okay; there is some difficulty communicating respect and understanding regarding the mother's and grandmother's insistence that their involvement is less critical now that Arturo will be receiving early childhood special education services 5 days per week.

3rd Space: This is the toughest area. There is difficulty finding and exploring complementary aspects of diverse perspectives (i.e., contradictions) related to parenting and family's continued involvement in Arturo's program. We tended to present the early childhood special education perspective as superior, and family also seemed to buy into that idea.

Figure 22.   Skilled Dialogue Self-Assessment completed by Arturo's early intervention team.

continued involvement not seen as the best option? What did continued involvement mean to them? The team decided to clarify this by following the second principle for Anchored Understanding: Establish interactions that allow equal voice for all perspectives. The team members decided on a more open agenda for the next collaborative meeting, which would give the family members more time to discuss their perspective. The team members also decided to communicate more explicitly their acceptance of the family's right to hold that perspective. They thought of statements that

Critical Incident Analysis Sheet

Child's name: _Arturo_   Date: _1/17/03_   Completed by: _Early childhood team (Brown, Devon, and Blake)_

Incident description: _During the meeting with Arturo's family, the practitioners were concerned about the mother's and grandmother's view that they could be less involved now that Arturo would receive services 5 days per week. They were also concerned about the great-grandmother's dichotomizing academic and social learning._

Quality	Anchored Understanding of Diversity	3rd Space
Respect	Key Principle: Acknowledge the range and validity of diverse perspectives. • _Review questions for identifying potential culture bumps._ • _Clarify meanings of a continuing level of participation for the family._	Key Principle: Stay with the tension of differing perspectives. • _Listen._ • _Observe differences without communicating disapproval or a need to change while clearly presenting our perspective._ • _Acknowledge differences._
Reciprocity	Key Principle: Establish interactions that allow equal voice for all participants. • _Maintain an open-ended agenda._ • _Elicit the family's views._ • _Listen without reiterating the early childhood special education perspective._	Key Principle: Develop opportunities for equalizing power across interactions. • _Stay open to topics that the family brings up._ • _Talk about how it is not an either-or choice; use the analogy of bilingualism._ • _Explicitly state that Arturo needs both the family's and the practitioners' perspectives if he is to participate competently in both cultures._
Responsiveness	Key Principle: Communicate respect and understanding of others' perspectives. • _Remember to explicitly communicate an acceptance of the family's perspective with statements such as "We really want to understand your point of view; we've watched you work with Arturo and know that you really want what is best for him."_	Key Principle: Create responses that integrate and provide access to the strengths of diverse perspectives. • _Rethink our understanding of participation as we listen to family. Does it have to mean what it has meant in the past (i.e., the family reinforcing the practitioners' strategies)? Can it mean something different (e.g., the family reinforcing one set of strategies and the practitioners reinforcing another? Are both complementary)?_

Figure 23. Critical Incident Analysis Sheet completed following home visit with Arturo's family.

118

would be helpful, such as "We really want to understand your point of view; we have watched you work with Arturo for several years now and know that you really want the best for him."

The team realized that using such statements immediately led to the first principle for establishing 3rd Space: Stay with the tension of differing perspectives. Rather than responding to the family's statements by clarifying their own perspective or giving additional reasons for continued involvement, the team members realized that they should simply listen and observe the differences between the two perspectives. This listening, even more than the explicit statement that they had crafted, would strongly communicate their respect for the family.

Examining and discussing the second principle for establishing 3rd Space—develop opportunities for equalizing power—yielded two results. The first was the team's decision to use the analogy of bilingualism to communicate how two different views (i.e., two different "languages") can work together to create better options. The family had significantly more experience with bilingualism than the team members. Thus, this analogy could equalize power by explicitly placing the team in the position of being learners as well as teachers. As the family described the process of using two languages, the team members would look for opportunities to compare that situation to the concept of two views on participation. A second result was the softening of their previous belief that the family's perspective was incompatible with their own. In preparing the bilingual analogy, the team members realized the potential for integrating diverse perspectives into a richer and stronger whole.

As they worked through the Critical Incident Analysis Sheet, the team members also realized that whatever happened, their interactions with the family would truly be more collaborative. Their earlier sense of tension lessened considerably. They could now think about possible 3rd Space responses. Even so, they remembered that family input was critical to assessing the viability of these options.

This sample scenario illustrates three steps essential to the third phase of Skilled Dialogue (see Figure 13). The first step is interacting with the child and family. The second step involves reflecting on the degree to which that interaction was respectful, reciprocal, and responsive. The third step is adjusting future interactions to diminish or eliminate culture bumps and to enhance respect, reciprocity, and responsiveness. The third phase is, in many ways, the "maintenance" phase of Skilled Dialogue. Respect, reciprocity, and responsiveness become integral parts of all early intervention/early childhood special education services as each of its three steps are followed. However, the third phase is not as clear cut as the other two. It does not take place in relation to a clear set of procedures or explicit protocols (i.e., assessment or plan development) as does the second phase, for example. Skilled Dialogue strategies are not intended to eliminate the "messiness" of unstructured and ongoing interactions. Rather, they are designed to help practitioners navigate through them with increasing respect, reciprocity, and responsiveness. Again, all three phases—establishing forestructures, setting the stage for Skilled Dialogue, and conducting ongoing Skilled Dialogue—work in a reiterative fashion to ensure the establishment of Anchored Understanding of Diversity and the creation of appropriate 3rd Space options. Their linear presentation in this chapter is not intended to communicate a rigid sequence. Revisiting Sections I and II may also be helpful in implementing this chapter's suggestions for learning and practicing Skilled Dialogue.

Finally, it is important to remember that Skilled Dialogue is a process-oriented skill. Like riding a bicycle, it cannot be acquired before it is practiced. The material in Chapters 7, 8, and 9 is intended to provide glimpses into how Skilled Dialogue might occur. In each example, one set of variables has been chosen, and one "conclusion" has been reached. These scenarios are not necessarily the best or only ones for ensuring respect, reciprocity, and responsiveness. Others can be equally valid in many cases. As in other human endeavors, there is seldom a single right answer. Therefore, it is important to focus as much on the process used to arrive at the "answer" as on the answers themselves (i.e., the outcomes). The key to cultural competency lies in this process, not in the answers. With that caveat, the authors wish the reader happy adventuring in Skilled Dialogue and invite the reader to share with them any aspects of that adventuring.

Respectful, Reciprocal, and Responsive Assessment

The challenge is not simply becoming aware of the framework from which a culturally different family operates, but . . . becoming aware of the cultural assumptions from which professionals derive their judgments. (Harry, 1992, p. 334)

As discussed in Chapter 7, early intervention/early childhood special education practitioners must develop forestructures and practice Skilled Dialogue on an ongoing basis. Practitioners cannot wait until they begin working with a family to develop and utilize these practices. Perhaps nowhere are the potential problems or dilemmas of waiting more evident than in the arena of assessment.

The evaluation and assessment of infants, toddlers, and preschoolers has presented significant challenges to the early childhood special education field (McLean, 2001). This is particularly true when families' cultural linguistic backgrounds differ from those of practitioners (Moore & Beatty, 1995; Santos de Barona & Barona, 1991). During any assessment process, a child's abilities must be considered within the family's cultural context and home environment. In an ideal situation, practitioners determine the degree of cultural consonance and the corresponding need for Skilled Dialogue prior to conducting any formal child assessment activities; however, this is not always the case. Even when other programs or individuals have already conducted assessments, it is important to determine the degree of cultural consonance between families and early childhood special education services, as well as the corresponding impact on specific procedures and interactions.

Sections I and II examine the potential dilemmas that practitioners may experience because of culture bumps. Some bumps revolve around communicative-linguistic issues related to language(s) spoken, nonverbal communication, and the perceived status of languages other than English and bilingualism. Common personal-social culture bumps stem from limited acculturation into and familiarity with ENC and the early childhood special education culture, as well as from differences in how individuals perceive their own identity and competence. Sensory-cognitive culture bumps arise because the types of knowledge deemed valuable and necessary vary substantially across cultures, and the value attached to certain learning and decision-making approaches can differ significantly between practitioners and families.

This chapter returns to many of these culture bumps by examining several assessment dilemmas that early intervention/early childhood special education practitioners and families commonly experience. Suggested research-based responses are provided to help practitioners consider ways to respond to the challenges that they may encounter in serving diverse children and families. However, these suggested responses do not comprise a complete list. Consistent with the concept and practice of 3rd Space, it is important to note that other appropriate responses exist.

COMMON ASSESSMENT DILEMMAS AND SUGGESTED RESPONSES

Common assessment dilemmas may be categorized into four broad categories: 1) determining language and language differences, 2) gathering assessment information, 3) interpreting assessment results, and 4) reporting and using assessment results. The following subsections present each dilemma as well as suggested responses. At the end of the chapter, several vignettes show how Skilled Dialogue can support practitioners and families as they confront these common assessment dilemmas and work through responses.

Language and Language Differences

The most common assessment dilemmas result from the fact that many culturally diverse families in the United States are also linguistically diverse. That is, they speak a language other than English with their children. These families and their children may be monolingual in a language other than English or speak one or more languages in addition to English. Such linguistically diverse home environments necessarily affect both the knowledge that children bring to assessment tasks and the language in which they hold and can express that knowledge. Consequently, two aspects of assessment are especially challenging:

1. The assessment of language proficiency, especially when families' languages cannot be incorporated into assessment (i.e., when personnel fluent in languages other than English cannot be identified)

2. The assessment of general knowledge/skills when items and directions can only be presented in English and/or when existing knowledge and concepts are not equivalent across languages

By utilizing the processes presented in Chapter 7, early childhood special education practitioners can determine the extent to which language differences should be factored into assessment. Specifically, as practitioners assess the degree of linguistic diversity, it may be necessary to conduct home visits and interview family members to determine how and when a child uses a variety of different languages. For example, they could use the Home Language Usage Profile (see Chapter 7, Figure 17, and the blank form in Appendix C). Practitioners should utilize the RLP Profile to support the analysis of a child's receptive and expressive skills in each language (see Chapter 7, Figure 16, and the blank form in Appendix C). As noted in the following suggestions, the relative language proficiency of children should always be assessed at the beginning of the assessment process. The following suggestions directly address such language-related issues.

Suggested Responses   It is critical that as a standard part of the assessment process, information about the language background and experience of all children be gathered from families using respectful, reciprocal, and responsive dialogue (i.e., Skilled Dialogue). The following suggestions are provided in order to support early intervention/early childhood special education practitioners engaged in the process of assessing young children from cultural and linguistic backgrounds different from their own.

Assess for Language Proficiency First   A child's language proficiency needs to be assessed first to determine which language(s) to use in presenting assessment tasks. Assessment for language proficiency is distinct from a comprehensive language assessment. Its purpose is to determine the degree to which a child understands and uses a particular language rather than to obtain a detailed profile of language skills within a single language. Although assessment of a child's language proficiency supports comprehensive language assessment, it cannot and should not replace it.

It is crucial to know a child's level of proficiency in English, as well as in other language(s) used in the home, even when the referring concern has nothing to do with language. Only with such knowledge can assessment tasks be properly planned and assessment results be properly interpreted. The Individuals with Disabilities Education Act (IDEA) Amend-

Table 5.   Language assessment decision matrix

Consideration	Type of assessment			
	Balanced bilingual assessment	Bilingual-dominant language assessment	Modified single language assessment	Single language assessment
Child's relative language proficiency	Similar proficiency in both languages	Partial bilingual	Receptive bilingual	Monolingual
Home language usage	Both languages used to similar degrees	Consistent use of one language with regular but limited use of the other	Some use of language other than English	Only one language used in the home
Child's language usage and preference	Consistent use of both languages	Evident preference for or dominant use of one language	Dominant use of one language with only occasional use of the other (e.g., with grandparents)	No receptive or expressive use of the second language
Emotional/cognitive considerations	Both languages important for interactions with significant caregivers	Elimination of the less proficient language would preclude access to a particular fund of knowledge	Understanding of particular concepts/vocabulary tied to the less proficient language	No use of the less proficient language by family members or other caregivers

ments of 1997 (PL 105-17) require administering assessment in the child's native language. If the child is bilingual, then many agencies choose to assess in the child's dominant language (Moore & Beatty, 1995). The results of an RLP Profile or other similar tools can help determine whether there is a dominant language or whether the child is similarly proficient in two or more languages (see discussion in Chapter 5). Table 5 presents a matrix to assist early childhood practitioners in selecting the most appropriate type of assessment. (For more information, see the discussion of the four language options in Chapter 9 and Figure 29.)

Seek Bilingual/Multilingual Practitioners and Other Individuals   Whenever possible, practitioners who assess children from diverse cultural and linguistic backgrounds should be 1) proficient in both English and the other language(s) spoken by child and family, 2) familiar with the child's home culture(s), and 3) knowledgeable about first- and second-language acquisition and development in bilingual or multilingual environments. Many practitioners believe that individuals with these qualifications do not exist in their geographic area; however, it is important to avoid this assumption. Early intervention/early childhood special education practitioners and programs need to establish connections with other early childhood programs in their community (e.g., child care centers, preschools, Head Start programs) as well as with a variety of experienced community personnel (e.g., military spouses who may not be working, practitioners with professional licenses from other countries). Families with cultural and linguistic backgrounds that differ from ENC typically live in communities with other families from similar backgrounds. Connecting with community programs can help practitioners identify individuals who share the language and culture of the families who seek early childhood special education assistance. The search for bilingual or multicultural personnel should be ongoing and may need to include the development of preservice or in-service materials to extend the skills of those identified (see the next suggestion).

Prepare and Utilize Knowledgeable Individuals   It may not be possible to identify bilingual staff immediately, but it is almost always possible to locate non–family members who are proficient in the desired languages and cultures. (Note: The practitioner may need to provide professional development specific to assessment of infants and young children). Word of mouth often elicits more responses in the community than written ads. Although family members can provide invaluable help, they must have a choice regarding the degree to which they act as translators and interpreters (see the "Challenges of Relationship" discussion in Chapter 1). In addition, it is important to use people's skills judiciously. Bilingual practitioners typically comment on how programs expect them to translate papers and conversations with little notice. One Spanish- and English-speaking practitioner from Puerto Rico who was working in the Southwest United States said that she was expected to translate despite her unfamiliarity with the local culture and dialect. For additional information, see Appendix D and sources such as Hamayan and Damico (1991).

Meet Beforehand with the Person Who Is to Assist   Before beginning the assessment process, make sure that everyone involved knows the tasks and items being used and what is being assessed. Ensure that interpreters[7] are knowledgeable about the language, culture, values, and traditions of both the family and the service provider. It is equally critical that the interpreter understands the terms and concepts likely to arise during assessment. If necessary, the interpreter should first observe the practitioner conducting another evaluation. Remember that interpreters should not be expected to assume the practitioners' roles and responsibilities.

---

[7]The authors recognize that *interpreter* and *translator* have distinct meanings. For the purposes of this text, however, the terms are used interchangeably to refer to any person who assists practitioners in bridging linguistic differences.

That is, they should not independently facilitate play situations or administer test items without specific guidance from appropriate early interventionists/early childhood special educators. Although translators and cultural guides may assist in understanding cultural and linguistic issues that may arise during the assessment process, early interventionists/early childhood special education practitioners remain responsible for making clinical judgments. For further information, see Appendix D.

Avoid Simultaneous Interpretation   It is best to avoid saying something in one language and then immediately having it interpreted in the other. This type of interpretation makes it difficult to determine which language a child is responding to and, thus, confounds the assessment results. Sequential interpretation—completing a portion of the assessment in one language before switching to the other—is usually more appropriate. Although standardized procedures should always be followed, valid alterations to these procedures (e.g., using another language) can be made following their completion. For example, after administering items in a standardized manner and obtaining a valid ceiling, practitioners can revisit missed items and re-administer them in another language or through the use of prompts. Responses to these latter items cannot be used in computing standard scores; nevertheless, they provide valuable information on a child's knowledge and skills. Additional suggestions are provided below in the section on reporting results.

Use the "One-Person, One-Language" Rule   When possible, one practitioner should speak one language with the child and another practitioner should speak the other language. The practitioners may speak English with each other, although they must do so cautiously because this may communicate that English is preferable or more valuable than the other language. Young children quickly learn what it takes to communicate with individuals; however, they do not grasp the abstract concept of language until after the age of 7 or so. This was demonstrated during a screening of bilingual children in a Head Start program. During this program, several English monolingual children approached the table where the screening materials were laid out and said that they wanted to play, too. On being told that only children who spoke Spanish were "playing" that day, one child replied, "We speak Spanish." The practitioner assented and began speaking to them in Spanish. The children responded readily—in gibberish, which is probably what the practitioner's words sounded like to them! It was clear that they could not yet grasp the distinction between languages.

Use an Observer/Recorder   When feasible, one person should observe and record while the other interacts with the child. Practitioners must acknowledge that their own observations can never be truly objective because people make evaluations based on personal and sociocultural "lenses" (Barrera, 1993). An observer who considers how the information is gathered can highlight the assessor's unconscious values and assumptions. Similarly, videotaping can also be useful for collecting accurate data that go beyond mere scores. In addition, if an assessment is videotaped, then a careful review of the translation and transcript can be conducted at a later date.

Assess Items in a Variety of Languages Early childhood special education practitioners should always present items missed in one language in the other language, although only after standardized procedures are completed (if these are being used). Many children from bilingual homes know some items in only one of their languages (e.g., they may know colors in English and kinship terms in their other home language). Children who are bilingual may lag behind monolingual children when assessed in only one language yet may possess a total vocabulary and language skills similar to those of monolingual children when assessed across both or multiple languages.

Note the Language(s) Used in Assessment Always note the language(s) used by the evaluator and the child when recording responses to assessment tasks. Practitioners should especially note when multiple languages were used. This information is important for the correct interpretation of assessment results (see the "Interpreting Assessment Results" section for more detail).

Discriminate Between Items that Tap Academic Readiness and Those that Tap Language Proficiency Readiness and academically oriented items such as color and number awareness 1) test a child's knowledge base rather than his or her language proficiency and 2) may not have the same developmental value in other cultures as they do in ENC. Rather than demonstrating ability, responses to these items may reflect the knowledge that a family values or the time when a family believes it is necessary to acquire these skills (which may vary greatly from ENC's expected age). Being able to label geometric shapes, for example, may not be highly valued before age 6, but naming second and third cousins may be expected by age 4.

These suggested responses to dilemmas related to language and language difference are not comprehensive. Nonetheless, it is important that practitioners consider each one. These responses provide a critical link to how assessment information is gathered and interpreted and, ultimately, to how it is used.

Gathering Assessment Information

Other common assessment dilemmas can result from culture bumps related to the content, format, and inherent values of assessment items, which may be unfamiliar or negative to children not from the population(s) on which the items were standardized. If items are unfamiliar, then children will be less likely to demonstrate the target skills during the assessment process. Clearly, responses to individual items will be severely affected for children whose cultural background does not include or value those items. Most tests cannot incorporate these issues in the final score and interpretation because their corresponding manuals outline specific standardized procedures for reporting scores.

Perhaps even more important, if the inherent values of the assessment process run counter to the values, beliefs, and customs of particular families, the families may passively or directly refuse intervention services. Families may demonstrate their concerns about the process by simply missing assessment appointments or not being home when the assessment team arrives. Other families undergo the initial assessment process but choose not to follow through on suggested intervention strategies based on the outcomes of the assessment. Clearly, how assessment information is gathered can have a significant impact on a family's decision to participate in early intervention/early childhood special education services and on the delivery of appropriate services and intervention strategies for children and families.

Suggested Responses   Although standardized measures play a valid role in assessing young children, practitioners should gather additional information from families and other caregivers about children's backgrounds and development. Having an Anchored Understanding of the differences that exist between families and practitioners significantly influences the quality of assessment information collected. Regular and periodic assessment and observations of children in multiple settings provide much more accurate depictions of children's skills and knowledge than a one-time administration of standardized measures. See the following suggestions for gathering assessment information from young children and their families.

Note Other Possibilities in Test Scoring   Children may not demonstrate a skill when a test item is culturally or linguistically unfamiliar. If a practitioner uses standardized procedures and reports scores according to the test manual, he or she should add comments on items that a child passed when adapted and translated. For example, the practitioner might note the score obtained if adapted items could have been scored as correct: "Obtained score was 'X'; had the translated items been credited, John would have obtained a score of 'Y.' " Such statements alert the reader to the fact that obtained scores may underestimate children's knowledge and abilities.

Practitioners should not limit themselves to the information collected during standardized procedures. The information yielded by these procedures may be accurately interpreted only when combined with information obtained through other assessment methods. More discussion on these issues is provided in the sections on interpreting and reporting results.

Delineate Between Language Functioning and Language Proficiency
Overall language functioning is not the same as proficiency in any particular language. A child's overall language functioning is best reflected by scoring *all* items passed, regardless of which language was used for presenting or responding to individual items. Proficiency in a particular language, conversely, is reflected by items passed in only that language. Of note, a speech or language delay or disorder refers to deviations in learning and using language, not to limitations in a specific language. A child may even have limited proficiency in two languages yet not have a language delay or disorder when "mixed" use of two languages is the norm in his or her community. As they gather assessment information, practitioners must differentiate between language delays/disorders and simple differences in language proficiency. Hamayan and Damico (1991) and Metz (1991) provided information and references related to these differences.

Utilize Information Gathered by Alternative Means   As stated previously, standardized results in themselves cannot sufficiently describe a child's abilities and skills. Parent reports and observations of same-age peers should be taken into account in determining a delay or disorder, even when statistically normative data are available. Even when scores indicate below-age performance, a language delay may not truly be present when a child's language is peer commensurate and normative within his or her social environment. Determining that a child's language corresponds with that of peers does not, however, preclude the presence of other developmental issues.

Regardless of the assessment method(s) used, practitioners should avoid placing children in artificial situations. To the maximum extent possible, children's typical home and preschool routines and activities should be used to obtain assessment information.

Distinguish Between Expressive and Receptive Language Delays   It is critical that practitioners work with the child and family to distinguish between expressive and receptive language delays. Research shows that mild-to-moderate expressive delays without co-occurring receptive delays often are not a sign of language disorders in children from bilingual environments (Metz, 1991). Children who demonstrate moderate-to-severe receptive language delays should be immediately referred for a comprehensive language assessment, as receptive delays tend to be more closely linked to communication disorders.

Interpreting Assessment Results

After assessment information is gathered, the assessment team is tasked with interpreting the results. In addition to psychometric interpretations, the team must also carefully consider the child and family's cultural linguistic context(s) as well as their broader environmental context. For example, some children lose a primary language spoken during early childhood because they may not have had opportunities to maintain it after entering preschool or primary school. These children become English monolingual or they may demonstrate limitations in both English and their early home language (Mattes & Omark, 1984). The first case results from decreased use and lack of opportunity to advance proficiency and vocabulary; the second case results from insufficient learning time or an overly abrupt language shift.

Language limitations due to limited exposure can be differentiated from true delays or disorders on the basis of 1) knowledge about the child's language learning history and 2) a practitioner's clinical experience with similar children. When it is not possible to definitively distinguish between language differences and language disorders, a follow-up evaluation should be recommended after interventions such as speech therapy or speech-language improvement classes, English for Speakers of Other Languages (ESOL) lessons, or bilingual instruction. These services result in significant progress for children whose limited proficiency stems solely from the loss of their home language, as their language learning abilities are not compromised. Children with true communication delays or disorders will continue to exhibit significant difficulties despite these interventions. For additional information on the interpretation of children's language performance, see Erickson and Omark (1981), Hamayan and Damico (1991), and Taylor (1986a, 1986b).

Suggested Responses   To the maximum extent possible, the entire assessment team should be involved in interpreting the assessment results. This may require utilizing Skilled Dialogue to ensure that 1) all diverse perspectives are acknowledged (respect), 2) an equal voice for all participants is present (reciprocity), and 3) responses are created that integrate and provide access to the strengths of diverse perspectives (responsiveness). The following suggestions offer support for interpreting assessment results.

Consider the Primary or Natal Language   A judgment of language delay or disorder must *always* take into account a child's proficiency in primary or natal language. Behaviors that seem to indicate a language disability or delay may have cultural or linguistic interpretations (Billings, Pearson, Gill, & Shureen, 1997). True communication delays and disorders cross languages and cultures. Their impact can be assessed across linguistic and cultural contexts.

It should never be assumed that a bilingual child with a moderate command of English can fully demonstrate his or her skills and knowledge in English. The differences between the language skills necessary for basic oral communication and those necessary for more abstract and decontextualized communication are well described by Chamot and O'Malley (1994).

Use Test Results Across Multiple Languages   When interpreting assessment information, the results of testing in a second or less familiar language should be added to total language performance or used only as indicators of second-language learning level. Judgments of delay or disorder should never be based on performance in a second or less familiar language. Children who are learning a second language may retain significant pockets of knowledge in their first language or may switch between two (or more) languages. Assessments that are conducted only in one language are unlikely to reflect the true skills and abilities of these children across most domains.

Differentiate the Reasons Behind Missed Items   The content, format, and inherent values of assessment items may be unfamiliar or negative to a child who is not from the population(s) on which these items were standardized. Behavior(s) that might appear indicative of disability or delay may, in fact, stem from cultural or linguistic differences (e.g., inability to ask questions in the "proper" verbal form) (Billings et al., 1997). It is therefore critical to obtain information on primary language and home culture to differentiate between items missed as a result of limited linguistic skill and items missed for other reasons (e.g., lack of familiarity with item/context, limited English proficiency, misinterpretation of item). When a team interprets assessment results, multiple perspectives can be voiced. It is important to acknowledge that there is a range of diverse perspectives that reflects both home and early intervention/early childhood special education settings, that each team member has an equal voice in the discussion, and that the responses integrate and provide access to the strengths of each of the perspectives present.

Increase Awareness of Typical Language Development in Bilingual/ Multilingual Environments   All languages contain both common and distinct features at all levels: phonologic, semantic, syntactic, morphologic, and pragmatic. Features within a particular language may vary according to dialectal usage. Practitioners should be aware that the mixing of two or more languages (i.e., code mixing or code switching) is strongly rule bound. Its presence may actually indicate strong metalinguistic skills rather than weak language proficiency. In addition, code switching or code mixing can reflect the following:

1.   Local usage norms

2.   Affective–motivational factors

3.   Differences between what one wishes to express and one's knowledge or skill in a particular language or in the structure/vocabulary of the language itself

4.   The structure or vocabulary of the language itself (e.g., *rapport* was taken from French to express a concept that no English word could adequately express)

Before a delay or disorder is determined, these features of language development in bilingual/multilingual environments must be carefully considered. Bilingual or multicultural language development is more than monolingualism in stereo.

Reporting and Using Assessment Results

The most important—and perhaps the most challenging—component of assessment revolves around reporting and using this information to improve the quality of intervention. Although many standardized measures may delineate methods for tabulating assessment results, early intervention/early childhood special education practitioners nevertheless struggle with how to report these results to families in a clear and comprehensible manner that is responsive to the unique parameters of cultural and linguistic diversity. Reports that contain large amounts of ENC professional jargon are unreadable for families as well as for professionals from other disciplines (Moore & Beatty, 1995). In addition, it is clear that most reports written by practitioners may fail to mention in a meaningful way the procedures used to adapt and respond to children's cultural linguistic needs or backgrounds. It is not uncommon, for example, to read reports of bilingual children's vocabulary levels without finding specific information on whether translators were used or on whether levels are similar or different between languages. Unless this information is provided, the meaning of the assessment results remains unclear. Similarly, each section of the report for children who speak multiple languages should consider how language differences affected both the selected procedures and the results of the assessment, as well as the implications for needed services. Simply put, the goal of any report should be to describe the measures used, the modifications to the measures, and the rationale for how the examiner(s) derived the assessment interpretation.

Meisels and Provence (1989) also advocated that practical suggestions for supporting a child's development be included in all reports. Effective early childhood practitioners continually assess individual and groups of children and revise the activities and interactions based on the results of that assessment. Unfortunately, many of the assessment tools and procedures used by practitioners do not make clear links between the results of the assessment and the implications for intervention. As practitioners increase their understanding that assessment must be inextricably linked to intervention, so too must they realize that the results and interpretation of assessment are inextricably linked to a cultural milieu. Brown and Barrera (1999) noted that from a developmental perspective, a child may show a developmental delay. From a cultural perspective, however, that same delay may indicate "diversity rather than disability" (p. 39).

A well-written report can serve as a powerful catalyst for change (Billings et al., 1997). This is true whether assessment results determine that a child has a developmental delay or disability. As discussed previously, children whose culture and language differ from ENC—and, therefore, from populations on whom many of the standardized tests were norm-referenced—are at risk for inappropriate referral and classification (Hamayan & Damico, 1991). Assessment results are a valuable and valid tool for early childhood educators only when appropriate time and effort have been taken to assemble a thorough, sensitive representation of a child.

Suggested Responses   Most states specify a minimum requirement for reporting assessment information, especially if it relates to information used for an initial evaluation and eligibility determination. When adaptations to standardized procedure require a greater degree of professional judgment, the entire assessment team should give input regarding the following components to be included in assessment reports (Billings et al., 1997):

1. A rationale for departing from the procedures and instruments commonly used to assess same-age peers with similar developmental concerns

2. Specifications of the alternative strategies used for assessment

3. A justification for use of the alternative methods

4. A statement of results

5. An explanation of an identified disability or delay that specifically rules out cultural and linguistic factors as the cause of atypical cognitive and behavioral performance OR an explanation of ineligibility, giving evidence of the specific cultural and linguistic factors that explain the cognitive or behavioral performance without identification of disability or delay

The following suggestions are provided to assist early intervention/ early childhood special education practitioners in reporting assessment results.

Consider the Format of the Results Report   The most helpful reports are free of professional jargon and use strengths-based language that notes the child's skills (Moore & Beatty, 1995). Every report should begin with clear identifying information, including the name, date of assessment, age and cultural background of the child, examiner(s) name, and language(s) in which the assessment was conducted. A short background should follow, which includes a brief overview of the family's cultural background along with a summary of the child's development across multiple domains and languages. Next, the results of the assessment should be clearly articulated. The results should note differences observed across settings, testing conditions, and language(s). The report also needs to contain a summary of the results. Finally, reports must include straightforward and comprehensible recommendations for environmental modifications, instructional practices, or intervention strategies that are responsive to the child's and family's cultural context(s).

Describe the Procedures Used to Respond to the Child's Cultural Linguistic Parameters   It is important that practitioners consider the cultural linguistic background of children in the assessment process. Because of the relational and contextual nature of diversity, cultural and linguistic diversity influence the assessment process of all children and families. If procedural changes are made or if specific items are adapted in response to culture and/or language, these changes should be clearly described. For a child in a multilingual environment, the report should describe how the assessment process responded to this factor. For example, such a report would detail any translation procedures that were used by an assessment team. Similarly, if an interpreter/translator was used, that person's background and training should be noted in the report. Statements such as

"Mary has a limited receptive vocabulary" must identify the language(s) in which limitations exist. It is important to know, for instance, whether Mary's entire receptive vocabulary, limited as it is, is Hmong. Or does she understand five words in Hmong and five words in English? Are they the same five words? Is her total vocabulary across Hmong and English five words or ten words? Such details immeasurably enhance the validity and usefulness of a report.

Indicate the Language(s) Used During the Assessment Process   When practitioners report performance levels, it is critical to indicate the language(s) in which items were presented. As previously discussed, language functioning is not the same as language proficiency in a particular language. A child's language functioning can best be reflected by looking at *all* items passed, regardless of the language used by the child or practitioner. Practitioners should note possible discrepancies in the score obtained through standardized procedure and the performance level that was assessed using the two (or more) languages.

For instance, an assessor might write, "Angie scored 'X' when items were presented in a standardized fashion. We could not credit the following items because of standardization violations. Had we been able to credit these items elicited using Tagalog (Angie's language other than English), the score would have been 'Y.' "

Ensure that the Report Includes the Child's Relative Language Proficiency   Identifying a child's Relative Language Proficiency (i.e., proficiency in all language[s] used) is an important first step in the assessment process. It is not sufficient to simply state whether a language other than English is spoken in the home. The assessment report should identify Relative Language Proficiency levels and describe which procedures were used to determine these levels. Chapter 5 introduced the RLP Profile, a tool to help early intervention/early childhood special education practitioners assess language proficiency (see also the blank version of this form in Appendix C).

Note the Degree to Which a Child's Background Matches the Assessment Instruments' Norming Samples   When standardized instruments are used, practitioners should report normed scores without qualification only when the child's experiential and linguistic background matches that of the norming sample (which is almost never!). In all other cases, the report should qualify the assessment results (e.g., "Assuming validity, Tariq's standard score would be 'X'; had the translated items been included in the total correct score, Tariq's standard score would be 'Y' "). It is also helpful to report an instrument's standard error of measurement, as cultural and linguistic differences heighten the probability that error will be present.

Clearly Identify Why Reported Performance Is or Is Not Interpreted as a Delay or Disorder   It is critical that reports explain why the child's performance during the assessment process was or was not identified as a disability or delay (e.g., it is a disorder because the child is unintelligible in both languages at age 4 years, it is a delay because the child's performance is markedly different from same-age peers with the same primary language). Specific information should be included about the cultural and linguistic factors that may contribute to seemingly atypical performance. In addition, an explanation of ineligibility should be provided when appropriate, giving evidence of specific cultural and linguistic factors that explain why performance does not indicate disability or delay (e.g., errors occurred in second language only, children from this population typically demonstrate a 3- to 6-month receptive delay). Disabilities or delays and cultural linguistic diversity are not mutually exclusive. Both may be present at the same time. When this is the case, each should be addressed in relation to the other.

Provide Recommendations that Address Children's Needs in All of Their Languages   If reports are going to support children and families, then tangible recommendations that link assessment to intervention must be provided. The recommended instructional practices and intervention strategies should address children's needs across both cultural and linguistic contexts.

ASSESSMENT IN PRACTICE: FOUR VIGNETTES

In the following section, four vignettes highlight several common assessment dilemmas and culture bumps that early intervention/early childhood special education practitioners are likely to encounter as they work with children and families from different cultural linguistic backgrounds. These vignettes are intended to illustrate how Skilled Dialogue tools and strategies may be used. Their "unfinished-ness" is purposely designed to raise questions and prompt further explanation. For each vignette, potential responses are examined. The vignettes vary in detail, reflecting the reality that contextual and background information vary for each child and family served. The most detail is given in the first vignette to provide an opportunity to consider a family from a variety of perspectives using several of the available tools presented in Chapter 7. The steps that practitioners should take relate directly to the amount and type of information available and the point in the assessment process. Each vignette closes with additional questions that practitioners may wish to consider.

Xee[8]

Xee Ly, a 4-year, 2-month-old child, was born to her parents in a suburban community outside of Philadelphia. Mr. and Mrs. Ly came to the United States in the late 1970s after the reunification of Vietnam. The Ly family currently lives in a three-bedroom apartment, and Mr. Ly works at a factory that is a 1½-hour drive from home. Xee has five older siblings and one younger sibling. Hmong is the family's cultural and linguistic heritage, and the family speaks Hmong as its primary language. Mr. Ly, however, is also fairly fluent in English.

At birth, Xee was diagnosed as having Hirschsprung disease (congenital megacolon). She had a colostomy after birth. At the age of 1 month, she was hospitalized due to seizures. The seizures have been controlled with anticonvulsant medication. The church that sponsored the Ly family's immigration made a referral to the local early childhood special education agency after Mr. Ly expressed concern to a fellow church member about Xee using only a few words in both Hmong and English. None of the professionals on the initial assessment team were familiar with Hmong culture or language.

A certain member of the congregation who was a veteran of the Vietnam conflict and had become friends with many Hmong families assisted the team in understanding Hmong culture. He then suggested a woman of the local Hmong community who might be willing to serve as a cultural mediator and translator. She attended the same church and was affiliated with a South East Asia Service Center program. The team met with the mediator to learn more about Hmong culture and to plan the assessment process.

An interview with Xee's parents was suggested as the first step. The goal was to determine the resources, priorities, and needs of the Ly family, as well as to complete an RLP Profile for Xee. The team decided that Mr. and Mrs. Ly should be present for the interview, as Hmong families emphasize the role of fathers in decision making. The interview would be conducted in Hmong by the mediator, and a member of the early childhood special education agency would be present. The mediator called the family to schedule the appointment.

The interview revealed that Xee's parents were concerned about Xee's failure to express herself verbally. Xee had limited receptive or expressive language in both Hmong and English. Her speech was often hard for family members to understand. Mr. Ly said that he wanted Xee and her younger brother to learn English because he thought it was important for them to do well in American schools. He expressed interest in having his wife learn ways to help with interventions at home so that Xee could enter a preschool program. Xee,

---

[8]Source for the Chapters 8 and 9 vignettes about "Xee": Pennsylvania Department of Education (1994).

however, was often fearful outside the home. She was most comfortable around other Hmong children with whom she played at church functions.

It was recommended that a speech-language pathologist assist in determining Xee's language needs, and Xee's parents agreed to have such an evaluation. Assessment team members were to include Xee's mother and father, the mediator, the case manager, the speech-language pathologist, an occupational therapist, and a Head Start teacher. Xee's skills in both Hmong and English would be assessed. During the interview, the mediator and the parents suggested several additional people who may be able to assist in the assessment and intervention processes.

This vignette describes many challenges that early intervention/early childhood special education practitioners may encounter as they assess children from diverse cultural and linguistic backgrounds. Cultural and linguistic diversity was clearly present in Xee's case (the first step of Phase II in Figure 13). Xee's case manager asked herself, "How likely am I to understand and attach the same meaning to behaviors as would Xee's family and/or others from similar cultural backgrounds?" and determined that she probably would understand behaviors differently and attach different meanings to them. Therefore, Skilled Dialogue was likely needed. Then, she assessed the nature and degree of the cultural linguistic diversity between the practitioners and Xee's family (the second step of Phase II in Figure 13). She and the ECSE team completed a Cultural Data Table, an RLP Profile, and a Cultural Consonance Profile to identify potential culture bumps and to consider approaches and responses for limiting the impact of these bumps. An initial Cultural Data Table for Xee (Figure 24) revealed a significant number of probable bumps in all three developmental/curricular areas. To respond to these potential bumps, the team determined the need to observe language usage for Xee and her family in a variety of settings as well as to observe and consider rules and values for behavior and communication in Xee's home and neighborhood.

After considering the information in the initial Cultural Data Table, the team recognized that further language assessment was needed to determine more precisely Xee's level of proficiency in Hmong and English. Following a play-based assessment, which included both an extensive observation of Xee playing with other adults and children and a parent interview, the team completed Xee's RLP Profile (Figure 25). The RLP confirmed that Xee's receptive and expressive language skills were significantly limited in English and Hmong. She was equally limited in both of the languages available to her.

As they examined this information, Xee's team recognized the need to complete a Cultural Consonance Profile (Figure 26). Xee's Cultural

Cultural Data Table

Child's name: _Xee_   Date completed: _12/1/02_   Completed by: _J. Sosa and M. Talbott_

Directions: Fill in responses to questions from the Guide to Identifying Cultural Data Related to Potential Culture Bumps.

Developmental/curricular area	Comments
Communicative-Linguistic	
Language(s) of child's primary caregiving environment(s)	Xee is 4 years old. Her family speaks Hmong as the primary language. In addition, her father speaks fairly fluent English.
Child's relative language proficiency (degree of proficiency in English and other language[s] used)	Xee uses only a few words in both Hmong and English. *Proficiency information (see Relative Language Proficiency [RLP] Profile) English: receptive (2) expressive (2) Hmong: receptive (2) expressive (2)*
Patterns of language usage in child's primary caregiving environment(s)	*Discussion among adults in the home is entirely in Hmong. Conversations between the children and their mother are in Hmong; their father speaks both English and Hmong to them. In addition, the children use both English and Hmong at church.*
Relative value placed on verbal and nonverbal communication	*Interactions within the community demonstrate a strong value on nonverbal communication. Within the home, however, both parents encourage extensive verbal communication in English and in Hmong.*
Relative status associated with languages other than English and with bilingualism	*The interview with the family showed that Mr. Ly places a high value on having his children learn English but hopes that they will maintain Hmong as well. The early childhood programs reflect a stronger value on English.*
Personal-Social	
Degree of acculturation into EuroAmerican Normative Culture (ENC)	*Mr. Ly has a fair amount of familiarity with ENC; however, Mrs. Nia Ly generally interacts with other Hmong families from her clan who live in the same community. All of her friends speak Hmong. The children who are school age have a greater familiarity with ENC.*

(continued)

Figure 24. Cultural Data Table for Xee.

139

Figure 24. (continued)

Degree of acculturation into U.S. early intervention/early childhood special education culture	No one in the family has any significant degree of acculturation into the U.S. early intervention/early childhood special education culture. To this point, Mr. Ly has been the primary contact with ENC, interacting with other social service agencies in times of unemployment.
Sense of self (e.g., relative weight on independence, dependence, and interdependence)	The family apparently places a strong value on interdependence. However, as Xee is approaching school age, Mr. Ly expressed his desire for Xee to begin assuming greater responsibility for her own behaviors and increasing her personal-social and self-help skills.
Perceptions of identity and competence	Initial assumptions from family observations depicted Xee as an extension of her parents. Although Mr. Ly expressed concern about how Xee's delay reflects on the family, he is anxious for her to function successfully in American schools.
Roles and rules associated with parenting and child rearing	During the family interview, Mr. Ly and Mrs. Nia Ly discussed that their primary ties and responsibilities were to their children. Their role is to make sure that the children "listen and obey."
Knowledge and experience regarding power and social positioning	The family views itself as lower-middle class. Mr. Ly explained that because of prejudice, many Hmong families in the community, including members of their extended family, are struggling to find and maintain employment.
Values/beliefs/skills associated with instrumental and emotional support (e.g., gaining access to external resources and getting personal support)	Mr. Ly indicated that up to this point, the family has relied on personal support from the Hmong community. However, he believes that there is great value in gaining access to other community services, such as Head Start, to help Xee and her siblings succeed in school.
Sensory-Cognitive	
Funds of knowledge: what type of knowledge is valued; concept structures and definitions (e.g., how family is defined)	The knowledge and support of the immediate and extended family is most valued. The family's ancestry and ancestors are often discussed. In the family interview, Mr. Ly repeatedly expressed his concern that Xee and her siblings understand their roles within the family structure as well as in the larger society.
Preferred strategies for acquiring new learning	Most of the learning strategies tend to be nonverbal. Teaching strategies generally revolve around methods like modeling.
Preferred strategies for problem solving and decision making	Mr. Ly is the primary decision maker in the family, especially for issues that affect the family outside of the home. It appears that Mrs. Nia Ly has more influence on the decisions that affect what happens within the home.
Worldview (i.e., assumptions about how the world works and about what is "right" and what is "wrong")	Mr. Ly seems to have a bicultural view. Although Mrs. Nia Ly's views were not explicitly stated, they appear to be more traditional. Although Mr. Ly wants Xee and her siblings to follow the Hmong social and family order and responsibilities, he also wants them to learn English and to succeed academically at school and within ENC.

Relative Language Proficiency (RLP) Profile

Child's name: _Xee_   Date: _12/13/02_   Date of birth: _12/10/97_

Chronological age: _5 years_   Completed by: _W. Bircher_

Site: _Child's home_   Instrument: _Informal_

Proficiency in Language Other than English (Specify language: _Hmong_)

	5	4	3	2	1
Receptive:				(2)	
	Good: No significant errors	Mildly limited: Some errors	Moderately limited: Consistent/ significant errors	Severely limited: Frequent and significant errors	Nonverbal and/or unintelligible
Expressive:	5	4	3	(2)	1

Comments:

Xee's mother and father indicated that she speaks approximately 10 words in Hmong.

English Proficiency

	5	4	3	2	1
Receptive:				(2)	
	Good: No significant errors	Mildly limited: Some errors	Moderately limited: Consistent/ significant errors	Severely limited: Frequent and significant errors	Nonverbal and/or unintelligible
Expressive:	5	4	3	(2)	1

Comments:

Xee's use of English is also limited to fewer than 10 words.

Relative Language Proficiency (Write language other than English in blanks below)

Hmong Monolingual	Receptive Bilingual	Partial Bilingual	Bilingual	Partial Bilingual	Receptive Bilingual	English Monolingual
Has had minimal exposure to English	_Hmong_ dominant; understands some English	_Hmong_ dominant; limited English	_Hmong_ and English about the same	English dominant; limited _Hmong_	English dominant; understands some _Hmong_	Has had minimal exposure to _Hmong_

Comments:

Xee's environments—home and child care—are bilingual in Hmong and English. She communicates, and is communicated with, equally in each of these languages.

Figure 25. Relative Language Proficiency (RLP) Profile for Xee.

Consonance Profile made it even clearer that extra attention was needed to limit the number of culture bumps (especially in the personal-social and sensory-cognitive areas) that might arise in gathering assessment information. To acknowledge the parents' competence in child rearing, for example, the practitioners needed to recognize their knowledge and skills

Cultural Consonance Profile

Child's name: _Xee_____   Date: _12/16/02_____   Completed by: _J. Sosa and M. Talbott_

	Highly similar to early childhood environment(s)/ practitioners' profiles ⟷ Highly dissimilar from early childhood environment(s)/ practitioners' profiles

I. Communicative-Linguistic Area

Comments

Item	5	4	3	2	1	Comments
Language(s) used in child's home	5	4	3	(2)	1	_____
Child's relative language proficiency	5	4	3	(2)	1	_____
Patterns of language usage	5	4	3	2	(1)	_Few words_____
Relative value placed on verbal/ nonverbal communication	5	4	(3)	2	1	_____
Relative status of language other than English and bilingualism	5	4	3	(2)	1	_Family values highly as compared with ENC_

II. Personal-Social Area

Item	5	4	3	2	1	
Family's degree of acculturation	5	4	3	(2)	1	_____
Sense of self/perception of identity/competence	5	4	3	(2)	1	_____
Parenting/child-rearing roles and rules	5	4	3	(2)	1	_____
Knowledge/experience regarding power and positioning	5	4	(3)	2	1	_____
Values and beliefs regarding support	5	4	3	(2)	1	_____

III. Sensory-Cognitive Area

Item	5	4	3	2	1	
Funds of knowledge/concept definition/structures	5	4	3	(2)	1	_____
Preferred learning strategies	5	4	3	(2)	1	_____
Preferred problem-solving/ decision-making strategies	5	4	(3)	2	1	_____
Worldview	5	4	3	(2)	1	_____

Degree of consonance with early childhood environment(s)/practitioners' profiles

Area	High	Moderate	Low	Minimal
Communicative-linguistic area	High	Moderate	(Low)	Minimal
Personal-social area	High	Moderate	(Low)	Minimal
Sensory-cognitive area	High	Moderate	(Low)	Minimal

Comments:

Figure 26. Cultural Consonance Profile for Xee.

with Xee. Similarly, activities and dialogue needed to be planned to build the family's sense of competence in navigating early childhood special education culture. Throughout this process, the family would be given extra time to consider all of the available choices.

In addition to these considerations, the team members considered whether translation of assessment materials into Hmong was appropriate and, if so, how they would do this. They had to choose formal assessment strategies based on the family's funds of knowledge, child-rearing beliefs and values, and preferred strategies for learning and problem solving. It was decided that each team member would work with volunteers from the Hmong community and Head Start staff to lessen or eliminate potential culture bumps identified by the Cultural Data Table. The goal of this process was to determine Xee's skills and needs, as well as appropriate intervention strategies regarding family priorities. Finally, the team created an Assessment Cultural Linguistic Response Plan for Xee (Figure 27).

Xee's story illustrates the principles and strategies of Skilled Dialogue in relation to a specific child and family. Forestructure is built prior to meeting with a family by means such as reading about first- and second-language acquisition. This information leads to the formulation of possible responses to the family. The stage is set for Skilled Dialogue as initial information is collected and potential culture bumps are reviewed through tools like the Cultural Data Table. Further information is gathered using these tools and the strategies designed to develop Anchored Understanding of Diversity between the practitioners and the family (see Figure 9 in Chapter 5). Based on this understanding, Cultural Linguistic Response Plans for both assessment and intervention are developed (see discussion in Chapter 7).

The questions and exercise below are provided to help practitioners further explore the application of Skilled Dialogue in relation to Xee and her family.

Questions for Reflection

1. Review Xee's Cultural Data Table and Cultural Consonance Profile. To what degree would cultural linguistic diversity be present if you were working with this child and family? What potential culture bumps would be critical to address?

2. Consider the assessment procedures that you typically use. What changes or adaptations would you have to make as a member of Xee's assessment team?

3. What additional information, if any, would you need to make these changes or adaptations?

Assessment Cultural Linguistic Response Plan

Child's name: _Xee_   Date: _12/18/02_   Completed by: _J. Sosa and M. Talbott_

Specific Assessment Considerations

RE: *Language and language differences*

1. Assess Xee's language proficiency in both English and Hmong.

2. Utilize and train, as necessary, a cultural mediator for the interpretation needs of the family and early childhood special education team.

3. Assess in Hmong all items that Xee missed in English.

4. For the items missed during assessment, discriminate between the items that test academic readiness and language proficiency.

RE: *Data-gathering procedures*

1. Consider a play-based approach to assessment that utilizes toys and materials with which Xee is familiar.

2. Discriminate between Xee's overall language functioning and her language proficiency in both English and Hmong.

3. Consider parent reports and observations of other Hmong children who are similar in age and development to Xee before determining a delay or disability.

4. Determine if Xee has both receptive and expressive language delays.

RE: *Interpretation of assessment information*

1. Consider the results of testing in both English and Hmong to get a total language performance.

2. Determine why Xee might miss any items during the assessment.

3. Work with the cultural linguistic mediator to increase awareness of any code switching.

RE: *Reporting assessment results*

1. Gain awareness about the funds of knowledge for Xee's family.

2. Clearly indicate when English is used for assessment purposes and when Hmong is used during the process.

3. Report assessment results in both Hmong and English to ensure that Xee's family understands the results of the assessment.

Underlying Process Reminders

	Anchored Understanding of Diversity	3rd Space
RESPECT	Acknowledge the range and validity of diverse perspectives.	Stay with the tension of differing perspectives.
RECIPROCITY	Establish interactions that allow equal voice for all participants.	Develop opportunities for equalizing power across interactions.
RESPONSIVENESS	Communicate respect and understanding of others' perspectives.	Create responses that integrate and provide access to the strengths of diverse perspectives.

Figure 27.   Assessment Cultural Linguistic Response Plan for Xee.

4. What might a Critical Incident Analysis Sheet look like for Xee? Complete one in preparation for a home visit (see Chapter 7).

Amad[9]

Amad is a 4-year-old African American with mild-to-moderate autism. He was recently evaluated for a center-based special education preschool program in his urban community. Amad's mother and grandmother expressed their concern that members of the interdisciplinary team discussed "school learning" (cognitive growth) but not Amad's happiness. Amad's mother and grandmother want him to "have friends and like people and be okay when he goes outside when he is bigger." The family wants to hear how the program will nurture Amad's emotional and social development so that he can fit in with the community and take care of himself. Amad's grandmother wants Amad to learn to deal with the difficulties in their community and be happy.

This shorter vignette is used to illustrate use of Critical Incident Analysis Sheets. Only limited information was initially available to the early childhood special education practitioners about the cultural background, beliefs, and values of Amad's family. This is not unusual, of course; practitioners will likely feel that they have very little information on many families as they begin working with them. However, the mother and grandmother's reaction to comments of certain interdisciplinary team members makes it clear that culture bumps were already present. The team decided to complete a Critical Incident Analysis (Figure 28) sheet prior to gathering more information from the family. They realized that this was necessary to make respect, reciprocity, and responsiveness the foundation of their dialogue with Amad's family.

Questions for Reflection

1. Review the Critical Incident Analysis Sheet (Figure 28) that Amad's early intervention team developed. Do you agree or disagree with its content? Would you add any other considerations? If so, what would they be?

2. Review the questions on culture bumps (see Figure 8 in Chapter 5). Which ones might be playing the most significant role in the interaction

---

[9]The Chapters 8 and 9 vignettes about "Amad" were created by Lucinda Kramer, Ph.D., at National University, La Jolla, CA.

Critical Incident Analysis Sheet

Child's name: _Amad_   Date: _12/06/03_   Completed by: _B. Johnson_

Incident description: _Amad, a 4-year-old African American boy with previously diagnosed mild-to-moderate autism, was recently evaluated. Amad's mother and grandmother expressed their concern that the other members of the interdisciplinary team are talking about "school learning" and not about Amad's happiness. The practitioners will focus on explicit communication of respect, reciprocity, and responsiveness._

Quality	Anchored Understanding of Diversity	3rd Space
Respect	Key Principle: Acknowledge the range and validity of diverse perspectives. • Obtain information on Amad's culture. • Set a tone of respectful curiosity for conversation. • State the purpose of the visit: to get the best picture of Amad's skills and potential. • Allow time for informal conversation; be somewhat less direct in responding to the family's preferred strategies.	Key Principle: Stay with the tension of differing perspectives. • Remember to remain nonjudgmental and not try to change family beliefs or practices. • Notice which aspects of behavior or beliefs are difficult to accept or validate.
Reciprocity	Key Principle: Establish interactions that allow equal voice for all participants. • Ask open-ended questions that allow the family to take the lead. • Ask the family members about their experiences and views regarding early intervention/early childhood special education. • Look for the positive and for what the family can teach or offer in the way of resources. • Ask family members to describe their understanding of happiness and school learning—how are these different?	Key Principle: Develop opportunities for equalizing power across interactions. • Use topics/analogies/metaphors that equalize participation; do not use unfamiliar vocabulary without explanation. • Communicate that family members are also experts and that early intervention/early childhood special education knowledge is not superior to family knowledge.
Responsiveness	Key Principle: Communicate respect and understanding of others' perspectives. • Reflect an understanding of the family's perspective with explicit statements (e.g., "I see how that makes sense"). • Check for understanding by paraphrasing and asking the speaker if that's what was meant.	Key Principle: Create responses that integrate and provide access to the strengths of diverse perspectives. • Explicitly state that we are seeking to gain access to family strengths and to integrate them with program and practitioner strengths; give examples of how these might complement each other. • Explore ways to focus on Amad's socioemotional well-being within the early childhood special education curriculum.

Figure 28. Critical Incident Analysis Sheet for Amad.

between Amad's family and the practitioners? Which developmental/ curricular areas (communicative-linguistic, personal-social, sensory-cognitive) seem key to the current issues?

3.   How might you integrate the family's emphasis on Amad's happiness as a resource to strengthen his "school learning" (i.e., find 3rd Space)? Review key principles for 3rd Space on Amad's Critical Incident Analysis Sheet.

4.   What additional information, if any, would you need to work effectively with Amad and his family?

Abrish[10]

Abrish is a 2-year, 4-month-old boy who lives with his parents and two younger sisters in a rural area of central Pennsylvania. Abrish's family recently immigrated to the United States from Hungary. He attends a community child care program three mornings per week. Although Abrish is active, he is quiet in public. During the past year, he has made few communicative attempts at the child care center. His mother and staff at the child care center noticed that Abrish has difficulty initiating communication or responding to directions and is quite fearful in new situations. Abrish rarely plays with other children at the child care center. He spends much of his time following the child care staff around and clinging to a toy cloth owl. Abrish's mother called the local early intervention agency because she was concerned about Abrish's development. She thought that Abrish might need special help to encourage interaction and the acquisition of skills for successful participation in preschool.

Although no forms (e.g., Cultural Data Table) accompany this discussion, readers are encouraged to practice completing these forms, to consider how they would approach the assessment process with Abrish and his family, and to consider how this approach resembles or differs from typical procedures. The early intervention agency responded to Abrish's mother by scheduling a developmental screening. A speech-language pathologist and an early intervention specialist completed the screening, which took place in Abrish's home. Methods of screening included a parent interview, administration of a developmental checklist, an informal language sample in both English and Hungarian, and a brief observation of Abrish playing with his toys. In addition, Abrish's mother provided background information about home language usage and Abrish's birth history, medical history, and language development in both languages.

---

[10]Source for the Chapters 8 and 9 vignettes about "Abrish": Pennsylvania Department of Education (1994).

The screening results indicated that Abrish had age-appropriate cognitive, problem-solving, and adaptive skills. It also identified possible developmental delays in receptive language development (in both English and Hungarian) and social skill development. Abrish's parents and the early intervention team agreed that further evaluation was warranted to develop a more thorough understanding of Abrish's functioning and developmental needs. Before additional evaluation procedures were conducted, however, the team decided to complete a Cultural Data Table, an RLP Profile, and an Assessment Cultural Linguistic Response Plan for Abrish and his family.

As part of the Assessment Cultural Linguistic Response Plan, the practitioners assembled a team that included Abrish's parents, an early intervention specialist, a speech-language pathologist, Abrish's child care provider, and a cultural linguistic mediator to translate language and potential culture bumps. At the meeting, an informal structured interview was used to elicit the parents' perceived resources and needs related to Abrish's development. An assessment battery was then selected, and various team members agreed to complete specific assessment tasks. The speech-language pathologist would administer several instruments and take a communication sample in English and Hungarian. The speech-language pathologist was not proficient in Hungarian, so the mediator, who was bilingual in English and Hungarian, assisted with the Hungarian communication sample. In addition, the early intervention specialist planned to administer several additional developmental instruments, including observations of Abrish's interactions with his peers at the child care center, a rating of Abrish's participation and communication at the child care center and at home, and his level of general engagement in structured activities. The child care provider was asked to provide brief anecdotal records of Abrish's social interactions and behaviors related to his receptive language skills in English. Abrish's parents agreed to record an at-home language sample and to record how often Abrish initiated communication in certain situations, noting when communication attempts occurred and which language Abrish used for which purposes.

Initially, the early intervention specialist tried to conduct certain assessments without Abrish's mother present. When Abrish accompanied the specialist (who only spoke English) to a small room in the child care center, he became tearful, clung to his toy owl, and kept his head down. The specialist and the speech-language pathologist found it difficult to conduct the assessment due to Abrish's fearfulness. The cultural linguistic mediator made the critical observation that Abrish's fearfulness likely resulted from his lack of acculturation into ENC and was compounded by separation from his mother, who was his secure base in unfamiliar situations. Eventually, the specialist noticed that Abrish became more cooperative when his mother was allowed to remain with him and when playful assessment processes were used in place of the initial highly structured tasks. For example, Abrish refused to complete a two-piece form board when he was directly asked to do so; when his mother was present, however, he eagerly completed the task while playing with his toy owl. Task compliance was achieved by Abrish's mother handing him the pieces, which they pretended were cookies to be put on a cookie sheet so that Owl could have a snack.

The early intervention specialist told the speech-language pathologist about the effectiveness of this play-based approach. The speech-language pathologist then re-administered some of her earlier tasks by having Abrish put his owl in a toy car and point to certain pictures in a book. With the help of the interpreter, the speech-language pathologist collected information in both English and Hungarian. Abrish enjoyed this game and cooperated for 30 minutes. In their reports, both practitioners indicated that the scores were tentative because of the adaptive, nonstandardized administration techniques used. They focused on describing the abilities that Abrish showed in completing the tasks across both languages.

In these additional assessments, Abrish's play behavior and performance on nonverbal reasoning tasks indicated age-appropriate cognitive skills. Likewise, although Abrish was hesitant to interact with other children and unfamiliar adults, the team believed that his social skills were age appropriate in both ENC and home cultural contexts. Abrish's auditory comprehension in English and Hungarian and basic concept skills also appeared to be age appropriate, but his language and general communication skills in Hungarian and English were moderately delayed. He demonstrated an expressive vocabulary of approximately 25 words (15 in Hungarian and 10 in English), which were intelligible for his age. Abrish had difficulty answering various "wh-" questions in English.

Both practitioners felt more confident in the information that they gathered from direct observation than in the initial information that was collected in a more structured manner. Upon completion of all assessment procedures, the team reconvened to discuss Abrish's developmental functioning, his family's strengths, and his needs.

Questions for Reflection

1. Abrish's vignette brings up issues of respect, reciprocity, and responsiveness. Can you identify them? (Complete a Critical Incident Analysis Sheet and see Figure 9 in Chapter 5 and Figure 10 in Chapter 6.)

2. Review the phases of Skilled Dialogue (Figure 13 in Chapter 7). Which aspects of Skilled Dialogue, if any, do you believe Abrish's early intervention team overlooked?

3. Review the questions related to potential culture bumps (Figure 8 in Chapter 5). What part, if any, do cultural linguistic factors play in this situation?

4. How would you complete an Assessment Cultural Linguistic Response Plan for Abrish and his family?

Peter[11]

Peter is 4 years old. His father is a farm worker by day and cleans office buildings at night. Both of his parents were born in rural Mexico. They have lived in the United States for 4 years, immigrating just prior to Peter's birth. Peter's father has learned some English at work. He speaks Spanish to his wife and uses both English and Spanish with Peter. Peter's mother has very limited English. For the past 3 years, she has provided child care in their one-bedroom apartment for young children from other Spanish-speaking families in their neighborhood. With the additional responsibility of caring for her 4-month-old daughter, Maria, Peter's mother is very busy and has great difficulty keeping appointments.

A doctor at the county medical clinic referred Peter for assessment. Peter has a history of chronic ear infections (few were treated), is thin, appears depressed, and demonstrates very limited speech. He speaks to his parents and others only when he needs something. Peter's mother told the clinic doctor that her son is very shy. She is reluctant to have Peter evaluated, as she is adamant there is nothing "wrong" with her child, and has canceled six appointments. She was told that a Spanish-speaking staff member will assist her and Peter during the assessment activities. Peter and his mother have just arrived at the early intervention agency for the assessment.

In this case, the practitioners have to make sure that they are respectful of the decision by Peter's family to delay the assessment. Despite the previously canceled appointments, it is critical that the early childhood special education team members consider all of the approaches available to support the assessment in both Spanish and English and ensure that they are responsive to the needs of Peter's family.

Questions for Reflection

1. Complete a Cultural Data Table for Peter and his family. What specific information is needed prior to conducting the assessment?

---

[11]The Chapters 8 and 9 vignettes about "Peter" were created by Lucinda Kramer, Ph.D., at National University, La Jolla, CA.

2. Complete a Critical Incident Analysis Sheet in preparation for a conversation with Peter's mother regarding her reluctance to have him evaluated.

3. Review the assessment dilemmas discussed in this chapter. What dilemmas might be encountered during Peter's assessment? Of the suggestions reviewed in this chapter, which ones would be the most helpful at this point?

4. Which strategies would you use to determine the degree to which Peter's communicative behavior reflects cultural and linguistic diversity? Which strategies would you use to determine the degree to which Peter's behavior reflects a disability or delay? If you believe that diversity and a disability or delay play roles, explain why.

CONCLUSION

This chapter has reviewed culture bumps and dilemmas that practitioners and families commonly experience as they engage in assessment activities. It has described dilemmas related to language and language differences, as well as how assessment information is gathered, how assessment information is interpreted, and how results are reported. Vignettes and strategies have been provided to help practitioners consider various ways that they can respond to the issues that they will likely encounter as they serve diverse children and families. Given the enormous challenges of assessing young children, especially when their cultural linguistic background is different from that of practitioners, the importance of utilizing Skilled Dialogue cannot be overstated. Practitioners must work to anchor their understanding of the families that they serve and, as needed, create 3rd Space options alongside these families.

Respectful, Reciprocal, and Responsive Intervention and Instruction

Promoting cultural diversity rather than ignoring it . . . is an important classroom policy. On an individual level, the goal is to develop an extensive cultural repertoire. An individual who acquires understanding and develops competency in different linguistic and cultural systems is said to have an extensive cultural repertoire. . . . [The development of such repertoires] . . . is important to validate [a] child's experience, acknowledge linguistic and cultural differences, [and] integrate the community as a resource in development. (Perez & Torres-Guzman, 2002, p. 18)

As stated in the discussion on Phase I of Skilled Dialogue, practitioners cannot wait until they are asked to work with diverse children and families to begin using Anchored Understanding of Diversity and 3rd Space. It is relatively easy to have interactions in which behavioral and value differences exist because they are always present—even within the same cultural group. When differences arise that generate bumps (e.g., confusion, frustration, anger), practitioners should seek to anchor understanding of these differences and explore nondichotomized response options (i.e., 3rd Space).

Phase II of Skilled Dialogue focuses on determining the presence of cultural linguistic diversity and assessing its nature by gathering pertinent cultural and linguistic data. These data are essential to inform assessment and intervention and to anchor understanding of actual and potential culture bumps. Phase II ideally begins during initial referral; however, it often occurs later (e.g., when families come to programs after initial assessments have already been completed). Even so, it is critical that Phase

II begin prior to initiating intervention and instruction, as its results are intended to inform such services.

Phase II of the Skilled Dialogue process includes 1) determining the presence of cultural diversity, 2) assessing the nature and degree of cultural linguistic diversity, and 3) developing cultural linguistic response plans (i.e., identifying strategies for minimizing potential culture bumps and maximizing a family's cultural resources). Assuming that cultural linguistic diversity is present, this chapter focuses on the second and third steps in relation to the development and delivery of appropriate intervention and instruction. Practitioners should consider using a Cultural Data Table and the Cultural Consonance Profile to explore the nature and degree of cultural linguistic diversity in specific situations (see Chapter 7). Once those considerations have been used to design an Assessment Cultural Linguistic Response Plan, an Instructional Cultural Linguistic Response Plan should be developed. Of note, if Phase III of Skilled Dialogue is necessary, the process for critical incident analysis is the same whether it occurs in the assessment stage or the intervention and instruction stage.

It is important to recognize that many challenges are rooted in culture bumps. Examples include families apparently not following through on interventions, not being home for scheduled visits, or being vested in goals other than those outlined on an Individualized Family Service Plan (IFSP) or Individualized Education Program (IEP). If practitioners question why a family does not follow an intervention plan without determining whether culture bumps are present, they can miss critical opportunities to anchor their understanding of the child and family and to become truly responsive to their needs. Similarly, 3rd Space options that honor those needs cannot be created unless early intervention/early childhood special education practitioners gain awareness of their own perspectives in relation to families' perspectives. Culture bumps occur not only as intervention and instruction are planned, but also subsequently as practitioners interact with children and families to implement planned activities and services. Practitioners may thus want to complete a Critical Incident Analysis Sheet in addition to an Instructional Cultural Linguistic Response Plan. Critical Incident Analysis Sheets are designed to be used whenever interactions between practitioners and children or families are less positive than desired (see Chapter 7).

This chapter provides suggested responses for common intervention and instruction dilemmas that arise from culture bumps. Evidenced-based responses are suggested to help early intervention/early childhood special education practitioners develop strategies for embracing children's and families' culturally based strengths. (Included is a Cultural Linguistic Response Plan specifically designed to support practitioners' consideration of potential intervention and instructional issues for the children and families.) Practitioners should not consider the suggested responses a complete list. Indeed, the more skilled one becomes in the practices of anchoring understanding of families and creating 3rd Space, the longer one's list of possible responses becomes. The chapter also returns to the vignettes presented in Chapter 8 to illustrate how Skilled Dialogue supports practitioners and families as they move from assessment to intervention and instruction services. As in Chapter 8, these vignettes are intended only as a beginning illustration of how Skilled Dialogue can enhance interactions between practitioners and children and their families.

COMMON INTERVENTION AND INSTRUCTION DILEMMAS AND SUGGESTED RESPONSES

Dilemmas engendered by culture bumps typically arise in four areas: 1) language and language differences, 2) teaching and learning strategies, 3) instruction content, and 4) teaching and learning materials. The framework of the Instructional Cultural Linguistic Response Plan is specifically designed to respond to these four areas (see Appendix C for the blank form).

Language and Language Differences

The most overt instruction and intervention dilemmas result from the fact that many culturally diverse families speak languages other than English with their children, either exclusively or in addition to English. These children may be monolingual in a language other than English or may speak languages in addition to English. Their linguistically diverse home environments necessarily affect the knowledge they bring to learning tasks and the language in which they hold and express that knowledge. Consequently, two aspects of teaching these children are challenging. The first is developing language itself. The second is using language (one or more) to teach particular skills and knowledge. These issues require understanding and addressing not only the dynamics of dual language acquisition, but also the role of language in acquiring and expressing knowledge/skills across developmental and academic areas.

Many of the language and communication challenges related to assessment (see Chapter 8) also arise when practitioners consider intervention or instructional practices for diverse children and families in early childhood environments. In addition, personal-social issues—including children's familiarity with the values reflected in intervention settings and procedures and their understanding of identity or competence—may lead to culture bumps. Other diverse cultural parameters, including types of knowledge valued and preferred learning strategies, can lead to misunderstandings or interactions that are less than responsive. These considerations are discussed in more detail next.

Communicative-Linguistic Considerations   In many instances, the language(s) and/or communication style used in a child's home and community differs from the language and communication style used by early intervention/early childhood special education practitioners. These differences challenge practitioners to develop intervention and instructional strategies that recognize the multilingual environments that children must negotiate as they learn new skills. Planning effective instruction relies on collecting relevant information about the child's environment and language development during the assessment process.

Practitioners must use children's documented relative language proficiency in making decisions about the language of instruction, pace of an intervention, and ways to approach a child's performance errors. Children with limited or no English proficiency may be unable to respond to verbal instructions or interactions in English monolingual environments.

Similarly, early childhood and home environments may differ significantly in rules for nonverbal communication and expectations regarding appropriate behavior. For instance, some children are taught that when an adult speaks to them, maintaining eye contact for extended periods of time is a challenge to adult authority or a sign of inappropriate intimacy (Lynch & Hanson, 1992). Conversely, practitioners may view failure to maintain eye contact as a sign of disrespect or even a developmental deficit. In fact, maintaining eye contact is an item on many developmental scales (Frankenburg et al., 1990; Newborg, Stock, Wnek, Guidubaldi, & Svinicki, 1984). Practitioners may even say, "Look at me when I'm talking to you," or position themselves directly in front of children so that direct eye contact is the only option. These situations may cause much anxiety and confusion for children as well as for practitioners.

In addition, the language and communication style reflected in early childhood environments, (e.g., addressing adults by their title and first name) may differ from that used in the child's home (e.g., addressing adults only by kinship terms like "aunt" or "uncle"). These differences can make it difficult for the child to understand communicative intent appropriately. They can equally affect families' willingness to support and implement activities and interactions developed by practitioners. Differences in language and communication style also have the potential to make families feel unwelcome or shamed. Sending the message, even unintentionally, that a child's language is less desirable than English can severely affect the child's learning and the interactions with the family.

Personal-Social Considerations   Language is the primary medium for making connections with others. For instance, when 5-year-old Pierre visited an early intervention program, he was asked which child he felt more comfortable playing with: Sammy, a nonverbal child with autistic behaviors, or Tony, a verbal child whose hands were at his shoulders because of thalidomide exposure. Everyone expected Pierre to say he was most comfortable playing with Sammy, who was attractive and charming. Yet, Pierre immediately answered that he felt more comfortable with Tony, because he could play and talk with Tony. This incident highlights the critical role of communication in relationships, even early ones. The ability to communicate nonverbally and verbally plays a significant role in the ability to establish relationships—whether for playing, obtaining support, or gaining information. When a child's most proficient language is not understood or accepted in early childhood environments, personal-social bumps are sure to arise.

In addition to influencing the quality and quantity of relationships, language and communication bumps can negatively affect a child's sense of self. For example, a practitioner who cannot pronounce a child's name may go as far as changing the child's name without recognizing the value that cultures place on names. For the practitioner's convenience, the child's identity may be significantly altered.

As children leave familiar adults and comfortable environments and begin to interact with practitioners and other children, they likely experience both positive and negative feelings. In an English-only environment, children with limited English proficiency will be severely limited in their ability to express and communicate these emotions.

Sensory-Cognitive Considerations   Regardless of whether a child has a disability or developmental delay, early childhood practitioners must determine the degree to which developmental concerns relate to language and communication differences rather than to actual developmental delays and disabilities (Landurand & Cloud, 1991; Metz, 1991). In all cases, practitioners need to consider which bilingual instructional strategy is most appropriate (see the following suggested responses for various dual-language formats). Finally, it is important to recognize that exposure to or use of language(s) other than English never causes or contributes to a communication disorder (Arnberg, 1987; Harding & Riley, 1986).

Suggested Responses   In exploring potential communication and language dilemmas that practitioners may encounter in their work, it is evident that collecting information about a child's language environment and language skills should be a standard part of the assessment process. This information is critical for planning appropriate intervention and instructional strategies. If assessment information about a child and family's language background is insufficient or inappropriate, practitioners must gather the necessary information prior to extensive intervention or instructional planning. The following suggestions address the communicative and linguistic dilemmas that can arise as practitioners plan interventions and help practitioners foster respectful, reciprocal, and responsive interactions.

Ensure Optimum Communication   An obvious communicative-linguistic bump is the disparity between the language(s) used in early childhood environments and the language(s) used in a child's home. Practitioners should work with the family to select the communication format and language usage pattern that most closely match a child's relative language proficiency and home usage patterns. Depending on the family's goals, various approaches may be appropriate: 1) full bilingual, 2) dominant language bilingual, 3) modified single language, or 4) multicultural monolingual (see Figure 29).

For the purposes of this discussion, it is assumed that English is the dominant language of early intervention/early childhood special education programs even though the authors recognize that this is not always the case. The alternative (i.e., a program in which a language other than English is dominant) is no less valid or valuable. In fact, this alternative may be more valid and valuable from a research-based standpoint (Baca & Cervantes, 1990; Chamot & O'Malley, 1994; Cummins, 1989). Nevertheless, such programs are relatively rare and certainly are more challenging to implement, given available resources and the numerous languages other than English represented by children in many programs.

A *full bilingual approach* to instruction integrates children's home language(s) and English. For children who have limited or no English proficiency, this is often considered the best alternative when exposure to English is already taking place in the home. (Note that full bilingual approaches

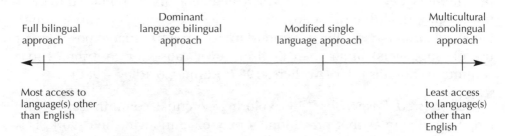

Figure 29.   A continuum of language approaches. (From "Effective and appropriate education for all children: The challenge of cultural/linguistic diversity and young children with special needs" by I. Barrera, 1993, *Topics in Early Childhood Special Education, 13*[4], 480. Copyright 1993 by PRO-ED, Inc. Adapted by permission).

may use a language other than English only for a period of time; it is not necessary to use the languages equally during each day and activity.) Children are encouraged to maintain the development of their language other than English while they acquire skills in English. Ideally, programs hire practitioners who are bilingual in the languages of the child. Cultural linguistic mediators and skilled translators are needed when this is not possible (Barrera, 2000). It is important to note that for a majority of countries, being exposed to and learning more than one language from early childhood on is considered the norm. No research indicates that exposure to multiple languages affects language development detrimentally; in fact, research indicates the contrary (Miller, 1984).

In the *dominant language bilingual approach,* one language is used more frequently. Legitimate interpretations of the dominant language bilingual approach include both home language–dominant with less English (e.g., a Spanish-dominant program) and English-dominant with less of the child's home language. For consistency and ease of understanding within this discussion, the approach is interpreted as English-dominant, meaning that it is the main language for instruction. English for Speakers of Other Languages (ESOL) and other such strategies must be used carefully to ensure comprehension and full access to existing skills. It is critical that the language other than English is not merely used informally but is also used in a planned manner to support learning and teaching. This approach is generally considered most appropriate for children who retain understanding of particular funds of knowledge in a language other than English yet have sufficient English proficiency to benefit from significant amounts of instruction in English. Similar to the full bilingual approach, the dominant bilingual approach requires teachers or skilled cultural linguistic mediators who can understand and respond to children regardless of which language they use.

The *modified single language approach* relies primarily on English as the language of instruction. The language(s) other than English is used occasionally only to clarify or reinforce instruction. Practitioners using this approach with children who understand and speak a language other than English need to explicitly reassure children that they can still use languages other than English to communicate as necessary. This approach is most appropriate for children with strong proficiency in English yet with continued exposure to another language in the home (e.g., Hmong may be used at home but is not dominant).

Practitioners should be aware that bilingual or multilingual children often appear to have greater English proficiency than they actually do (Harding & Riley, 1986). Although these children may initially appear fluent in English, their ability to use it in an academic context may be much more limited. See also considerations under the subheadings "Realize that Expressive Skills May Exceed Comprehension" and "Recognize that Basic Interpersonal Communication Skills are Distinct from Cognitive Academic Linguistic Proficiency."

A *multicultural monolingual approach* uses only one language (typically English), with diverse aspects of several cultures integrated into the curriculum. All early childhood programs should at least implement this approach, even when significant linguistic diversity is not present, as it sensitizes children to the existence and positive nature of cultural diversity. A multicultural monolingual approach is also appropriate for working with culturally diverse children and families when there is little or no linguistic diversity (i.e., both children and families are highly fluent in English). Under carefully structured conditions, it also may be used when such diversity is present. If access to children's language(s) other than English has yet to be identified, then practitioners may use an ESOL approach with limited or no use of language(s) other than English. However, practitioners must pay close attention to the children's language development and concept comprehension when this is the case. See also the next suggested response in this chapter and "Distinguish Between Expressive and Receptive Language Delays" in Chapter 8's discussion of dilemmas related to interpreting assessment results.

The multicultural monolingual approach is never ideal because children with limited proficiency in English must simultaneously deal with two different needs: 1) attending to the language itself (e.g., "What did she just say? What did it mean? Was she asking or telling me to do something?") and 2) attending to the content of instruction (e.g., "What is a square? What is a community helper?"). Children who are already proficient in English only need to attend to the latter. See also this section's subheading "Distinguish Between Situations in Which Language Is the Medium and Those in Which Language Is the Teaching Topic."

Whenever this approach is used, it is critical that implicit and explicit messages about diversity communicate strength, not deficit. All children should be encouraged to explore multiple languages and ways of communicating and thinking (e.g., have audiotapes in a variety of languages, bring in children's family members who speak languages other than English). For additional information on instructional approaches for linguistically diverse children, see Baca and Cerventes (1998), Barrera (1993), and Winzer and Mazurek (1994).

Respond to Children's Communication Efforts with Words or Behaviors They Understand   Children with limited proficiency in the language of instruction need to become familiar with an early childhood program's routines and environment before they are approached with questions or directives. Tabors (1997) noted that teachers initially may choose to include a child by using his or her name without directly asking questions that require responses (e.g., "How about we give Chun a chance," "Let's show Erich how to put this puzzle together"). Tabors referred to this strategy as a "low-demand" situation that gives the child time to adjust to the new cultural and linguistic environment. Using this strategy does not mean that practitioners should not respond to the child's communicative efforts. On the contrary, practitioners should respond even if they do not fully understand the child's attempted message, as recommended with nonverbal children.

Use a Variety of ESOL and Other Language Improvement Strategies Early intervention/early childhood special education practitioners need to consider a variety of communication strategies as they work with children and families whose primary language differs from their primary language. Many of these strategies are similar to those used with children who are nonverbal or have communication impairments. For example, practitioners can combine verbal (e.g., "Please get that truck") and nonverbal prompts (e.g., gesture, directed gaze). Other such strategies include the following:

- Repeat instructions to give a child more opportunities to understand.

- Ensure that communication focuses on the "here and now" so the child has a better chance of narrowing down what is being discussed.

- Expand communication attempts. For example, if a child says "cracker," the practitioner may say, "These crackers taste good. Would you like another cracker?"

Cheng (1995), Echevarria and Graves (1998), and Tabors (1997) provided additional effective ESOL strategies. Ventriglia (1982) also provided a wealth of language development strategies designed especially for young English language learners. These strategies can augment more familiar language development strategies.

Determine Relative Language Proficiency   Early intervention/early childhood special education practitioners should always assess relative language proficiency (i.e., proficiency in English and in language[s] other than English) prior to assessment or intervention. Sometimes the phrase *identifying language dominance* is used to characterize this step. The point, however, is to establish a working knowledge of the child's receptive and expressive skills in all languages used, rather than to single out one language as dominant. Determining relative language proficiency, as opposed to dominance, is particularly critical for young children. Bilingual or multilingual children often do not have a clearly dominant language but, rather, use two or more languages separately or in combination, depending on context and purpose.

Relative language proficiency may be judged either formally through bilingual language screening/evaluation tools or informally through observations and parent interviews. In addition to probing the child's language usage, which may be minimal if severe disabilities are present, it is also important to probe language usage by others in the home (i.e., how much of which language is used by whom and in what contexts). See also the Chapter 7 discussion of relative language proficiency and the Home Language Usage Profile.

Distinguish Between Situations in Which Language Is the Medium and Those in Which Language Is the Teaching Topic (e.g., whether one is teaching the concept of "up" or teaching the English word "up") Practitioners need to understand the purpose of language to determine when to use which language(s). New concepts and unfamiliar material are taught most effectively in the language that the child understands best. The less familiar language should be used primarily when the purpose is to teach known concepts and structures. For example, the *concept* "up" should be introduced and taught in the most familiar language. If English is the less familiar language, the English word "up" could then be taught and associated with that concept. The less familiar language is best used, at least initially, only for teaching the language itself.

Learning both content and form (language) is simultaneously less efficient and more difficult for anyone, especially a child. Therefore, basic vocabulary for familiar items and actions should be known in the less familiar language prior to using it for instruction. Presentation of new concepts or skills, and demands for demonstrating learning of those concepts and skills, should be made in the more proficient language whenever possible. When this is not possible, which should rarely be the case, systematic ESOL strategies should be used to ensure optimal learning. As stated previously, languages in which one has limited proficiency are poor tools for learning anything other than the language itself.

Connect New Language and Content with Known Language and Familiar Contexts Keeping the context familiar allows children to connect the unknown with the known. This connection maximizes the transfer of existing knowledge and skills to the new situation or language and enhances comprehension. Examples include using familiar discourse, behavior rules, and objects found in the child's home.

Create a Physically and Emotionally Safe Environment   Consider setting up learning environments as "safe havens" in which children can play. For instance, practitioners can select materials that are readily available for children (e.g., Legos, puzzles, blocks). Space should be available for children to interact independently with these materials if so desired. Coming into an unfamiliar environment with unfamiliar expectations and demands, in addition to lacking proficiency in that environment's language, can be a daunting experience for anyone. How much more daunting might it be for a 3- or 4-year-old whose problem-solving skills and experiential repertoire are only beginning to form? In many ways, Igoa's (1995) statements about immigrant children are equally applicable to all young, culturally linguistically diverse children entering unfamiliar and "foreign" environments where demands to respond to an unknown language prevail:

> *When immigrant children leave the country [i.e., environment] that was their home—a familiar language, culture, community, and social system—they experience a variety of emotional and cognitive adjustments to the reality of life in a new country. How dry and clinical that sentence sounds! It doesn't even begin to convey the paralyzing fear in a little boy from Afghanistan that he will never fully understand English, that he will always be on the outside looking in. It doesn't explain why an achievement-oriented girl from Vietnam will intentionally fail tests that might advance her in the educational system. (p. xi)*

Is this true only for children who are immigrants? Countless children born and raised in the United States have also lived that forced shift from the familiar to the unfamiliar. The first author entered first grade (in a school that was 100% Hispanic through the fourth grade) already speaking some English. Yet, the effects of cultural dissonance and needing to quickly master an unpredictable cultural and linguistic environment remain with her to this day (see Epilogue). Similar stories abound in culturally linguistically diverse communities of second- and third-generation U.S. citizens (e.g., Garcia, 2001). Appendix A examines some ways in which unsupported acculturation can be traumatizing. Delays and disabilities that delay or impede language and problem-solving abilities can further compound the trauma.

Expect a Silent Period   Children should be given ample time and opportunities to orient themselves to the expectations of the early childhood providers and environments. Children entering an environment where their home language is not dominant will speak little or not at all, depending on their personalities and other factors (Díaz-Rico & Weed,

1995). It is important to let them simply observe and/or interact nonverbally if they wish. Demands for verbal expression should be kept to a minimum until the child demonstrates spontaneous attempts at verbal interaction. Such attempts typically appear fairly quickly; if they are not evident in interactions with peers within 3–4 weeks, other factors may be precluding them and practitioners should look more closely at the situation.

Avoid Direct Correction of Verbal Errors   As children begin to express themselves in English, their utterances should be accepted without correction, although they may be asked to repeat something if it is not understood. Approximations should be accepted to encourage continued expression. Children whose verbalizations are corrected may feel shame and decrease or stop attempts to communicate. In addition, many errors in a second language are developmental, responding more to time and practice than to correction (Díaz-Rico & Weed, 1995).

Provide Comprehensible Input   Practitioners should provide comprehensible input whenever a child's less familiar language is used. *Comprehensible input* refers to making the language directed to the child as easy to understand as possible by providing as many cues as possible (e.g., pictures, objects, gestures, familiar contexts and routines). The idea is to pair the spoken language with these cues to facilitate comprehension. This type of language exposure is very effective in helping children acquire communication skills in a second language (Cummins, 1984, 1989). Translating immediately after speaking is not effective for this purpose, although it is effective for learning concepts or content.

Realize that Expressive Skills May Exceed Comprehension   It is generally assumed that a child who says something in a language understands the content and has mastered the requisite language structures. For example, a child who says, "What is your name?" might be assumed to understand that question and to have mastered the forms for questions and pronouns. Bilingual children, however, frequently learn language in chunks and may be able to express more that they can understand. For example, they may have learned "What is your name?" as a single utterance without really understanding individual words or grammar. Therefore, they may sound more proficient than they actually are in their second language. It is important never to assume understanding based on expressive skills. Understanding should always be specifically assessed, especially across a variety of situations.

Recognize that Basic Interpersonal Communication Skills Are Distinct from Cognitive Academic Linguistic Proficiency   There are two distinct levels or facets of language skills (Chamot & O'Malley, 1994; Cummins,

1984). On the one hand, basic interpersonal communication skills (BICS) are present in face-to-face, informal, interpersonal interactions (e.g., talking with a friend about what one did yesterday). This type of communication is characterized by the availability of strategies and cues such as facial expressions, repetition or revision, shared referents, and suprasegmentals (vocal pitch, stress, loudness). On the other hand, cognitive academic linguistic proficiency (CALP) skills are necessary for competent functioning in academic environments. Preliteracy and literacy skills are major components of CALP, as is the understanding of formal oral discourse (Díaz-Rico & Wood, 1995). Many strategies and cues common to BICS are not common to CALP, for which reliance on extralinguistic cues is greatly reduced and the need to understand literate strategies (e.g., story grammars) is increased. A child may be very proficient at a BICS level and still have significant difficulty with academic work (e.g., following abstract discussions or directions, interpreting text).

Validate the Language Other than English   Children quickly learn to associate a particular language with a particular person, environment, and/or activity. It is important, therefore, to pay attention to how often a language is being used in certain situations. It is especially critical to avoid communicating that English is a higher status language than the child's other language(s). This message may be inadvertently communicated when English is used in school and by professionals while Spanish, for example, is used only when English cannot be used. This message devalues languages other than English and can inhibit a child's progress in those languages and in English. Languages other than English are validated when modeled by a variety of persons—professional and nonprofessional—in a variety of environments. Exposing the child to literature and recordings in those languages is another effective strategy for validating them.

Cue Language Contexts   Although language use should not communicate a difference in status, it should be predictable, at least in the early stages of learning (see the section "Use the 'One-Person, One-Language' Rule" in Chapter 8). A child who is first learning English should be cued when English is to be used. For example, one person may speak English and another Spanish, or English may be used exclusively during a particular activity or time period every day. Puppets may also be used as visual reminders of which language is to be used at a particular time.

Teaching and Learning Strategies

Other dilemmas are related to the use of specific teaching strategies that may be unfamiliar to or not similarly valued by culturally linguistically diverse children and families. The following discussion clusters strategies into the three developmental/curricular areas used to discuss culture bumps.

Communicative-Linguistic   Teaching is based on effective communication. Language is a primary medium for the transmission of information as well as for the self-talk that can be a critical aspect of learning. The language differences, dilemmas, and suggested responses are also highly relevant to this examination and should be considered in addition to the ones discussed in this section.

One of the initial factors that practitioners should consider when working with bilingual or multilingual children is the language(s) in which a child can best learn a new skill. Determining this may be especially challenging in early childhood special education environments in which children may come from a multitude of linguistic backgrounds. In these instances, practitioners need to consider how to incorporate all of the children's languages into the classroom.

Because it is impossible for practitioners to be competent in the languages of all of the children and families with whom they work, they are challenged to recognize the limitations that they bring to the dialogue. Practitioners must realize that it is not just the children or families with limited proficiency in English who are "limited." Practitioners' low proficiency in the families' primary language is an equal limitation. This realization is critical to establishing reciprocity, a key characteristic of Skilled Dialogue. For example, it is important to communicate that translators/interpreters are necessary not because families have limited English proficiency but because practitioners have limited proficiency in the families' language(s).

A good guide to creating multicultural/multilingual early childhood environments is the ALERTA curriculum (Williams & DeGaetano, 1985), which contains suggestions and protocols for practitioners' use. This curriculum contains forms and concrete suggestions for areas such as identifying and using community resources; preparing multicultural, bilingual language environments for young children; integrating strategies for language learning throughout the program; and observing children's interests, developmental levels, and language use.

Personal-Social   Teaching is in many ways a relational endeavor. The importance of emotional intelligence in both teaching and learning is increasingly being recognized (Goleman, 1995; Greenspan, 1999). Practitioners need to examine how well their teaching strategies are responsive to children's personal-social funds of knowledge.

Practitioners tend to develop interventions and instructional practices based on the theoretical constructs accepted by their formal education and training. However, these constructs often do not account for different child-rearing practices (Bhagwanji, Santos, & Fowler, 2000). "Appropriate" social and instructional interventions are culturally defined (Fewell, 1996). For instance, Schneider, Parush, Katz, and Miller noted that families differ in the "the amount of auditory, visual, or tactile stimulation, whether play and movement are encouraged and in what way, and whether certain skills are actually taught or practiced" (1995, p. 20). Cintas (1995) stated that the cradleboards used by the Navajo and Hopi people illustrate a culturally based child-rearing practice designed to shape infant behavior for the parent's and the child's benefit. Practitioners must consider and incorporate such practices as they develop interventions and instructional practices for children and families. As Bhagwanji et al. (2000) noted, intervention activities aimed at increasing a young child's independence without also addressing interdependence and shared caring may conflict with the social and cultural preferences of many groups. See the discussions in Chapters 5 and 7 on the Guide to Identifying Cultural Data Related to Potential Culture Bumps for other personal-social aspects that tend to differ across cultures.

Sensory-Cognitive How practitioners present information highly influences the ability of children and families to understand the concepts or information provided. Similarly, how children and families communicate information may strongly influence the ability of practitioners to comprehend what is being communicated. Practitioners need to consider families' funds of knowledge and the types of knowledge valued within these funds. Are these primarily personal or communal? To what degree are funds of knowledge contained orally? To what degree are they contained in written form? Asking families that primarily value oral information to rely on written documents (e.g., IFSPs, IEPs) may lead to significant culture bumps.

Practitioners must also consider families' preferred strategies for acquiring new knowledge (e.g., modeling, questioning), as well as for problem solving and decision making. Practitioners must assess the degree to which learning strategies used at home are direct, indirect, explicit, or implicit. Observing how family members teach children what they consider important can give insight into which approaches are valued.

Suggested Responses The need for culturally and linguistically responsive intervention and instruction procedures is receiving a great deal of attention in early childhood education. However, only a limited amount of research exists to help practitioners accomplish this. Fortunately, the practices of Skilled Dialogue can support practitioners in ensuring that they present culturally and linguistically sensitive information in a respectful, reciprocal, and responsive manner. The following suggested responses can limit the impact of dilemmas that may arise from how information is presented to diverse children and families.

Establish a Relationship   Practitioners take time to build rapport with children and their families before beginning assessment or intervention. Although it is critical that a positive relationship be established to support the learning of all children, it is even more imperative that this occur when the cultural and/or linguistic background of practitioners differs from those of the children and families with whom they work. When families realize that they are respected, that they have ample opportunities to voice their perspectives, and that practitioners truly attempt to respond to their needs, many potential bumps are eliminated before they occur. Acknowledging that this process takes some time is an important first step. To the maximum extent possible, practitioners should work to build in opportunities for establishing this rapport prior to initiating academic instruction.

Set a Stable and Predictable Routine   Interacting with children via a consistent routine is one of the most helpful ways for practitioners to support children in managing a new or less-familiar language and communication environment. Routines make it easier for children to pick up subtle cues and use other children and adults as models of the expected behaviors. A stable routine gives children the opportunity to predict certain communications and instructions.

Use Teaching and Learning Strategies Familiar to and Valued by the Child and Family   Activities that are carefully selected to match the patterns of a child and family's environment yield the greatest gains in overall development and early literacy (Kame'enui, Carnine, Dixon, Simmons, & Coyne, 2002; Williams & DeGaetano, 1985). Any attempt to address the learning strategies of a diverse group of children must offer a wide range of options. Gardner's (1993) multiple intelligences framework recognizes differences while reducing the risk of stereotyping children's abilities based on their cultural background. The materials developed and used by the Capitol School in Tuscaloosa, Alabama, provide an example of the application of this framework to early childhood (B. Roundtree, personal communication).

Match Communication Styles   To the maximum extent possible, practitioners should match a family's pacing, level of directness, nonverbal behaviors, and other communication aspects. Such matching requires that practitioners have developed a strong forestructure and an anchored understanding of specific differences based on the actual communication structures of the families with whom they work (see discussion on Skilled Dialogue Phases I and II in Chapter 7).

Be Responsive to a Family's Funds of Knowledge   Practitioners must closely examine the vocabulary and concepts used in intervention tasks and other communications for the degree of match with a family's funds of knowledge. If there is not a match, there may be insufficient connections between the home and early childhood environments, making it difficult to transfer knowledge from one environment to the other. When unaddressed, this lack of continuity can put children at risk for academic problems as well as limit opportunities to develop the attitudes and skills necessary to succeed in a variety of environments.

Encourage the Continued Home Use of the Language Other than English   Some practitioners may believe that placing a child in an English-only environment is the best way to ensure fast acquisition of English (Quiñones-Eatman, 2001). Yet, research does not validate the belief that children who are second-language learners should be exposed to as much English as possible (Baca & Cervantes, 1998). Research with both monolingual and bilingual children indicates that the richer the home language environment, the better the child's language development and school achievement. Cummins (1984) reported on a study of 108 Hispanic fifth and sixth graders, in which the relationship between maintaining Spanish as the home language and academic performance was examined. Results indicated that children from homes where Spanish usage was not maintained had "significantly poorer academic performance . . . in comparison to students who had maintained Spanish as the main home language" (p. 112). Cummins reported on another study of 53 Chinese American 9- and 10-year-olds, which showed that increased exposure to Chinese outside the home correlated with better performance on a particular standardized test. Even more significant, the "amount of English used in the home was unrelated to [test] scores" (1984, p. 112). Unfortunately, few studies like these target younger children. Nevertheless, their implications cannot be ignored.

To provide an optimum home language environment, parents should be encouraged to use the language with which they are most comfortable and in which they are most proficient. The richer the language environment they can provide—regardless of which language(s) they use—the better their children will be able to develop and acquire new information. Home language patterns are also tied to self-identity and esteem, so the perceived demand to change them can have a significantly negative emotional impact.

Instruction Content

What practitioners teach in early childhood special education environments is often unfamiliar—and perhaps even inappropriate—for some children, based on their cultural and/or linguistic backgrounds. In these instances, culture bumps are likely regarding what practitioners and families expect and want in the learning environment. What practitioners value as individuals can strongly influence the content of instruction and the implementation of interventions. As practitioners learn to acknowledge and understand their own cultural lenses, they can begin to see beyond their particular frameworks. Thus, as practitioners incorporate Skilled Dialogue in their work, they can select content that is developmentally appropriate within ENC and respectful of diverse cultural values and beliefs.

Communicative-Linguistic Considerations Language, language level, and language style should be important parts of any content selection for instruction. To maximize the appropriateness of selected content, children and families need regular and frequent opportunities to communicate and share their ideas.

It is critical that practitioners avoid sending the message, either implicitly or explicitly, that one language holds a higher status than another. Rather, they need to ensure that all children learn the value of bilingualism and multilingualism. Similarly, practitioners should recognize the relative value that is placed on verbal versus nonverbal communication in the selected content for instruction. Finally, practitioners must understand that meaningful communication is essential to learning. It is difficult for young children to learn through an insufficiently developed communication medium. Stunting the development of one language to develop a second language in order to initiate instruction in that second language is an ineffective method both for developing communication skills and teaching concepts.

Personal-Social Considerations Practitioners must be aware that what they teach can either support or hinder the development of children's self-esteem and self-confidence. Instructional materials should offer many opportunities for learning activities that develop social responsibility and interpersonal skills in ways that honor and extend the values and beliefs of families. It is in these very early years that practitioners and families lay the groundwork for young children's competence in Skilled Dialogue. At no point should families be made to feel that they must choose between what they know and value and what practitioners recommend. Equally important, children should never be taught that their language, knowledge, beliefs, and values are anything less than assets that can help them learn the unfamiliar.

Sensory-Cognitive Considerations   The curricula or content of instruction should confirm that diversity in all of its facets is an asset to be tapped and not something that needs remediation. The content of instruction should reflect how children develop ways of observing, thinking, and experimenting within their environment and should support the funds of knowledge valued by their families. At an age-appropriate level, instructional content should engage children in determining an appropriate response to solving problems by using a variety of different decision-making strategies.

Suggested Responses   Practitioners must consider which intervention and instructional content can best respond to culturally and linguistically diverse children and families. Using Skilled Dialogue and examining these suggested responses can assist practitioners in selecting which information and skills they present to young children and families.

Teach the Value of Diversity   Practitioners should work to ensure that instruction content reflects the value of cultural linguistic diversity (e.g., through the stories and pictures used). Even in the youngest years—perhaps especially in these years—children are sensitive to what it feels like to be respected, to have reciprocal communication, and to have responsive caregivers. The actions that practitioners model and the content of instruction reveal their values to children and families.

Encourage the Continued Home Use of the Language Other than English   Children and families should be supported to continue using language(s) other than English at home. As noted previously, research with monolingual and bilingual children indicates that such continuity improves a child's language development and school achievement. Parents should be encouraged to use their preferred language with each other as well as with their children. In addition, home language patterns are tied to self-identity and self-esteem, so continuing them is important.

Allow for Exploration   The instruction content should encourage children to explore and draw conclusions in a risk-free environment. Doing so allows practitioners to build an environment in which children can safely try new things in a manner that is consistent with their cultural practices. Some toys and play materials that children use at home should also be a part of the environment to the maximum extent possible. As discussed previously, making children feel secure is a critical component for learning new skills. Early childhood environments should be structured so that children can choose which parts of their environment to explore (or not explore). It is important to note that in some cultures, exploration in infants and toddlers is not valued. Therefore, practitioners need to create an environment where all children are not expected to conform to the same cultural practices and daily routine.

Provide Frequent and Varied Opportunities for Children to Communicate in English and Other Home Languages   To the maximum extent possible, instructional content should allow children to share information about their feelings, knowledge, values, and beliefs in whichever language and communication style is most comfortable. Communication should be thought of in a broad manner. Children who speak multiple languages may have a preferred language to communicate certain ideas or topics. In addition, children may prefer to communicate in nonverbal ways. Children who are learning a new language may begin expressing themselves with incomprehensible utterances. These should be accepted without correction, as correcting early communicative attempts may shame a child and decrease or stop further attempts to communicate.

Ensure that Assessment Information Is Ongoing During Teaching   Learning activities provide assessment information and help practitioners determine the extent to which children have processed information and can apply it to problem-solving strategies. As practitioners consider what to teach, how to assess the impact of what is taught should be simultaneously considered. This assessment process should help practitioners craft the next steps in the instructional process.

Many tools presented in Chapter 7 support practitioners as they continue to gather information about the children and families with whom they work. As an example, the Cultural Data Table can capture information about which teaching strategies seem to be consistent with a child's cultural linguistic background. Responses to the information noted on these tools should be considered dynamic. For instance, as children learn and develop, their expressive and receptive skills in English and other languages are likely to change. Therefore, these tools should be periodically reviewed and updated as part of an ongoing assessment process to help practitioners make decisions about what and how they teach.

Teach the Practices of Skilled Dialogue The concepts of Skilled Dialogue could serve as a core for nearly any early childhood curriculum. It is never too early for children to learn about dialogue that is based on respect, reciprocity, and responsiveness. This is taught to infants and toddlers primarily through modeling. Early childhood special education practitioners can help preschoolers begin to understand the rich variety of cultural expressions (i.e., to anchor their understanding of differences). It can also be immensely helpful to teach children that there is always a third choice—the basic component of creating 3rd Space options. The ability to find third choices can be important developmentally (e.g., when one child wants to play and the other does not). It is also important culturally to emphasize that it is never necessary to lose one behavior (e.g., speaking Hmong) in order to gain another (e.g., speaking English).

Teaching and Learning Materials

Despite increased awareness that practitioners must respond to the impact of culture and language on the educational process, teaching materials and curricula that adequately address diversity remain limited (Lynch & Hanson, 1992). Early childhood professionals face the challenge of finding quality early childhood materials to share with children, families, and their communities. To work effectively with diverse children and families, it is imperative to find or adapt materials with contents that respect, reflect, and include these families' values, beliefs, and customs (Santos, Fowler, Corso, & Bruns, 2000). Although authors and publishers of educational materials may increasingly acknowledge cultural and linguistic diversity, practitioners still have the responsibility of selecting which materials to use. No one item is totally responsive to the full range of values and beliefs that exist across cultures. Therefore, the most challenging part of finding and effectively using materials is reflecting on their content and, subsequently, considering ways to adapt content to increase its cultural and linguistic appropriateness for the individuals with whom the materials will be used.

Communicative-Linguistic Considerations The format of possible materials (e.g., print, video, audio) should be evaluated based on families' or children's preferred learning styles. In addition, the materials should be assessed to ensure the comprehension level is appropriate for the intended audience. Practitioners should specifically consider the degree to which technical terminology or early intervention/early childhood special education jargon is used in the material and whether it is adequately defined.

Many more efforts are underway to provide materials in languages other than English, but practitioners must carefully consider these materials. The vast majority are translations of materials originally developed in English (CLAS Early Childhood Research Institute, 2001). In an effort to provide materials in the family's preferred language, practitioners may be tempted to use any available resources in that language. As Santos, Lee, Valdivia, and Zhang wrote,

> In our quest to provide information that the family will access, comprehend, and implement, we may be inadvertently disseminating outdated, inaccurate, or even offensive information. Instead of setting the stage for an improved relationship between early intervention professionals and family members, we may further alienate the family by giving them inappropriate materials. (2001, p. 26)

According to Santos et al., effective translations

1. Match the material's comprehension level with the intended audience's reading ability, education, social and economic status, and acculturation level

2. Reflect regional and dialectical differences in the language spoken by the intended audience

3. Recommend activities and examples that are familiar to the intended audience

4. Use real stories and authentic voices and include visuals and photographs that are representative of the intended audience

5. Make appropriate accommodations for the use of novel words and borrowed terms (e.g., *Individualized Family Service Plan*)

6. Do not distort, delete, or change the information

Personal-Social Considerations   To be responsive to children and families served, materials must reflect families' characteristics, roles, backgrounds, and geographic location (Santos et al., 2000). Practitioners should consider children's or families' degree of enculturation in ENC and early intervention/early childhood special education culture as well as their skill in negotiating these cultures. Other issues that may affect which teaching and learning materials practitioners select pertain to the different roles that family members may play in child rearing, a family's experience regarding social and personal power, and the degree to which a family belongs to and identifies with a group with "minority" status.

Sensory-Cognitive Considerations   Practitioners must assess the extent to which the materials reflect and acknowledge families' funds of knowledge. That is, do they address the diversity found in their community? Or can they be adapted to acknowledge a specific group's concerns, beliefs, and practices? Materials that were once viewed as supporting best practice in the early intervention/early childhood special education field and other widely used materials may contain strategies that would offend some cultural and linguistic groups (e.g., to question adults, to solve problems without adult assistance). Practitioners have to determine the degree the worldview described in the material matches the worldview of the child or family with whom the material will be used. They must consider whether the material's basic assumptions about how the world works and about what is considered right and wrong challenge or support the beliefs of a child or family. Appendix C contains a Funds of Knowledge Worksheet for Story Assessment. This form or one like it can be used to assess the types of knowledge reflected in stories and other print materials (e.g., materials that show and discuss only nuclear families).

Suggested Responses   All materials inherently contain implicit and explicit judgments about which beliefs, practices, and funds of knowledge should be valued (e.g., by the persons depicted or the events highlighted). Instructional materials influence what and how teachers teach, and, subsequently, what children and families learn. Selecting culturally and linguistically appropriate instructional materials implies that the content presented is congruent with local cultural and environmental knowledge. The material also should reflect current research. These two aspects may appear at odds in certain materials, but this does not necessarily mean the materials are not worthy of use. Instead, this situation may challenge practitioners to find 3rd Space to hold the seemingly contradictory information together. The following suggested responses can support practitioners as they face dilemmas about teaching materials.

Use Materials that Include Multiple Populations   An initial challenge for practitioners or programs often begins with simply finding up-to-date materials and information on specific topics. However, several projects and professional organizations have done much of the work to create substantial collections of materials (e.g., Catlett & Winton, 2000; Perry & Duru, 2001; Culturally and Linguistically Appropriate Services [CLAS] Early Childhood Research Institute, see http://clas.uiuc.edu). These collections allow practitioners to make informed choices about which materials are most appropriate.

Carefully Consider the Selection of Materials   To the maximum extent possible, practitioners should ensure that materials and resources in the children's primary languages are accessible to the children and their families. Books, videotapes, posters, and other materials that are part of the early childhood environment should reflect the diverse languages of the children. When selecting materials, it is important that practitioners develop forestructures to become knowledgeable about the children, families, and community groups with whom they will share the material. Early intervention teams must realize that individuals and families are members of multiple cultures (Kalyanpur & Harry, 1999). Kalyanpur and Harry noted that "children are raised within a cultural framework that imposes rewards and sanctions for efficient learning of the group's norms and expectations" (p. 3); however, intragroup differences are often as large as intergroup differences. Therefore, there is not a simple "recipe" approach to selecting materials and practices with which practitioners can assume that a family from a particular culture should receive certain materials.

Practitioners must evaluate the overall strengths and limitations of the material's content. Practitioners should especially consider whether the material is responsive to the cultural and linguistic background of the intended audience. Specifically, teams need to determine whether the values, beliefs, and practices highlighted in the material support or conflict with those of the children and families receiving the materials.

Practitioners also should determine whether the material's presentation and format are appropriate for the needs of the intended audience. For instance, families may prefer a videotape to printed material or material written in Spanish to English. If the material is translated, teams should assess the accuracy and quality of the translation.

Adapt Materials to Make a Match   After weighing the strengths and limitations of certain materials, practitioners will likely find something that approximates their needs. Instead of simply using a certain item as is, practitioners should reflect and consider how it can be made more suitable for the children and families receiving it. That is, how can practitioners create a match between materials and the values, beliefs, and practices of children and families? Although the content of some materials may be used as originally produced, others may need to be adapted to meet the intended objectives. It is important to keep in mind which kinds of adaptations can be made. Copyrighted materials may not be altered without permission from the copyright holder (typically the author or publisher); however, this generally does not prohibit teams from using parts of the original material or using it in conjunction with other materials. Teams have more freedom to adapt materials in the public domain (e.g., a government publication) as needed. It is always a good practice to credit by citing the original source.

When considering adaptations to a material, several questions can help the community team determine what adaptations, if any, are necessary. Some questions that practitioners may ask themselves include

- Does the content match the child's learning needs?

- Is the content sensitive to diverse learning styles, values, and practices?

- Are there better ways to present the material to children or families (e.g., in print, in face-to-face interactions, electronically)?

- Can I address my concerns and identify appropriate ways of using the material through supplemental activities, discussion, or other materials?

- Can I use some but not all of the material and still produce desired outcomes?

- Can I use the material as a model to develop a new document, given my current resources?

Practitioners should rely on the benefits of the multiple voices in their agencies and communities to spark ideas and provide direction for adapting the materials that they have selected.

In adapting a material, practitioners should consider the values, assumptions, and beliefs represented as well as those of the participants and families with whom the material will be used. Adapting a material's presentation often enhances the material's clarity, comprehension level, format, and graphics, possibly making it more user friendly or efficient. As the process of selecting and using materials unfolds, practitioners may continually refer to the question "How can I adapt this material to best reflect the unique strengths and needs of children and families in this community?"

Allow Family Members to Interact with Materials   Too often, materials are simply given to families with no explanation about their content or purpose and with no follow-up. Ideally, practitioners should consider a process that encourages the families to interact with the materials. Practitioners can specifically highlight portions of the material that may not be consistent with the family's beliefs and practices. This may facilitate dialogue between the family and practitioners around issues raised by the material's information.

Solicit Questions or Comments About Materials   Children and families should be asked what they liked about the material and what they think needs to be improved. With this input, practitioners can decide whether to continue using a material. In this reciprocal process, it is important to engage the voices of as many diverse stakeholders as possible. This allows the selection and adaptation of materials to be a shared responsibility, thus increasing the potential to use a material more appropriately with diverse populations.

INTERVENTION AND INSTRUCTION IN PRACTICE: FOUR VIGNETTES

This section returns to the four vignettes introduced in Chapter 8 to discuss the culture bumps that practitioners are likely to encounter when implementing interventions and instructional practices. The components of Skilled Dialogue are explored to illustrate practices that might support the implementation of effective interventions. Again, each vignette is purposely "unfinished." Questions are provided at the end of each vignette to help practitioners consider potential next steps for working with the child and family.

Xee

After Xee's assessment was completed, Mr. Ly requested that Xee be enrolled in a morning early childhood special education preschool and in an afternoon Head Start program. The team immediately realized that to plan effective instruction, it was critical to review all relevant assessment information about Xee's environment and language development. The team decided to return to the completed Cultural Data Table and RLP Profile (see Figures 24 and 25 in Chapter 8). From this information, the team developed an Instructional Cultural Linguistic Response Plan to support intervention planning (see Figure 30).

Communicative-Linguistic Data

From the initial assessment information, the practitioners ascertained Xee's communicative-linguistic data. It was determined that Xee lives in a Hmong-English home environment, with Hmong as the dominant language. Yet, family observations and interviews revealed that Xee's older siblings often speak English when their mother is not present. Xee's RLP Profile showed that receptive and expressive language were very limited in Hmong and English. Her receptive and expressive skills in English were roughly the same. Nonetheless, the information gathered did reveal that Xee is partially bilingual.

The presence of a language other than English alerted the team that bilingual instructional strategies needed to be considered for Xee. Before they engaged in any detailed intervention planning, the Head Start teachers and the early childhood special education preschool teachers worked with the family to

Instructional Cultural Linguistic Response Plan

Child's name: _Xee_ _____ Date: _12/19/02___ Completed by: _J. McCarelle_____

Specific Intervention and Instruction Considerations

RE: *Language and language differences*

1. Determine how the language and communication styles used in Xee's home can overlap with the language and communication styles used in the preschool and Head Start environments.
2. In both of the early childhood environments, consider using a modified single language approach that primarily uses English as the language of instruction but is supported by Hmong.
3. Allow Xee to initially experience "low-demand" situations that give her time to adjust to the new early childhood environments.
4. Work with the preschool and Head Start staff to support all of Xee's communication attempts, avoiding the correction of any errors in Xee's communication efforts.

RE: *Teaching and learning strategies*

1. Use modeling and other indirect teaching strategies as much as possible, as these seem to be the preferred strategies for acquiring new knowledge in Xee's home.
2. Support the family's oral emphasis when presenting new information.
3. Maintain stable classroom routines that help Xee predict upcoming events and feel safe in the new early childhood environments.
4. Support the Ly family's continued use of both Hmong and English at home.

RE: *Instruction content*

1. Ensure that all children in the preschool and Head Start environments experience a variety of languages.
2. Give Xee frequent opportunities to share information about her feelings or experiences in either Hmong or English.
3. Provide regular and ongoing assessment of Xee's learning based on the different teaching styles and approaches used.

RE: *Teaching and learning materials*

1. Utilize materials that reflect the characteristics and background of Xee's family.
2. Consider how current materials can be adapted to include the beliefs and practices of Xee's family.
3. Find materials in Hmong and English that allow the family to support the intervention strategies used in the preschool and Head Start environments.

Underlying Process Reminders

	Anchored Understanding of Diversity	3rd Space
RESPECT	Acknowledge the range and validity of diverse perspectives.	Stay with the tension of differing perspectives.
RECIPROCITY	Establish interactions that allow equal voice for all participants.	Develop opportunities for equalizing power across interactions.
RESPONSIVENESS	Communicate respect and understanding of others' perspectives.	Create responses that integrate and provide access to the strengths of diverse perspectives.

Figure 30.   Instructional Cultural Linguistic Response Plan for Xee.

develop as ample an understanding as possible of the communication envi-
ronment in Xee's home. Because none of the teaching staff were fluent in
Hmong, they were concerned about Xee's ability to handle verbal instructions
and classroom interactions. Having worked with other Hmong children and
families in the community, some team members had developed their forestruc-
tures sufficiently to realize that nonverbal communication rules in Xee's home
and in the classroom could be very different.

Mr. Ly clearly expressed that he believed English was critical to Xee's par-
ticipation in school and the larger community. Through additional family in-
terviews, the teachers determined that the primary language used outside the
home was English; however, the family considers speaking and understand-
ing Hmong important for communication within the family and with other
Hmong speakers.

Personal-Social Data

Xee's family did not have a long association with either the Head Start pro-
gram or the early childhood special education preschool, so only a small
amount of personal-social data were initially available. Therefore, Xee's team
gathered additional information through some informal observations and in-
terviews with family members. In addition, the team gathered information
from the cultural mediator that was found through Xee's church.

Overall, the Ly family had a moderate level of acculturation to ENC. Mr. Ly
was the first family member to acquire any degree of familiarity with ENC.
Neither he nor his wife attended school outside of their country of origin, so
their only connection with the U.S. public school system was through their
children. Mrs. Nia Ly had maintained her original way of life and beliefs to
a large extent.

Family observations and interviews taken during a 4-week period revealed
that some of the team's initial assumptions were more accurate than others re-
garding family members' understanding of sense of self, perceptions of iden-
tity and competence, and roles and rules associated with parenting and child
rearing. The family members did consider themselves minorities relative to the
larger culture of ENC. Because of the large Hmong population in their com-
munity, however, their sense of identity was not significantly affected by this
feeling of minority status. The team initially believed that the family strongly
valued interdependence. Yet, during the family interviews, Mr. Ly expressed a
desire for Xee to begin assuming greater responsibility for her own behaviors,
personal-social skills, and self-help skills. Xee's parents repeatedly discussed
that their primary ties and responsibilities were to their children, and their
role was to make sure that the children "listen and obey."

Sensory-Cognitive Data

The team realized the need for sensory-cognitive data beyond those that were
collected during the initial assessment. These data were especially important

to the preschool teachers, who wanted to plan and implement instructional strategies that supported the family's funds of knowledge (i.e., the skills and knowledge that they bring to early intervention/early childhood special education environments) and the teaching and learning strategies modeled in Xee's home.

In their work with the early childhood special education team, Xee's family tended to discuss as their priorities the cognitive knowledge and skills typically valued in ENC environments. Inside the family's household, however, the team noted that the social skills were highly valued. For instance, the children were expected to support their immediate and extended families above all else and to follow traditional Hmong beliefs about social and familial order. Modeling was the preferred strategy for acquiring new knowledge, as Mrs. Nia Ly seemed to rely more on indirect teaching strategies. It was clear from interviews with family members that Mr. Ly was responsible for all decisions outside of the home, while Mrs. Nia Ly was the primary decision maker for issues that affect child rearing within the home.

The family's worldviews differed across family members. Mrs. Nia Ly and the two younger siblings had worldviews that reflected more traditional Hmong beliefs. Mr. Ly and the older siblings tended to have worldviews that reflected both ENC and Hmong beliefs. For example, although Mr. Ly wanted Xee and her siblings to follow the Hmong social and family order and responsibilities, he also wanted them to learn English and succeed academically at school and within ENC.

As the teachers planned their initial instruction strategy, they realized that the best course of action was to build rapport with Xee and to let Xee get comfortable in her new environments. Although the language of instruction would be primarily English, the team included some children's stories written in Hmong. The team decided to ensure that Xee was not initially put into situations in which her language delays would increase her anxiety. To the maximum extent possible, the teachers would combine verbal and nonverbal strategies to help Xee negotiate the classroom. In addition, special attention would be given to ensure that they responded immediately to any of Xee's communication efforts.

Questions for Reflection

1. Review Xee's Cultural Data Table. Which learning strategies might be important to incorporate?

2. Given the family's level of acculturation, do you anticipate some culture bumps once intervention begins? What might they be?

3. What strategies could be used to ensure that Hmong is included in Xee's early childhood environments?

Amad

As noted in Chapter 8, Amad is a 4-year-old African American boy with the diagnosis of mild-to-moderate autism. Amad's mother, Regina, and grand-mother, Doretha, expressed concern that members of the interdisciplinary team were more interested in Amad's "school learning" than his happiness. Regina and Doretha want to ensure that Amad has friends and is prepared to interact with people in his community. They want to hear how the early childhood spe-cial education program would nurture his social and emotional development.

Working with Amad during the ensuing year gave the early childhood spe-cial education team members numerous opportunities to enhance their un-derstanding of the family's goals and cultural values. Regina and Doretha were very involved in the implementation of the team's intervention strategies. They also were instrumental in helping the team gather information about Amad's receptive and expressive language in English and his social function-ing. Similar to many young children with autism, Amad had a much higher level of expressive language than receptive language. This led to many con-cerns about Amad's ability to follow verbal instructions. Amad had great dif-ficulty communicating with his teachers and other children in the early child-hood program. Despite the family–program staff interactions and increased awareness about Amad's learning styles, the team did not believe much un-derstanding existed between Amad's family and the practitioners.

This vignette illustrates how the principles and strategies of Skilled Dia-logue come into play when planning interventions with specific children and families. As discussed in Chapter 8, members of Amad's early child-hood special education team recognized that they were likely experienc-ing some culture bumps. These bumps had generated confusion and frus-tration between the team and Amad's family. They completed a Critical Incident Analysis Sheet, then realized that significant discrepancies ex-isted between intervention and instruction goals for Amad. The prac-titioners recognized the need to find 3rd Space so that the family's in-tervention goals could be integrated with and complement the team's academic goals.

The early childhood special education staff engaged in the process of Skilled Dialogue to craft respectful, reciprocal, and responsive interactions with Regina and Doretha. To anchor their understanding of Amad's fam-ily, they built in time for more informal conversation and worked to es-tablish interactions that allowed equal voice for all perspectives. The prac-titioners worked to communicate respect and understanding of the family's perspective. They team also revisited the questions about culture bumps (see Figure 8) and decided to review several questions with Regina and Doretha. To improve their understanding of the family's "sense of self," the team members decided to explore the question "How is autonomy defined by the family, and to what degree is it valued?" In addition, the team believed that it was important to gather more information to answer "How do the family members like to define themselves (e.g., by ethnic, professional, or other labels)?" Specifically, the team believed a key area of understanding that they needed to develop was related to "What characteristics denote competence for Amad's family?" The early childhood special education team was beginning to think appropriately about the skills and definitions that led to competence in Amad's family and community.

Questions for Reflection

1. What do you think are some of the key challenges in this case?

2. What strategies could you use to develop Anchored Understanding of Diversity regarding Amad's family? (Hint: See Figure 8.)

3. Which of this chapter's strategies and suggested responses would best integrate the family's concerns with the early childhood special education team's concerns during intervention planning?

Abrish

Abrish's family recently immigrated from Hungary and lives in a small community in central Pennsylvania. Abrish attends a community child care center a few mornings each week but is reserved and makes few communicative attempts with anyone other than his parents. His mother and his caregiver have noticed that Abrish had difficulty initiating communication or responding to directions and was fearful in new situations. Abrish's mother called the local early intervention agency because she was concerned about Abrish's development. Abrish was 2 years old when he started receiving early intervention services.

Abrish's assessment results indicated age-appropriate cognitive skills, problem-solving skills, and adaptive skills. The results also showed developmental delays in expressive and receptive language development in both English and Hungarian, as well as in social skill development. As part of the assessment process, the team completed a Cultural Data Table, an RLP Profile, and an Assessment Cultural Linguistic Response Plan (see Appendix C for blank versions of these forms).

Prior to initiating any long-term instructional strategies, the early intervention developmental specialist and the speech-language pathologist observed Abrish's interactions with peers at his child care program. Abrish was hesitant to interact with other children and unfamiliar adults, but his social skills were otherwise age appropriate. From the assessment, Abrish's language and general communication skills were found to be mildly delayed (see Chapter 8). A particularly important finding was that his auditory comprehension and basic concept skills appeared to be age appropriate.

Despite the efforts to gather complete assessment information, the early intervention team decided that more information was needed to determine Abrish's language use patterns. This would assist the team to decide on the best format for instruction. In addition, the team wanted to review the early childhood environment to recommend how to create a physically and emotionally safe environment for Abrish—one that would allow him to explore his environment at his own pace and in his own way.

Abrish's "silent period" lasted for several weeks, but the early intervention team worked with his child care staff to find ways for him to interact verbally and nonverbally. Similarly, the practitioners discussed ways to ensure a consistent classroom routine. This would support Abrish in managing the early childhood environment more easily so he could concentrate on the communication in his environment. Although Abrish's child care program was primarily monolingual (English), the team encouraged his family to continue using the language (generally Hungarian) with which they were most comfortable at home. The team understood the importance of a child's home language and language's relationship to a child's self-identity and self-esteem.

Questions for Reflection

1. Contrast Abrish's culture with early childhood special education culture. In which areas might major culture bumps occur? (Hint: See Chapter 5.)

2. Which of the strategies in this chapter might be responsive to the culture bumps you identified?

3. How could you help Abrish's mother develop Hungarian language skills at home so that existing funds of knowledge could be tapped and general language skills strengthened?

Peter

Peter's parents moved from Mexico to the United States shortly before Peter's birth. His father, Nelson, is a farm worker during the day and a janitor at night. Nelson has learned some English through his work but speaks Spanish to his wife, Yolanda, whose English is very limited. To make extra money,

Yolanda provides child care for neighborhood children. Caring for Peter's 4-month-old sister, Maria, makes it difficult for Yolanda to keep appointments with practitioners.

Peter, now 4 years old, has a history of chronic ear infections but has received limited medical care. He demonstrates very limited speech—speaking to others only when he needs something. Yolanda has credited his limited speech to shyness and insisted that nothing is "wrong" with her child. Peter's case manager, Milagros, is fluent in Spanish and assisted during the assessment. Once the assessment was completed, Peter was diagnosed with a moderate hearing impairment.

Despite Milagros' presence at meetings, Yolanda had great difficulty sharing information about interventions for Peter's condition with Nelson. Although Milagros tried to explain the technical terms used by the audiologist at the clinic, Yolanda requested written information in Spanish that she could take home. The medical team discussed the possibility of tubes for Peter's ears or—even more confusing to Yolanda—cochlear implants. Yolanda felt frustrated by the team's focus on Peter's problems and deficits. She wondered if they saw Peter as she saw him.

Milagros was aware that some culture bumps were present and decided that Skilled Dialogue might help determine the degree to which they were caused by cultural and linguistic differences between Peter's family and the clinic staff. During the assessment process, Milagros worked with the clinic team to complete a Cultural Data Table, an RLP Profile, and a Cultural Linguistic Response Plan. As the discussion moved to planning intervention, Milagros encouraged the team to develop an Instructional Cultural Linguistic Response Plan. Milagros searched for materials in Spanish that might help explain the medical procedures to Yolanda and Nelson. Unfortunately, all of the materials available at the clinic were only available in English.

Milagros searched the Internet for materials that explained these procedures in Spanish. She found several web sites with material that looked appropriate. Before she gave them to Peter's family, however, she reviewed the materials. In her review, Milagros noticed several points in which the implicit values of the material might conflict with the family's values.

Questions for Reflection

1. Where might Milagros have found resources to share with Peter's family? Identify specific web sites and other resources in your community.

2. Which issues might Milagros have considered before selecting materials to share with Yolanda and Nelson? (Hint: See the CLAS Institute web site at http://clas.uiuc.edu)

3. If selecting materials that have been translated into Spanish from another language, what special issues should Milagros consider?

4. After selecting materials to share, what should Milagros consider in using this material with Peter's family? (Hint: See "Suggested Responses" under the heading "Teaching and Learning Materials.")

CONCLUSION

Several vignettes have been used in this chapter to illustrate some of the most common dilemmas that stem from culture bumps related to intervention and instruction. Suggested responses to the dilemmas posed by these culture bumps have been offered to show how practitioners can develop strategies that embrace children's and families' culturally based strengths. In addition, the chapter has provided an Instructional Cultural Linguistic Response Plan that is designated to support practitioners' consideration of potential intervention and instruction issues. As practitioners become more comfortable using these processes and more skilled in the practices of anchoring their understanding of families and creating 3rd Space, they will greatly improve their ability to enhance intervention and instruction for the children and families they serve.

Afterword

ISAURA BARRERA

At its core, this book is about recognizing the need to remember individuals for who they are and honoring their identities. Skilled Dialogue's focus on Anchored Understanding of Diversity responds to remembering who individuals are. Its focus on 3rd Space addresses honoring multiple identities in mutual and collaborative ways.

Remembering identity and honoring the surrounding, rich diversity of all identities is as important for practitioners themselves—whatever their culture(s)—as it is for the children and families they serve. Failing to recognize and honor diverse identities has implications that reach far beyond early childhood. Palmer's observation is critical:

> *Remembering ourselves and our power can lead to revolution, but it requires more than recalling a few facts. Re-membering involves putting ourselves together, recovering identity and integrity, reclaiming the wholeness of our lives.* When we forget who we are [because there is insufficient validation] we do not merely drop some data. We "dis-member" ourselves, with unhappy consequences for our politics, our work, our heart. *(1997, p. 20, emphasis added)*

Sociological and scientific data expand our understanding of these "unhappy consequences." Quinn quoted a poignant statement by a Peruvian elder: "I dream in Chamicuro, but I cannot tell my dreams to anyone. Some things cannot be said in Spanish. It's lonely being the last one" (2001, p. 9). Failure to honor culture as an integral part of identity results in the loss of more than words and behavioral rules; also lost are dreams and unique funds of knowledge that unlock perspectives otherwise unknown. In addition, data on the need to recognize and preserve diversity at the biological and environmental levels are a red flag for the need to recognize and preserve diversity at the human and cultural levels. Nabhan eloquently presented the delicate and utterly complex interdependence of "cultural diversity, community stability, and the conservation of biological diversity" (1997, p. 2).

Data at a human developmental level show the "dis-membering" consequences of culturally discontinuous or invalidating early environments. Validating and culturally continuous environments that support unique, individualized experiences are a crucial requirement for all children's development and well-being (Brazelton & Greenspan, 2000). The need to believe that all persons have worth and that the world is a safe and nurturing place is basic (Janoff-Bulman, 1992). One of culture's primary purposes is to ensure and protect this need. Culturally invalidating experiences can shatter a person's sense of self and of the world's safety and meaning, leaving him or her with no secure base on which to stand.

Once diversity is recognized, its preservation must follow. Doing so, however, is seldom easy. Skilled Dialogue proposes 3rd Space as a mindset and skill that can facilitate preserving others' diverse identities without sacrificing one's own identity, which is also unique (i.e., diverse from theirs). Recognizing diversity invariably presents contradictory assumptions about how the world works and about how persons should behave within it. Fletcher and Olwyer (1997) pointed out that accepting contradictions and mining them for their potential strengths expands one's value of oneself and of others. In conceptualizing 3rd Space, the authors have referred to the phrase "Janusian thinking: the ability to conceive of two or more opposites existing simultaneously [and in a complementary manner]" (p. 10).

My encounters with radically contradictory roles and rules drew and continue to draw me to the study of such thinking. Three specific anecdotes illustrate this experience. The first one illustrates my discovery that the academic environment (i.e., the "English-speaking world," as I perceived it) operated by a very different set of rules than my familial "Spanish-speaking world":

- *"Always sit in the front row."*
- *"Always raise your hand even if you don't know the answer (the teacher never calls on those who raise their hands repeatedly)."*
- *"Always smile and nod your head as the teacher is talking."*

These three rules and a basic vocabulary of approximately 100 English words were my mother's gifts to me the summer before I started first grade—and my first recognition that reality might not be as seamless as I believed. As a teacher herself, my mother had some familiarity with academic environments and their demands on strong-willed Mexican American 6-year-olds who spoke only Spanish.

Consequently, as described in the second anecdote, I learned that being competent in one world was not enough in the eyes of the other world:

At age 6, I learned quickly that there was a sharp contrast between the roles and rules of the reality I had lived from birth and the roles and rules common to academic environments. The divide between these two sets of roles and rules was further reinforced as I left home for college. My father, who had lovingly shared his knowledge of the world with me as I grew up, told me in the only letter he ever wrote me that I was going into a world within which he could no longer mentor me. The message was clear: Knowledge from one world was neither valued nor useful in the other. Unlike my mother, he did not perceive himself as having both sets of knowledge.

The third anecdote describes my realization that in certain cultures, it is not only possible but also advisable to split one's emotional reality from one's professional reality:

Approximately 5 years later, while I was in graduate school, the message that echoed the degree of contradiction between my worlds was "official"—it issued from academia itself. I was struggling amid rather unsettling personal events to meet the demands of rigorous clinical training as a speech-language pathologist. I sometimes exhibited less than the calm, "objective" professional demeanor expected of everyone in that environment (which should come as no surprise to anyone who knows me)!

One day I was explicitly told that this could not continue. I no longer remember what exactly happened. I do remember my supervisor's instructions: Imagine a basket at the classroom door; then, drop all of your frustrated, upset, and other negative emotions into that basket, and enter the room with a calm, professional demeanor. Up until that time, I had never been explicitly asked to split my subjective emotional self from my professional self. To me, the message was clear: Leave your personal way of being outside of the professional environment; only a professional role determined by others is allowed in.

In many ways, this book is an outcome of these and other similar experiences, of what I discovered and came to value in my journey of "recovering identity and integrity, reclaiming the wholeness of [my] life"

(Palmer, 1997, p. 20). The material presented in this book is designed to help practitioners strengthen and sustain (i.e., "remember") families' and children's identities and integrity across environments in ways that are life enhancing. As Langer stated in her book on mindful learning,

> *The rules we are given to practice are based on generally accepted truths about how to perform the task and not on our individual abilities. . . . Even if we are fortunate enough to be shown how to do something by a true expert, mindless practice keeps activity from becoming our own. If I try to serve exactly like Martina Navratilova serves, will I be as good as she (apart from differences in innate gifts), given that my grip on the racket is determined by my hand size, not hers, and my toss of the ball is affected by my height, not hers, and given the difference in our muscles? (1997, p. 14)*

In practicing Skilled Dialogue, we recommend what Langer termed "sideways learning," or "learning a subject or skill with an openness to novelty and actively noticing differences, contexts, and perspectives" (1997, p. 23). Ultimately, cultural competency as defined in this book cannot be prescribed. Each situation, no matter how similar to the illustrative vignettes, will have its own unique complexities. We hope that the information in this book provides a framework for exploring those complexities in ways that are respectful, reciprocal, and responsive. These qualities can only truly emerge when, in Palmer's words,

> *We embrace the promise of diversity, of creative conflict, and of "losing" in order to "win". . . [and] face one final fear—the fear that a live encounter with otherness will challenge or even compel us to change our lives. . . . Otherness, taken seriously, always invites transformation, calling us not only to new facts and theories and values but also to new ways of living our lives—and that is the most daunting threat of all. (1997, p. 38)*

Isaura Barrera

References

Althen, G. (1988). *American ways: A guide for foreigners in the United States.* Yarmouth, MA: Intercultural Press.

Archer, C.M. (1986). Culture bump and beyond. In J.M. Valdes (Ed.), *Culture bound: Bridging the cultural gap in language teaching* (pp. 170–178). New York: Cambridge University Press.

Arnberg, L. (1987). *Raising children bilingually: The preschool years.* Philadelphia: Multilingual Matters.

Baca, L.M., & Cervantes, H.T. (1984). *The bilingual special education interface.* St. Louis, MO: Times Mirror/Mosby.

Baca, L.M., & Cervantes, H.T. (1998). *The bilingual special education interface* (3rd ed.). Columbus, OH: Charles E. Merrill.

Banks, J.A. (1988). *Multiethnic education.* Boston: Allyn & Bacon.

Banks, J.A., & Banks, C.M. (1993). *Multicultural education: Issues and perspectives.* Boston: Allyn & Bacon.

Barrera, I. (1993). Effective and appropriate education for all children: The challenge of cultural/linguistic diversity and young children with special needs. *Topics in Early Childhood Special Education, 13*(4), 461–487.

Barrera, I. (1996). Thoughts on the assessment of young children whose sociocultural background is unfamiliar to the assessor. In S.J. Meisels & E. Fenichel (Eds.), *New visions for the developmental assessment of infants and young children* (pp. 69–84). Washington, DC: ZERO TO THREE: National Center for Infants, Toddlers, and Families.

Barrera, I. (2000). Honoring differences. *Young Exceptional Children, 3*(4), 17–26.

Barrera, I., & Corso, R. (2000, December). *Cultural diversity and early childhood: A critical review of literature with implications for ECSE research, evaluation, and practice.* Research Roundtable presented at the Division of Early Childhood (DEC) National Conference, Albuquerque, NM.

Barrera, I., & Kramer, L. (1997). From monologues to skilled dialogues: Teaching the process of crafting culturally competent early childhood environments. In P.J. Winton, J.A. McCollum, & C. Catlett (Eds.), *Reforming personnel preparation in early intervention: Issues, models, and practical strategies* (pp. 217–251). Baltimore: Paul H. Brookes Publishing Co.

Benson, R. (Ed.). (2001). *Children of the dragonfly: Native American voices on child custody and education.* Tuscon: The University of Arizona Press.

Bhagwanji, Y., Santos, R.M., & Fowler, S.A. (2000). *Culturally and linguistically sensitive practices in motor skills interventions for young children* (Culturally and Linguistically Appropriate Services [CLAS] Technical Report #1). Champaign: University of Illinois at Urbana-Champaign, Early Childhood Research Institute on Culturally and Linguistically Appropriate Services.

Billings, J.A., Pearson, J., Gill, D.H., & Shureen, A. (1997). *Evaluation and assessment in early childhood special education.* Olympia, WA: Office of the Superintendent of Public Instruction.

Bowers, C.A., & Flinders, D.J. (1990). *Responsive teaching: Ecological approach to classroom patterns of language, culture, and thought.* New York: Teachers College Press.

Bowman, B.T., & Stott, F.M. (1994). Understanding development in a cultural context. In B.L. Mallory & R.S. New (Eds.), *Diversity and developmentally appro-*

priate practices: Challenges for early childhood education (pp. 119–134). New York: Teachers College Press.

Brazelton, T.B., & Cramer, B.G. (1990). *The earliest relationship.* Reading, MA: Addison-Wesley.

Brazelton, T.B., & Greenspan, S.I. (2000). *The irreducible needs of children: What every child must have to grow, learn, and flourish.* Cambridge, MA: Perseus Books.

Bredekamp, S., & Copple, C. (1997). *Developmentally appropriate practice in early education programs.* Washington, DC: National Association for the Education of Young Children.

Brice, A.E. (2002). *The Hispanic child: Speech, language, culture, and education.* Boston: Allyn & Bacon.

Brown, W., & Barrera, I. (1999). Enduring problems in assessment: The persistent challenges of cultural dynamics and family issues. *Journal of Early Intervention, 12*(1), 34–42.

Bush, R.A.B., & Folger, J.P. (1994). *The promise of mediation: Responding to conflict through empowerment and recognition.* San Francisco: Jossey-Bass.

Catlett, C., & Winton, P. (2000). *Selected early childhood/early intervention training manual* (9th ed.). Chapel Hill, NC: The Systems Change in Personnel Preparation Project's Resource Guide.

Chamot, A.U., & O'Malley, J.M. (1994). *The CALLA handbook: Implementing the cognitive academic language learning approach.* Reading, MA: Addison-Wesley.

Cheng, L.L. (1995). *Integrating language and learning for inclusion.* San Diego: Singular Publishing Group.

Childs, C. (1998). *The spirit's terrain: Creativity, activism, and transformation.* Boston: Beacon Press.

Cintas, H.L. (1995). Cross-cultural similarities and differences in development and the impact of parental expectations on motor behavior. *Pediatric Physical Therapy, 7,* 103–111.

Clandinin, D.J., & Connelly, F.M. (2000). *Narrative inquiry.* San Francisco: Jossey-Bass.

CLAS Early Childhood Research Institute. (2001, February). *CLAS annual report.* Champaign: University of Illinois at Urbana-Champaign, Early Childhood Research Institute on Culturally and Linguistically Appropriate Services.

Cole, M. (1998). Culture in development. In M. Woodhead, D. Faulkner, & K. Littleton (Eds.), *Cultural worlds of early childhood.* New York: Routledge.

Cummins, J. (1984). *Bilingualism and special education: Issues in assessment and pedagogy.* Philadelphia: Multilingual Matters.

Cummins, J. (1989). A theoretical framework for bilingual special education. *Exceptional Children, 56*(2), 111–119.

Cushner, K., & Brislin, R.W. (1996). *Intercultural interactions: A practical guide* (2nd ed.). Thousand Oaks, CA: Sage Publications.

Damen, L. (1987). *Culture learning: The fifth dimension in the language classroom.* Reading, MA: Addison-Wesley.

Darder, A. (1991). *Culture and power in the classroom: A critical framework for bicultural education.* Westport, CT: Bergin & Garvey.

de Bono, E. (1970). *Lateral thinking.* New York: Harper & Row.

Delpit, L. (1995). *Other people's children: Cultural conflict in the classroom.* New York: The Free Press.

Deskin, G., & Steckler, G. (1996). *When nothing makes sense: Disaster, crisis, and their effects on children*. Minneapolis, MN: Fairview Press.

deVries, M.W. (1996). Trauma in cultural perspective. In B.A. van der Kolk, A.C. McFarlane, & L. Weisaeth (Eds.), *Traumatic stress: The effects of overwhelming experience on mind, body, and society* (pp. 398–413). New York: The Guilford Press.

Díaz-Rico, L.T., & Weed, K.Z. (1995). *The crosscultural language and academic development handbook: A complete K–12 reference guide*. Boston: Allyn & Bacon.

Donovan, D.M., & McIntyre, D. (1990). *Healing the hurt child*. New York: W.W. Norton.

Dunst, C., Trivette, C., & Deal, A. (1988). *Enabling and empowering families*. Cambridge, MA: Brookline Books.

Echevarria, J., & Graves, A. (1998). *Sheltered content instruction: Teaching English language learners with diverse abilities*. Boston: Allyn & Bacon.

Edwards, C., Gandini, L., & Forman, G. (1995). *The hundred languages of children: The Reggio Emilia approach to early childhood education*. Westport, CT: Ablex Publishing.

Erickson, J., & Omark, D.R. (Eds.). (1981). *Communication assessment of the bilingual child*. Baltimore: University Park Press.

Fewell, R. (1996). Intervention strategies to promote motor skills. In S.L. Odom & M.E. McLean (Eds.), *DEC recommended practices: Indicators of quality in programs for infants and young children with special needs and their families* (pp. 245–258). Arlington, VA: Council for Exceptional Children.

Fletcher, J., & Olwyer, K. (1997). *Paradoxical thinking: How to profit from your contradictions*. San Francisco: Berrett-Koehler Publishers.

Frankenburg, W.K., Dodds, J.B., Archer, P., Bresnick, B., Mashka, P., Edelman, N., & Shapiro, H. (1990). *Denver II*. Denver, CO: Denver Developmental Materials.

Freedman, J., & Combs, G. (1996). *Narrative therapy: The social construction of preferred realities*. New York: W.W. Norton.

Fritz, R. (1989). *The path of least resistance*. New York: Fawcett Books.

Garcia, E. (2001). *Hispanic education in the United States: Raíces y alas*. Lanham, MD: Rowman & Littlefield Publishers.

Gardner, H. (1993). *Frames of mind: The theory of multiple intelligences*. New York: Basic Books.

Goleman, D. (1995). *Emotional intelligence*. New York: Bantam.

Gollnick, D.M., & Chinn, P.C. (1990). *Multicultural education in a pluralistic society*. Upper Saddle River, NJ: Prentice Hall.

Gonzalez-Mena, J. (1993). *Multicultural issues in child care*. Mountain View, CA: Mayfield Publishing Co.

Gonzalez-Mena, J., Herzog, M., & Herzog, S. (2000). *Diversity: Reconciling differences*. Crystal Lake, IL: Magna Systems.

Greenfield, P. M., & Cocking, R.R. (1994). *Cross-cultural roots of minority child development*. Mahwah, NJ: Lawrence Erlbaum Associates.

Greenspan, S. (1999). *Building healthy minds*. Cambridge, MA: Perseus Books.

Groome, T. (1980). *Christian religious education*. New York: Harper & Row.

Hamayan, E.V., & Damico, J.S. (1991). *Developing and using a second language*. Austin, TX: PRO-ED.

Harding, E., & Riley, P. (1986). *The bilingual family: A handbook for parents*. New York: Cambridge University Press.

Harry, B. (1992). Developing cultural self-awareness: The first step in values clarification for early interventionists. *Topics in Early Childhood Special Education,
12*(3), 333–350.

Hall, E.T. (1977). *Beyond culture.* New York: Anchor Books.

Haviland, W.A. (1993). *Cultural anthropology.* New York: Harcourt Brace.

Igoa, C. (1995). *The inner world of the immigrant child.* New York: St. Martin's Press.

Individuals with Disabilities Education Act (IDEA) Amendments of 1997, PL 105-17,
20 U.S.C. §§ 1400 *et seq.*

Jahn, G. (2002, January 6). Second generation is also haunted by Holocaust. *Arizona Republic,* p. A24.

Jalava, A. (1988). Mother tongue and identity. In T. Skutnabb-Kangas & J. Cummins (Eds.), *Minority education: From shame to struggle* (pp. 168–169). Philadelphia: Multilingual Matters.

Janoff-Bulman, R. (1992). *Shattered assumptions.* New York: The Free Press.

Josselson, R. (1994). Identity and relatedness in the life cycle. In H.A. Bosma, T.L.
Graafsma, H.D. Grotevant, & D.J. de Levita (Eds.), *Identity and development* (pp.
81–103). Thousand Oaks, CA: Sage Publications.

Kalyanpur, M., & Harry, B. (1999). *Culture in special education: Building reciprocal
family–professional relationships.* Baltimore: Paul H. Brookes Publishing Co.

Kame'enui, E.J., Carnine, D.W., Dixon, R.C., Simmons, D.C., & Coyne, M.D.
(2002). *Effective teaching strategies that accommodate diverse learners.* Columbus,
OH: Charles E. Merrill.

Karr-Morse, R., & Wiley, M.S. (1997). *Ghosts from the nursery: Tracing the roots of violence.* New York: Atlantic Monthly Press.

Katie, B. (2002). *Loving what is.* New York: Harmony Books.

Kendall, F. (1996). *Diversity in the classroom.* New York: Teachers College Press.

Klein, G. (1998). *Sources of power: How people make decisions.* Cambridge, MA: The
MIT Press.

Kramer, L.K. (1997). *Cultural perspectives on developmentally appropriate practice in a
model inclusive Navajo preschool.* Unpublished dissertation, University of New
Mexico, Albuquerque.

Koplow, L. (1996). *Unsmiling faces: How preschools can heal.* New York: Teachers
College Press.

Landrine, H. (1995). Clinical implications of cultural differences: The referential
vs. the indexical self. In N.R. Goldberger & J.B. Veroff (Eds.), *The culture and psychology reader* (pp. 744–766). New York: New York University Press.

Landrine, H., & Klonoff, E.A. (1996). *African American acculturation.* Thousand
Oaks, CA: Sage Publications.

Landurand, P.M., & Cloud, N. (1991). *How disability can affect language acquisition.*
Educational Resources Information Center (ERIC) Clearinghouse on Disabilities and Gifted Education, ERIC Excerpt #12. Reston, VA: The Council for Exceptional Children.

Langer, E.J. (1997). *The power of mindful learning.* Reading, MA: Addison-Wesley.

Lanning, K.V. (1992). *Child molesters: A behavioral analysis.* Arlington, VA: National
Center for Missing and Exploited Children.

Lave, J., & Wenger, E. (1991). *Situated learning: Legitimate peripheral participation.*
New York: Cambridge University Press.

Lawrence-Lightfoot, S. (1999). *Respect.* Cambridge, MA: Perseus Books.

Lubeck, S. (1994). The politics of developmentally appropriate practice. In B.L. Mallory & R.S. New (Eds.), *Diversity and developmentally appropriate practices: Challenges for early childhood education* (pp. 17–43). New York: Teachers College Press.

Lynch, E.W., & Hanson, M.J. (1992). *Developing cross-cultural competence: A guide for working with young children and their families.* Baltimore: Paul H. Brookes Publishing Co.

Lynch, E.W., & Hanson, M.J. (1997). *Developing cross-cultural competence: A guide for working with children and their families* (2nd ed.). Baltimore: Paul H. Brookes Publishing Co.

MacIntosh, I.S. (2001). Plan A and plan B for cultural survival. *Cultural Survival, 25*(2), 4–6.

Malina, B.L. (2001). *The New Testament world: Insights from cultural anthropology.* Louisville, KY: Westminster John Knox Press.

Markus, H.R., & Kitayama, S. (1991). Culture and the self: Implications for cognition, emotion, and motivation. *Psychological Review, 98*(2), 224–253.

Mattes, L.J., & Omark, D.R. (1984). *Speech and language assessment for the bilingual handicapped.* San Diego: College-Hill Press.

McGinn, L.R. (1999). *Dancing in the storm: Hope in the midst of chaos.* Grand Rapids, MI: Fleming H. Revell.

McGoldrick, M. (Ed.). (1998). *Re-visioning family therapy: Race, culture, and gender in clinical practice.* New York: The Guilford Press.

McLean, M. (2001). *Conducting child assessment* (CLAS Technical Report #2). Champaign: University of Illinois at Urbana-Champaign, Early Childhood Research Institute on Culturally and Linguistically Appropriate Services.

Medina, V. (1982). *Interpretation and translation in bilingual B.A.S.E.* San Diego: San Diego County Office of Education.

Meisels, S.J., & Provence, S. (1989). *Screening and assessment: Guidelines for identifying young disabled and developmentally vulnerable children and their families.* Washington, DC: ZERO TO THREE: National Center for Infants, Toddlers, and Families.

Metz, I.B. (1991). Learning from personal experiences. In M. Anderson & P. Goldberg (Eds.), *Cultural competence in screening and assessment: Implications for services to young children with special needs ages birth through five* (pp. 8–10). Chapel Hill, NC: National Early Childhood Technical Assistance System.

Middleton-Moz, J. (1989). *Children of trauma: Rediscovering your discarded self.* Deerfield Beach, FL: Health Communications.

Miller, A. (1980). *The drama of the gifted child.* New York: Basic Books.

Miller, N. (Ed.). (1984). *Bilingualism and language disability: Assessment and remediation.* San Diego: College-Hill Press.

Mofina, R. (2001, Summer). 20,000 survivors of residential schools to seek compensation. *First Nations Drum.*

Moll, L.C., & Greenberg, J.B. (1990). Creating zones of possibilities: Combining social contexts for instruction. In L.C. Moll (Ed.), *Vygotsky and education: Instructional implications of sociohistorical psychology* (pp. 319–348). New York: Cambridge University Press.

Moore, S.M., & Beatty, J. (1995). *Developing cultural competence in early childhood assessment.* Boulder: University of Colorado at Boulder.

Nabhan, G.P. (1997). *Cultures of habitat.* Washington, DC: Counterpoint Press.

Nakkula, M.J., & Ravitch, S. (1998). *Matters of interpretation*. San Francisco: Jossey-Bass.

N.E. Thing Enterprises. (1993). *Magic eye: A new way of looking at the world*. Kansas City, MO: Andrews McMeel.

Neighbors, H.W., & Jackson, J.S. (Eds.). (1996). *Mental health in Black America*. Thousand Oaks, CA: Sage Publications.

Newberg, A., D'Aquili, E., & Rause, V. (2001). *Why God won't go away*. New York: Ballantine Books.

Newborg, J., Stock, J.R., Wnek, L., Guidubaldi, J., & Svinicki, J. (1984). *The Battelle Developmental Inventory (BDI)*. Allen, TX: DLM/Teaching Resources.

Palmer, P.J. (1997). *The courage to teach: Exploring the inner landscape of a teacher's life*. San Francisco: Jossey-Bass.

Paradise, R. (1994). Interactional style and nonverbal meaning: Mazahua children learning how to be separate-but-together. *Anthropology and Education Quarterly, 25*(2), 156–172.

Pennsylvania Department of Education. (1994). *Early childhood assessment guidelines* (Draft ed.). Harrisburg, PA: Bureau of Special Education.

Perez, B., & Torres-Guzman, M.E. (2002). *Learning in two worlds: An integrated Spanish/English biliteracy approach*. Boston: Allyn & Bacon.

Perkins, D. (2001). *The eureka effect: The art and logic of breakthrough*. New York: W.W. Norton.

Perry, G., & Duru, M. (2001). *Resources for developmentally appropriate practice: Recommendations from the profession*. Washington, DC: National Association for the Education of Young Children.

Philips, S.U. (1972). Participant structure and communicative competence: Warm Springs children in community and classroom. In C.B. Cazden, D. Hymes, & V. John-Steiner (Eds.), *Functions of language in the classroom* (pp. 370–394). New York: Teachers College Press.

Phillips, C.B. (1994). The movement of African-American children through sociocultural contexts. In B.L. Mallory & R.S. New (Eds.). *Diversity and developmentally appropriate practices: Challenges for early childhood education* (pp. 137–154). New York: Teachers College Press.

Polk, C. (1994). Therapeutic work with African-American families: Using knowledge of culture. *Zero to Three, 15*(2), 9–11.

Price-Williams, D., & Gallimore, R. (1980). The cultural perspective. In B.K. Keogh (Series Ed. & Vol. Ed.), *Advances in special education: Vol. 2. A research annual: Documenting program impact* (pp. 165–192). Stamford, CT: JAI Press.

Quinn, E.M. (2001). Can this language be saved? *Cultural Survival Quarterly, 25*(2), 9–12.

Quiñones-Eatman, J. (2001). *Second language acquisition in the preschool years: What we know and how we can effectively communicate with young second language learners* (CLAS Technical Report #5). Champaign: University of Illinois at Urbana-Champaign, Early Childhood Research Institute on Culturally and Linguistically Appropriate Services.

Remen, R.N. (2000). *My grandfather's blessings*. New York: Riverhead Books.

Rothstein-Fisch, C. (1998, June). *Bridging cultures: A pre-service teacher preparation module*. Material presented at the National Association for the Education of Young Children National Institute for Early Childhood Professional Development, Miami, FL.

Sanchez, S. (1999). Learning from the stories of culturally linguistically diverse families and communities. *Remedial and Special Education, 20*(6), 351–359.

Santos, R.M., Fowler, S.A., Corso, R.M., & Bruns, D. (2000). Acceptance, acknowledgement, and adaptability: Selecting culturally and linguistically appropriate early childhood materials. *Teaching Exceptional Children, 32*(3), 14–22.

Santos, R.M., Lee, S., Valdivia, R., & Zhang, C. (2001). Considerations when selecting and using early childhood materials translated from one language to another language. *Teaching Exceptional Children, 34*(2), 26–31.

Santos de Barona, M., & Barona, A. (1991). The assessment of culturally and linguistically different preschoolers. *Early Childhood Research Quarterly, 6,* 363–376.

Schneider, E., Parush, S., Katz, N., & Miller, L.J. (1995). Performance of Israeli versus U.S. preschool children on the Miller Assessment for Preschoolers. *The American Journal on Occupational Therapy, 49*(1), 19–23.

Schoepko, T., & Wham, M. (1995). *Hymn of peace.* Albuquerque, NM.

Seelye, H.N., & Wasilewski, J.H. (1996). *Between cultures: Developing self-identity in a world of diversity.* Lincolnwood, IL: McGraw-Hill/Contemporary.

Shafir, R.Z. (2000). *The Zen of listening.* Wheaton, IL: Quest Books.

Shavelson, R.J., & Stern, P. (1981). Research on teachers' pedagogical thoughts, judgments, decisions, and behaviors. *Review of Educational Research, 51,* 455–498.

Shelton, C. (1999). *Quantum leaps.* Woburn, MA: Butterworth-Heinemann.

Shem, S., & Surrey, J. (1998). *We have to talk.* New York: Basic Books.

Skutnabb-Kangas, T., & Cummins, J. (1988). *Minority education: From shame to struggle.* Philadelphia: Multilingual Matters.

Stettbacher, J.K. (1991). *Making sense out of suffering.* New York: Dutton.

Stewart, E.C., & Bennett, M.J. (1991). *American cultural patterns: A cross-cultural perspective.* Yarmouth, ME: Intercultural Press.

Super, C.M., & Harkness, S. (1981). Figure, ground, and gestalt: The cultural context of the active individual. In R.M. Lerner & N.A. Busch-Rossnagel (Eds.), *Individuals as producers of their development* (pp. 70–83). San Diego: Academic Press.

Tabors, P.O. (1997). *One child, two languages: A guide for preschool educators of children learning English as a second language.* Baltimore: Paul H. Brookes Publishing Co.

Takaki, R. (1993). *A different mirror: A history of multicultural America.* Boston: Little, Brown & Company.

Taylor, O. (Ed.). (1986a). *Nature of communication disorders in culturally and linguistically diverse populations.* San Diego: College-Hill Press.

Taylor, O. (Ed.). (1986b). *Treatment of communication disorders in culturally and linguistically diverse populations.* San Diego: College-Hill Press.

Trumbull, E., Rothstein-Fisch, C., Greenfield, P.M., & Quiroz, B. (2001). *Bridging cultures between home and school.* Mahwah, NJ: Lawrence Erlbaum Associates.

Vaill, P.B. (1996). *Learning as a way of being.* San Francisco, CA: Jossey-Bass.

van der Kolk, B.A., McFarlane, A.C., & Weisaeth, L. (Eds.). (1996). *Traumatic stress: The effects of overwhelming experience on mind, body, and society.* New York: The Guilford Press.

Vann, G. (1960). *The heart of man.* Garden City, NY: Image Books.

Velez-Ibañez, C.G., & Greenberg, J.B. (1992). Formation and transformation of funds of knowledge among U.S. Mexican households. *Anthropology & Education Quarterly, 23*(4), 313–335.

Ventriglia, L. (1982). *Conversations with Miguel and Maria.* Reading, MA: Addison-Wesley.

Wheatley, M.J. (1992). *Leadership and the new science.* San Francisco: Berrett-Koehler Publishers.

Wildman, J.M. (1996). *Privilege revealed: How invisible preference undermines America.* New York: New York University Press.

Williams, L.R., & DeGaetano, Y. (1985). *ALERTA: A multicultural, bilingual approach to teaching young children.* Reading, MA: Addison-Wesley.

Wilson, J. (2001). Looking closer. *Hope, 27,* 64.

Winzer, M.A., & Mazurek, K. (1994). *Special education in multicultural contexts.* Columbus, OH: Charles E. Merrill.

Yankelovich, D. (1999). *The magic of dialogue.* New York: Simon & Schuster.

Trauma from a Cultural Perspective

DIANNE MACPHERSON

This appendix strives to integrate two areas of literature whose relationship has received little attention within the early childhood special education field. The author realizes that in connecting discussions of cultural diversity and trauma, she risks being misinterpreted. Nevertheless, it is important to raise these issues if practitioners are to truly develop Skilled Dialogue and act in the best interests of the children and families with whom they work.

As discussed in this book, there are many challenges to understanding cultural diversity and developing Skilled Dialogue. The sociodemographic backgrounds of children in early childhood and early childhood special education settings are typically complex. Multiple experiences have already shaped these children's view of the world and themselves, including cultural diversity. For many of these children, traumatic and stressful experiences also have profoundly altered their lives. The prevalence and impact of trauma and stress are so significant that practitioners must consider these issues in any discussion designed to broaden understanding of the communication and interaction styles of children and their families. All efforts to develop respectful, reciprocal, and responsive interactions may be unsuccessful if trauma or prolonged stress is ignored or not sufficiently identified. Judgments and assumptions about individuals can be further complicated by the fact that trauma may be hidden or well disguised—sometimes even repressed beyond conscious awareness. There-

---

Much of the material in this appendix draws from years of work with culturally diverse individuals and families in a clinical mental health setting. Without changing the intent of the discussion, details of the vignettes have been altered for confidentiality. The observations and interpretations are based on such professional experiences as well as many hours of training and applying research-based material. Unless cited specifically, these observations and interpretations are presented as a professional point of view and may or may not be supported by research in the field of trauma and extreme stress.

fore, to develop the necessary skills for cultural competency, practitioners cannot assume that cultural diversity is the only issue that impedes establishing respect, reciprocity, and responsiveness.

Trauma can be a life-altering experience that generates a unique worldview, along with a set of beliefs and values that may equal or exceed cultural diversity in causing discord in interactions. The discussion that follows is designed to contribute more insight into this complex interrelationship. It is meant to sensitize early childhood and early childhood special education practitioners, as well as other related professionals, to the overlapping issues of trauma and cultural diversity. It is in no way a definitive or comprehensive treatise of these interrelated topics. Most important, this information is not intended to prepare practitioners to identify or diagnose trauma as a mental health or psychiatric condition in this or any other context.

TRAUMA DEFINED

Deskin and Steckler explained *trauma* as

> *An injury to the physical or psychological well-being of an individual or group. It means that the individual or group has been hurt or upset to the degree that the way they function, either mentally, emotionally or physically, or any combination of these, is severely affected. (1996, p. 6)*

Trauma tends to occur when an event or situation shatters basic assumptions about self, others, and/or the world. *Trauma* may refer to the event itself or to the event's sequelae (i.e., aftereffects). It also may relate to a single occurrence of extreme stress or to multiple stressful events that can break down the functioning of an individual, a community, or a society.

Incidents such as being in a car accident or witnessing a crime may cause an acute stress reaction that is characterized by shock and temporary disruption in thought, feeling, and behavior. If there is no opportunity to process the trauma sufficiently when it occurs, a delayed stress reaction may surface unexpectedly some time after the trauma. To process trauma adequately, certain factors must be in place: the ability and the opportunity to express one's thoughts and feelings, ample time to deal with these thoughts and feelings, and a validating environment. A very young child who experiences trauma lacks the verbal skills to express the associated thoughts and feelings, although art and play therapies may offer some preliminary opportunities. A woman who gives birth to her first child in a difficult delivery and then learns that her mother has died in a car accident the next day does not have time to deal with her mother's death. A young child who lives in an invalidating environment and begins to disclose details of abuse by a relative may be blamed for the abuse or not believed at all. When these types of situations occur, a delayed stress response is almost inevitable. A child who experiences verbal or physical abuse by others who are intolerant of his or her cultural or ethnic identity also may encounter disbelief or lack of support, especially outside the home. Though outwardly distinct, all of these situations can be traumatizing.

Prolonged and repeated exposure to extreme stress or trauma can result in Post-Traumatic Stress Disorder (PTSD). An individual with PTSD repeatedly recalls and reexperiences the trauma, perhaps throughout his or her life. The impact of a traumatic event is directly related to the individual's perceived threat and risk of harm, sense of responsibility (i.e., blaming self for having been victimized), and feeling of helplessness. Young children are particularly vulnerable to the effects of trauma because they lack the cognitive maturity to perceive and process these events accurately. The "magical thinking" and egocentricity of young children, as well as their tendency to idealize adults, form a collage of distorted perceptions and feelings that often persists into adulthood. Although young children may misperceive and misinterpret traumatic events, casting doubt on the validity of certain abuse allegations, some type of trauma probably has occurred in most cases. The exact details of the event, however, are subject to distortion and inaccuracy when reported by very young children who have been repeatedly traumatized.

TRAUMA AS A UNIVERSAL, CROSS-CULTURAL EXPERIENCE

Some form of trauma occurs at least once during the life span of most individuals and groups. Electronic, televised, and print media provide almost instantaneous news reports, with the result that individuals witness worldwide, traumatic events on a frequent, almost daily basis. This lessens people's ability to distance themselves from the images of war, terrorism, famine, and natural disasters. As with the attacks on and collapse of the World Trade Center towers on September 11, 2001, sometimes individuals even witness such horrors as they occur.

Just as all persons view the world through the lens of their cultural experiences, trauma also becomes a lens that may distort or impair the life experiences that follow the trauma. Many people agree that the September 11 attacks changed the world. The sense of safety and security of those living in North America probably has never been violated to such a degree in modern history. Not only did individuals experience the trauma of these events, but to some degree, various communities, cultural groups, and societies were affected as well. Arab Americans and others with a similar physical appearance became targets for discrimination, hatred, and even murder in retaliation for the acts of an extremist Islamic group. An American Muslim who lost a family member in the World Trade Center attacks might had have a much different experience with the trauma and its aftermath than a non-Muslim. This person may have felt cultural shame that significantly affected the grieving process. Although community support and validation existed for those who lost loved ones in this tragedy, this person may have experienced an invalidating environment. In addition, one can almost imagine a classroom of children struggling to make sense of this tragedy, talking about it with their teacher, ignorant of the private suffering—and perhaps even shame—of a student who is a Muslim and an American. Anchored understanding of different experiences with particular events is a critical component of ensuring emotional safety and lessening the sequelae of trauma for all children.

It has been said that "the song sung to the cradle is heard to the grave." In no case is this more true than for the child with stressful or traumatic early life experiences. By the time a child has reached 5 years of age, he or she may have experienced the extreme stress caused by one or more experiences common in modern society: poverty; homelessness; immigration; exposure to neighborhood crime; risk of death or injury; violent or premature death of a family member or friend; family violence; or physical, emotional, verbal, or sexual abuse. Also included are natural disasters, accidents, and vicarious exposure to trauma through family members who survived traumatic events (e.g., the Holocaust, the Vietnam War).

WHEN INVALIDATION OF CULTURE RESULTS IN TRAUMA

When children's cultural linguistic backgrounds differ from those of their peers and educators, many of their early life experiences may be traumatic. Such children may struggle to master developmental tasks in contexts that are not responsive to their cultural linguistic repertoire and, therefore, are confusing and nonsupportive. Differences in language, values, beliefs, and practices pose significant challenges for communication. In addition, when such diversity is not understood or respected, it alienates children from others in the environment, including peers and practitioners.

Children from "minority" groups, immigrant families, and oppressed cultures (i.e., politically oppressed or persecuted) may experience the social environment as foreign, invalidating, and nonsupportive—sometimes even threatening. They may be shunned or bullied because they are different and do not have the power and status of their peers from EuroAmerican Normative Culture (ENC). When young children's interactions with others are not respectful, reciprocal, and responsive to existing differences, they may feel disconnected, ashamed, and guilty for "causing" culture bumps. They may withdraw and try to blend into the crowd. They may become bullies to protect themselves from further victimization. Some children may retreat into their home culture, refusing to learn new customs and the accompanying language. Others may shun their home culture's language and traditions along with the skills and knowledge that those contain.

Children also may respond by becoming the communication facilitators between their families and the social environment, thrusting them into a role that is developmentally inappropriate (i.e., emotionally dissonant and cognitively premature). They become the adults to their parents, called on to act as translators and family spokespersons at an age when they should have limited responsibility and involvement in adult activities. Out of necessity, they become privy to information about family troubles, finances, and other matters in which younger children should not be involved. This involvement in adult matters can overwhelm and burden children with responsibility they often cannot handle. In addition, this role reversal further isolates them from their peers, who are just being children. Furthermore, they often have difficulty with authority figures, including parents and caregivers, who on many other occasions expect compliance with rules that are more age appropriate. These issues often are not recognized as inappropriate, much less traumatizing. Nevertheless, they place culturally diverse children with delays or disabilities at added risk for failure in early childhood settings. Using an adult translator to engage in Skilled Dialogue with families can be invaluable for determining the degree to which such issues are present and exploring ways to reduce their impact.

PROBLEMS IN DIFFERENTIATING TRAUMA AND CULTURAL DIVERSITY

Trauma and cultural diversity often co-occur (e.g., a child of parents who speak a language other than English is sexually abused by a neighbor). Distinguishing their associated issues may become problematic. Many sequelae of individual and societal trauma are strikingly similar to the issues that emerge when cultural diversity is present, further compounding the complexity of the situations that practitioners must address. The following vignette illustrates how the elements of trauma and cultural diversity need to be understood if respectful, reciprocal, and responsive interactions are to develop.

Chantel, an African American woman, lost custody of her children because her chronic drug and alcohol abuse resulted in allegations of neglect. The children were in the care of Caucasian foster parents, and the Child Protective Services (CPS) case manager was also Caucasian. One day, Chantel learned that the foster mother had cut her daughter's hair, and she rushed to her daughter's school despite a court order forbidding contact with the children. The school called the police to have Chantel removed and reported the incident to CPS. The case manager documented the mother's violation of the court order and cited this as another example of Chantel's noncompliance and failure to follow the CPS plan to regain custody of her children.

Chantel had been seeing a Caucasian counselor, to whom she reported a personal history of sexual abuse and rape in childhood and adolescence. Further investigation by the counselor revealed issues that may explain Chantel's behavior:

1. *From the moment her children were placed in foster care Chantel was very upset that they had not been placed with an African American family.*

2. *Chantel had been chronically concerned about her daughter's hair not being properly braided and conditioned because of the foster mother's lack of understanding of African American hair grooming practices.*

3. *Cutting a child's hair in the African American culture, especially without the mother's permission, appeared to be a traumatic violation. Chantel acknowledged somewhat shamefully that in stark contrast to a Caucasian child's hair, her child's hair may take an extremely long time to grow back.*

4. *This violation appeared to trigger memories of Chantel's past experiences with sexual violation, resulting in common symptoms of posttraumatic reactions: excessive irritability, rage, and desperate attempts to regain control.*

5. *Chantel insisted that she was not going to accept this situation without a fight, saying, "I'm nobody's slave." This statement also recalled another time and carried particular meaning in her culture's history.*

This vignette illustrates how the overt manifestations of trauma can often be confusing and difficult to identify when cultural diversity is also present, for there are many similar and overlapping sequelae. Traumatic elements of both personal and cultural history often interweave into a single, apparently seamless tapestry. Without understanding their various strands, responses become only reactions and intentions to be respectful are doomed to failure.

MANIFESTATIONS OF TRAUMA IN CHILDREN

Children who experience prolonged stress or trauma often develop predictable physical and emotional states and patterns of social interaction, as well as a certain cognitive style, which set them apart from their peers (van der Kolk, McFarlane, & Weisaeth, 1996). In many ways, their baseline funds of knowledge are permanently altered, as in the case of a young adult male who, as a child, was sexually abused by a male relative for many years. He described himself as homosexual but often wondered if the events of his childhood had influenced his sexual orientation and, ultimately, his entire life experience. The losses for some of these children are profound, including the loss of what their lives might have been without the trauma. Specific manifestations of trauma in children fall into five categories:

1. Social: Children may become withdrawn, avoidant, unable to tolerate being alone, aggressive, clingy, mistrustful, or too trusting. They may isolate themselves, act out, attempt to control and abuse peers, or demand excessive attention.

2. Physical: Children may experience chronic headaches, stomachaches, diarrhea and other somatic complaints, numbness and analgesia (the inability to feel physical pain), sleep disturbance and frequent nightmares, failure to thrive, poor appetite or overeating, or incontinence. They may daydream frequently, appearing dazed or in a trance. Or they may engage in self-injury and self-mutilation, repetitive reenactments through play, rituals, and compulsive behaviors.

3. Emotional: Children may be hypervigilant, hypersensitive, irritable, restless, hyperactive, depressed, angry, tearful, anxious, fearful, apathetic, or full of rage. They may also regress, develop new and sometimes irrational fears, act helpless, feel overwhelmed, feel excessive guilt and shame, or feel worthless.

4. Cognitive: Children may exhibit difficulty concentrating and focusing; experience memory lapses; appear confused, lost, or stuck in their thinking; deny or distort reality; live in a fantasy world; or have negative preoccupations.

5. Communication: Many children who have experienced trauma develop a code for telling their stories. As they become more verbally sophisticated, they may begin to speak in metaphors with hidden meanings. They may attempt to hide their true feelings by saying that everything is fine, or they may become silent or even mute. Their language is often detached, as they lack words for the overwhelming feelings that they are experiencing. Lack of maturity also may impair

children's ability to interpret and talk about traumatic experience. For example, when adults who were sexually abused as children are asked to report the age of their first sexual experience, few reply with the age at which they were sexually abused. Even adults have a hard time comprehending that their first sexual experience occurred at such a young age. To shift the focus from what is really wrong, children also may speak negatively about themselves or others.

In many ways, it seems that these patterns of thinking, feeling, behaving, and communicating form the basis for a disconnection and alienation from peers and other social contacts. This alienation and disconnection can be similar in many ways to the experiences of children from culturally diverse environments when the larger society does not understand or value these environments.

TRAUMA AS A CUMULATIVE EXPERIENCE

The best preparation for a bad experience is a *good* experience, not a bad experience. Those who function best under extreme stress have had minimal previous negative, stressful experiences and come from environments where they have been able to accumulate a reserve of resources, including self-esteem and effective coping skills. Individuals who have not had prior traumatic experiences are able to think and feel simultaneously and usually react appropriately to stressful situations. Conversely, those who still carry the sequelae of high-stress, traumatic environments have limited reserves and marginal coping skills; and they may even "fall apart" over time. Their thoughts and feelings have become disconnected, and subsequent traumatic experiences often immobilize them. For example, say that during a walk two individuals encounter a vicious dog. One of the individuals has been bitten by a dog; the other has not. It might be assumed that the first person would have an advantage in handling the situation because of previous experience. However, it is more probable that this person would freeze or react foolishly by running or hitting the dog. The person who has never been bitten may be more likely to stop, assess the situation, and perhaps recall previous warnings about what to do in such situations. In other words, the person who was not previously traumatized might be frightened but able to think rationally. Cumulative trauma exposure, therefore, may predispose individuals to evoke ineffective coping responses (van der Kolk et al., 1996).

A high number of individuals and families from oppressed or "minority" groups have lower socioeconomic status and, as a result, have higher rates of exposure to stress-producing factors. Some of these factors include poor diet, hunger, poor education, exposure to crime, traffic hazards (e.g., playing in the street), unreliable or inadequate transportation, substandard and overcrowded housing, low-paying jobs, unemployment and underemployment, lack of health insurance, limited access to services, untreated or poorly treated health and dental problems, inadequate prenatal care, greater exposure to disease, premature death, higher death rates, and inadequate child care provisions.

These conditions of prolonged stress may adversely affect the physical and mental health of a child and his or her immediate and extended family, neighborhood, community, and cultural or ethnic group for many generations. As a result, a child who experiences a traumatic event, such as the death of a parent or exposure to a violent crime, may be predisposed to greater suffering because of the cumulative trauma, not just the most recent traumatic event. It is no surprise that children are being hospitalized in psychiatric institutions at younger and younger ages as their coping skills become exhausted. Imagine the horror and disbelief at hearing a 5-year-old girl, hospitalized in a children's psychiatric unit, recount her efforts to kill herself by sitting on a swing and twisting its chains around her neck to strangle herself, expressing a desire to die. Although it seems unlikely that a 5-year-old would be developmentally able to fully comprehend the nature and finality of death, this child seemed so bent on her own self-destruction that one can only imagine her previous experiences with death and suffering. "Warrior Child," a poem by Nanci Presley-Holley, eloquently sums up the cumulative effects of years of trauma:

> I've never been a soldier
> But I know what war is like
> Having survived a childhood
> Besieged by enemies
> More dangerous and insidious
> Than those
> Armies face with guns
> My foes were alcoholism and child abuse
> And I was unarmed
>
> I never got just the one-year tour of duty
> In some battle torn country
> I was there for the duration
> From birth to age 18
> Escaping like a prisoner of war
> Only to be snapped back into the fold
> When they'd find out where I lived
> Or I broke down and told

Just like a soldier who has no life of his own
I was my family's possession
Theirs to send where they wished
Sometimes to grandma's, an aunt's, an uncle's
When the burden of raising three children
Pushed them to the limit
But it wasn't "rest and relaxation" for me
'Cause no matter where I went
The enemy had already crossed the lines
The disease ran rampant
Through my family

"Army issue" was hand me downs
Or poorly made clothes by a woman
Trying to maintain her sanity
'Cause dad had drank what little money there was
Or spent it on some floozy in town

Bedroom inspections were always on Saturday
If everything was perfect
We could go outside for the day
But a comic book out of place
    or a messy bed
We'd pay dearly
What does a 5 year old really know
About dust and hospital corners?

Normal childhood activities, like play?
Not this child
I was always combat ready
Training myself to survive
I had to be on guard, alert
For the fist in the stomach, a slap upside the head
Because I'd spoken when I was supposed to be quiet
Or asked for something to eat
Or even colored over the lines
I never knew when the flak would hit
There was never any warning
I wished there'd been someone
To scream "incoming"

Nighttime was the worst
But unlike armed camps
There weren't any sentries
Laying in my bed
Hovering between exhaustion and sleep
Listening for the whisper of the intruder
Just in case he crept toward my room
Or waking to find he'd already infiltrated
And was laying on top of me
How could I do anything else
    . . . Except play dead?

My childhood was a war zone
As frightening and devastating as Viet Nam
A battleground of fear
Where discord and conflict were the rule
Once in awhile
When I allow the feelings stored since childhood
To bubble to the surface
I have a hard time keeping them under control
I immediately want to fight or flee
Destroy something
Sometimes
  Even
   Me
(as cited in Middleton-Moz, 1989)

The hidden lives of many children come close to the nightmare portrayed in the "Warrior Child." These children become experts at surviving but have no opportunity for thriving. Their coping skills, which are learned in these environments, do not prepare them for a healthy life but, rather, to transmit a distorted view of the world to succeeding generations. Breaking the cycle of trauma becomes an even greater challenge when cultural diversity is present, because an equal level of shame, pain, and worthlessness can result from a lack of acceptance of one's culture and identity.

DIFFERING CULTURAL PERSPECTIVES ON CHILD MALTREATMENT

The roles of children can differ dramatically across cultures. In some cultures, children are allowed to express themselves freely; in other cultures, children are given very little freedom of expression. Certain cultures advocate protecting children until they reach maturity while others may do little about the sexual and economic exploitation of very young children. These norms often change over time and are influenced by factors such as the increasingly influential roles of women; population shifts with immigration; loss of economic status and power from war, unemployment, and natural disasters; or improved economic status. For instance, children begging in the streets may be the norm for a culture in which economic status has declined because of civil war.

Acceptable methods of disciplining children also vary widely among cultures and are subject to change. At one time in North America, the strap was an acceptable way to administer punishment in public schools, as was excessive corporal punishment at home. In the latter part of the 20th century, these practices were designated a form of child abuse subject to both criminal and civil penalties; however, some parents who were raised in these environments still believe that they have the right to discipline their children the same way. Many of these parents have so repressed the trauma of their own abuse that they are shocked when anyone suggests that they are mistreating their children. With therapy, these parents may begin to connect with their own feelings of pain and helplessness, allowing them to see the pain and helplessness in their own children (Miller, 1980; Stettbacher, 1991).

Now imagine what it must be like when a parent from a cultural group that continues to practice harsh discipline immigrates to a society or community where those practices have been outlawed. Such parents can quickly find themselves in serious legal trouble if, for example, they beat their children as a form of punishment. These parents can also lose custody of their children, perhaps permanently, when CPS and the courts intervene.

Some cultures practice noninterference when there is a problem within a family. For example, if a Native American child is being abused at home, the extended family or clan may find a way to quietly move the child into the home of other family or clan members. If the child lives on a reservation and traditional ways have been preserved, this resolution may be quite successful. If an outside teacher, counselor, or medical professional learns about the abuse, however, state and federal laws mandate filing a report with the authorities. This policy of interference may result in the child's being removed from the home as well as from the Native American community. Culture clash regarding the maltreatment of children occurs frequently, presenting a dilemma for teachers and service providers who must adhere to the law while serving families and children from many different cultures.

SECOND-GENERATION TRAUMA

It is important to note that many traumatic reactions are not the result of direct exposure to trauma. Trauma may be experienced vicariously through the lives of others, even those who are already deceased. These residual emotional reactions are often culture specific. People whose parents and grandparents lived through the Depression still may exhibit residual compulsive behaviors, such as not wasting food and turning out the lights when leaving a room (although there are certainly valid reasons for these behaviors in any time period).

Very often, trauma that is experienced vicariously is related to an event that is part of the history of an entire culture. One example of this phenomenon involves descendants of people who experienced the Holo-caust firsthand. These people may live under a cloud of unexplained sad-ness and doom, with a restricted range of feelings (i.e., blunted affect) and a sense of overwhelming shame whenever they make mistakes. At a Vi-enna outpatient clinic addressing trauma from the Nazi era, Dr. David Vys-soki said that some descendants live in an "oppressive climate of silence" (as cited in Jahn, 2002, p. A24). When the horrors are so unimaginable, sometimes there is no opportunity for catharsis by talking about what happened, and some survivors have no memories because they have com-pletely repressed details of the Holocaust. Their children and grandchil-dren may never feel that they have permission to have fun and play and are often workaholics as adults. They may describe often feeling guilty in their interactions with others, especially with members of their family, knowing that they escaped the hell that others experienced. When they connect these thoughts and behaviors to the past, it is as if their whole life begins to make sense for the first time. Their overreaction to things such as tattoos and the smell of barbeques, never before understood, finally begins to make sense in the context of second-generation trauma.

Another example involves Native American and First Nation Cana-dian[1] children whose parents and grandparents were taken from their homes on reservations and sent to boarding schools across the country. These parents and grandparents were often prevented from going home to their families until age 18, and in many cases, their families never knew where they were sent. Sadly, many of these children also suffered emo-tional, physical, and sexual abuse by the caregivers and teachers who were tasked with indoctrinating them into the "white man's ways." Mem-bers of succeeding generations frequently experience prolonged depres-sion, high rates of drug and alcohol addiction, and academic and behavior difficulties in school. The shame felt by the previous generations who ex-perienced the trauma is passed on to the children and grandchildren as a secret that is never discussed. Beginning in 1990, newspaper articles and lawsuits describing the horrors of these boarding schools began to expose the hidden traumas of multiple generations of native people (see Mofina, 2001). Because this unspoken burden has remained hidden for decades, the average American or Canadian is most likely unaware of these events and their resulting scars. Practitioners working with Native American or First Nation Canadian children in any school, whether on or off a reser-vation, should be aware of this legacy whenever home–school coopera-tion problems arise.

---

[1]*First Nation Canadians* is a term adopted in the 1970s, referring to the Indian people in Canada.

Frequently, a child who experiences trauma has a caregiver who was also traumatized as a child. This "double-jeopardy" situation requires the child to compete with the caregiver for limited resources to deal with the sequelae of trauma. The child almost always loses out. A caregiver whose own childhood was affected by trauma may be totally unavailable to the child, instead struggling with his or her own feelings of shame, anger, and low self-esteem. In addition, if the family lives in a high-stress environment where daily living is a struggle and danger lurks at every corner, the child has little hope of finding a "good enough" environment for recovery from current trauma and stress. Some practitioners also may struggle with their own traumas. If they do not address their own issues, these practitioners may

- Fail to read and respond to the child's distress
- Be insensitive to serious symptoms exhibited by the child, dismissing them as "normal"
- Avoid any discussions or experiences that might evoke memories of their own traumas, resulting in pressure to forget or "get over" the experience
- Rationalize that the child is too young to remember what happened
- Misinterpret aggression, especially in boys
- Fail to sense danger or intervene in dangerous situations
- Blame the child for what happened or excuse the adult
- Become so distraught that the child must tend to the adult's needs
- Focus on dangers outside instead of inside the home
- Force the child to suppress his or her feelings and "grow up"
- Create an environment of constant crisis and chaos

When dealing with the parents and families of children who have experienced trauma, it is important to be aware of the potential for multigenerational trauma. Many children who are sexually abused have a parent who was also sexually abused as a child and may be unable to protect the child or recognize danger. This occurs because of the tendency to repress or deny traumatic information. For example, a woman who was sexually abused by her father may leave her children in her parents' care without making the connection that her children also could be abused. Assuming that this mother would know better than to leave her children in the care of a known perpetrator amounts to a *cognitive error*—that is, a way of thinking based on a faulty belief system that is designed to protect one's view of the world. Practitioners who have experienced sexual abuse are more likely to make cognitive errors. They may believe that perpetrators would never repeat their crimes, especially if caught or confronted, but there is no known cure for such behavior and perpetrators often abuse multiple children (Lanning, 1992). Practitioners who have dealt successfully with their own traumas are much less likely to make cognitive errors and can show great sensitivity toward these children because of their own experiences.

CULTURAL DIFFERENCES IN HELP-SEEKING BEHAVIORS

Once a practitioner has identified that trauma or extreme stress and cultural diversity are co-occurring issues, the next step is to begin formulating appropriate intervention strategies. Intervention must account for many variables, including subjective, wide-ranging reports of well-being and various help-seeking behaviors. There is no single cross-cultural approach to dealing with problems and seeking solutions. ENC coping strategies are not universally endorsed by all cultures.

Both help-seeking behaviors and ways of disclosing problems are rooted in one's culture. The self-help movement has attracted mostly white, middle-class individuals who have become experts themselves on a variety of trauma-related issues (e.g., codependency, recovery). This new culture of help-seekers has spawned an explosion of print media and talk shows to support efforts to resolve childhood trauma. Conversely, individuals from "minority" cultures can be overrepresented in community mental health programs. These programs primarily serve individuals with low socioeconomic status or with chronic mental illness, as well as those whose treatment has been mandated by courts, Probation, CPS, or the Department of Social Services. The overrepresentation of minority cultures in these programs is not a function of culturally based help-seeking behavior. In reality, "minority" status frequently correlates with low socioeconomic status and limited access to care. Sadly, when these issues are misinterpreted or confused, individuals as well as entire groups may be labeled as having negative help-seeking behavior.

Suppression and/or denial of stress may be a function of an individual's mental illness as well as a coping strategy of a person who is oppressed. These two issues are frequently confused, and when the cultural aspects of self-disclosure are not considered, an individual may be labeled as resistant, manipulative, noncompliant, or controlling. Members of various cultural groups may perceive self-disclosure as unsafe or as a sign of giving up control and independence; therefore, the tendency toward nondisclosure may limit help-seeking behaviors. Admission of a problem may be perceived as an acknowledgement of weakness in some cultures, which could lead to more vulnerability, oppression, or victimization (Neighbors & Jackson, 1996).

Fear of outside authorities may also affect help-seeking behavior. An African American mother with limited financial resources may be less likely to request help when she cannot take care of her children, knowing that she may risk losing custody of them. Conversely, a Caucasian middle-class mother facing similar circumstances may be more aggressive about seeking help, knowing that the risks of losing custody of her children are much smaller. There is an inherent (and experience-based) mistrust of agencies and helping professionals among many cultures. Those with limited resources and less sophistication in dealing with "the system" are frequently treated poorly or unfairly while those with a greater degree of education, money, and access to legal aid have a distinct advantage. Justice is seldom blind for those who are disadvantaged and oppressed.

Many variables appear to predict the extent to which stress is denied as well as preferred types of help-seeking behaviors. Social status (income, education, access to resources and third-party insurance), social roles (gender, age, personal competence), and group identification (social supports, extended family, religious affiliation, cultural affiliation) seem to play significant roles in determining which individuals are likely to disclose problems and seek help voluntarily. Preference for specific helpers is also determined as much by prior individual experiences as by the experiences and beliefs of one's entire culture. Members of some groups (e.g., ENC) tend to seek outside professional help. Other individuals have been socialized to request help from nonprofessionals such as extended family, friends, and church or community healers (Neighbors & Jackson, 1996).

When children and families are in crisis, it is important to understand the normative help-seeking behaviors for their culture before drawing conclusions about their level of dysfunction or planning interventions. It is also important to understand that culturally based help-seeking behaviors that functioned well when a culture was intact often become ineffective or inadequate when individuals are displaced or relocate beyond the boundaries of their original culture. As shown in the following vignette, this frequently occurs when families immigrate to a new country and find that their new environment does not support their traditional help-seeking behaviors.

Rosa, a Hispanic woman in her mid-thirties, had been having thoughts of suicide, so she called the county crisis line. She was referred to a mental health crisis center for psychiatric assessment. Upon her arrival at the center, staff quickly determined that Rosa was a native of another country who spoke very little English. Because the center's evaluator did not speak Spanish, a male mental health worker was also present to translate. Rosa had to sign numerous forms to complete the evaluation, none of which were written in Spanish. She appeared anxious and hesitant, stating through the translator that she wanted to leave because no one was home to care for her four children, ages 2–10 years. The evaluator determined that Rosa had been very depressed since her husband's illness and death a year earlier.

Throughout the interview, Rosa was very guarded in her responses, but several inconsistencies emerged. The evaluator noted that Rosa began responding to questions before the translator finished the translation. The evaluator questioned this, and Rosa eventually responded in fluent English. She admitted that she had been living in the United States since she was a teenager and was not a legal immigrant. Several family members resided in the United States while others, including her father, remained in Rosa's native country. She acknowledged a previous suicide attempt in adolescence while living in her native country, but she never sought help, nor did she disclose this to her family. Rosa finally admitted that her father, as well as several male relatives, had sexually abused her. She stated that her mother knew what had happened but they never talked about it. Rosa believed that the move to the United States may have been an attempt to remove her and her siblings from the abuse and agreed that this might explain why her father never joined the family in the United States. She was shocked when asked if the abuse had ever been reported to the authorities in her native country; she believed that the police would then abuse her, too. When asked whether she thought some of her emotional distress was connected to the abuse, Rosa agreed that it might be possible. She said that she currently felt overwhelmed by grief regarding her husband's death and did not understand why she could not just "get over it" as her mother and aunts advised.

Rosa admitted that she was having trouble going to work because of her depression and because her family members refused to watch her children while she was at work. When asked for more information about her job, Rosa admitted that she worked for an escort service, which was why her family did not support her job. However, Rosa found that she could make a lot of money at this job even though she did not have papers to work legally in the country. In addition, the flexibility of her hours allowed her to spend more time with her children. Rosa then noted that her children were becoming defiant and unmanageable at school, adding to her stress. She also stated that her children could not receive any survivors' benefits from Social Security, as her husband never worked legally in the United States, either. She had no health or disability insurance and would probably qualify for little financial assistance for mental health services or prescription medications. When Rosa was

encouraged to apply for legal resident status in the United States, she said that
she did not want to take chances on being deported or losing the house that
she had purchased.

Several conclusions can be drawn from this example. Rosa's initial refusal to speak English and her refusal to consider becoming a legal resident indicated her distrust of "the system." She did not see herself as the
traditional U.S. worker with a need for benefits and security for herself
and her children. This worldview limited her access to services and resources in the United States.

Rosa's sociocultural background also did not support utilizing outside
professional resources to solve problems, as demonstrated by her family's
recommendation that she "just get over it." Rosa even appeared to believe
that seeking help from professionals is dangerous, based on her beliefs
about the police in her native country. Members of the U.S. psychiatric
community would suggest that Rosa was moderately depressed and possibly needed medication to stabilize her moods. Based on her past history,
she was at risk for another suicide attempt and possibly death.

Rosa did not view her job, working for an escort service, as a reen-
actment of her sexual abuse trauma, which was likely preventing her
from addressing her grief. Not only was she minimizing her trauma to
others but to herself as well. She never had an opportunity for catharsis,
as she had not talked about the trauma and the environment was very invalidating. Many immigrants believe that they have left their traumas behind, but the "geographical cure" rarely lessens the sequelae.

Rosa's coping skills and help-seeking behaviors were severely compromised by her illegal immigrant status, the stigma of her chosen profession, and unresolved trauma issues. She was beginning to see problems
with her children but probably did not realize just how unavailable she
was to them because of her own grief and her broken-down family support system. Her cultural beliefs made it unlikely that she would seek outside help from professionals for herself and the children. In addition, it is
possible that she would not recognize if her children were in dangerous
situations and would not report suspected abuse to the authorities. The
prognosis was not hopeful for Rosa's successful resolution of her mental
health issues and her children's challenging behavior.

It is likely that Rosa's children would begin to experience emotional
problems and receive little support from their mother or her extended
family. In a classroom, practitioners would probably have only limited information about the extensive trauma issues that so clearly influenced the

mother's coping skills and help-seeking behaviors. Engaging her in getting help for her children, if needed, would at least require a basic understanding of the interplay of cultural diversity and trauma issues.

CULTURE AS A PROTECTIVE FACTOR

Culture provides a structure for normalizing experiences, renders life predictable, and defines rules for emotional expression and grieving. Without this structure, the individual and the family may become more vulnerable to the effects of extreme stress and trauma. Unfortunately, some cultures and societies, especially those in the Third World, seem more prone to such experiences as a result of ongoing civil wars and limited resources to recover from natural disasters. When such catastrophic events occur, an entire culture may be severely disrupted or even devastated to the point that recovery seems impossible. In examining the aftermath of such events, one must begin to consider the following questions (deVries, 1996):

- When a culture is intact, does it protect against the effects of stress and trauma?

- What happens to individuals and families when the culture has been disrupted or destroyed?

- What happens to individuals and families who become separated from their culture?

- How are these issues relevant for early childhood and early childhood special education providers in the classroom?

In almost every classroom in North America, there are children whose families have experienced some disruption in their culture as a result of immigration or relocation. Catastrophic events elsewhere in the world often result in an influx of immigrants to North America, who are seeking sanctuary for themselves and their families. Many others come looking for a better life and the American Dream. The Native Americans were forced to relocate to reservations far from their established homelands and support structures. When individuals and families immigrate or relocate outside their culture, they often must rely on themselves to survive. Without the bond to their culture, there may be no mechanism to stabilize and restore functioning, especially when the events precipitating the immigration or relocation were extremely traumatic, perhaps even catastrophic.

Many factors protect individuals and families with a strong cultural affiliation from disintegration in times of extreme stress: norms and beliefs, rituals, social roles, prescribed tasks during the life cycle, stories, legends, ceremonies, concepts of emotional illness, a religious context that involves a belief in a higher power or a spiritual realm, rules for grieving, the support and involvement of extended family, and a medical treatment system. Many children from first-generation immigrant families come to school with these protective factors disrupted or distorted, thereby reducing the children's ability to adjust to their adopted culture. As a result, children may exhibit emotional problems and challenging behavior, and the family may be unable to cope without resorting to maladaptive responses. This situation is illustrated in the following vignette.

Anna and Jacob were well-educated professionals who had considerable professional status in their homeland and adequate financial resources despite the overall poverty in their country. Regardless of their success, they believed that the future was bleak for their two children in their native county. Jacob remained there, working to provide for his family, but Anna and their children immigrated to the United States. Anna was pregnant and determined to give birth to the child in the United States although she was not a legal resident. Jacob, reluctant to give up his job because he would have to learn English to work in his profession in the United States, was not present for the birth of their son. After 2 years, however, he eventually joined Anna. When the family's money ran out, Anna took a job that would allow her to obtain legal U.S. residency. Anna's employer promised to pay back wages as soon as she received her Social Security number but did not follow through. Thus, Anna was forced to work in a factory and clean houses to feed her family. During this time, Jacob refused to work, became increasingly depressed, and started drinking heavily. He said that he was too old to learn English, and he did not help with the children even though he was home all day. Jacob often got so frustrated that he screamed at the children, occasionally hitting them with a belt to get them to behave. Anna gave him an ultimatum: get a job or leave the family. Jacob finally got a menial job, and the oldest child, age 17, took over most of the family child care responsibilities. The youngest child, 8-year-old Joseph, was beginning to show signs of emotional disturbance, including hyperactivity, aggression toward his parents, oppositional and defiant behavior, and outbursts of rage. Anna told Joseph's teacher that she could no longer manage his behavior. She also explained that her only support in the United States was her husband, who left all of the disciplining to her and often undermined her authority by indulging Joseph despite his behavior. Anna had not established any relationships in her new community with persons from her culture. Although she stated that she was very proud of her culture, Anna did not encourage Joseph or her other children to participate in it or use its language.

This vignette demonstrates how cultural disconnection can result in individual and familial breakdown. Without familiar resources to restore functioning, the family members resorted to ineffective coping skills (e.g., excessive drinking, withdrawal, violence, neglect). A teacher or practitioner struggling to help such a family needs to consider cultural disconnection as a major factor in the family's inability to manage the stress of relocating outside its culture. One possible intervention is connecting the family to other families from this culture that have successfully made the transition.

Other Mediating Factors

It is important to recognize other protective factors—those for the individual child as well as those within the environment—that can affect the child's response to extreme stress and trauma. These mediating factors include

- A secure, predictable, stable home environment
- An independent, resilient personality (children with dependent, fragile personalities are more vulnerable to emotional upheaval)
- Advanced age and developmental stage (younger children are more affected by their parents' reactions)
- Birth order (older children may have access to more resources than their younger siblings)
- Physical and emotional well-being (physical and emotional vulnerability are risk factors for negative outcomes due to stress and trauma)
- Access to culturally responsive and validating environments in the classroom, at home, and in places of worship
- Access to accurate information and education about resources to address mental illness, addiction, abuse, and neglect
- Evidence of successful adjustment and good recovery from previous stressful events

CREATING HEALING
ENVIRONMENTS FOR YOUNG CHILDREN

It is assumed that all early childhood and early childhood special education practitioners strive to provide classroom environments that are conducive to learning and cognitive development. Addressing the overwhelming stress and trauma that many students struggle with daily presents an additional challenge. Yet, providing a healing environment for these children not only enhances their learning but also allows them to thrive rather than merely survive. The following elements may be part of such an environment:

- Sensitivity to changes in a child that may signal stress or trauma
- Respect for physical safety and boundaries
- Solution-focused rather than blame-oriented strategies
- Validation of feelings and experiences
- Safe opportunities to express feelings through talking, drawing, and playing
- Comfortable, familiar, and predictable routines
- Flexibility in routines when needed (e.g., special accommodations to allow a child to feel safe)
- Patience when attempting to decode the meanings and metaphors in a child's language and behaviors
- Permission for temporary regression when appropriate

Practitioners are often on the front line of intervention with young children and families who are struggling with extreme stress and trauma. Although these issues may also require intervention from mental health professionals, much can be done in the classroom to mediate some effects of stressful or traumatic experiences. The author hopes that this discussion will help educators and other practitioners who strive to understand the complexities of working with children and families from diverse backgrounds. For further information, see two sources that made significant contributions to this appendix: Neighbors and Jackson (1996) and van der Kolk et al. (1996).

Looking Closer

JON WILSON

It's too easy to assume that quick judgments and first impressions tell us all we need to know about each other.

I learned a great lesson, recently, in the risks of quick assumptions and the benefits of looking closer. It was during the meeting of our community reparations board, a group established to enable discussion between victims of minor crimes and their offenders. Reparations boards are gaining momentum in communities around the country as a way of helping victims feel a truer sense of justice by having the offenders face them (and the community) directly so they can understand and repair, to the extent possible, the effects of their behaviors. My lesson came when what I'd somewhat arrogantly presumed at first glance collided with the truth.

A mother of three had been arrested and later sentenced to a month in jail for driving without a license. She was in her late thirties, and she'd been designated a habitual offender. Since she had a couple of OUIs on her record, we'd assumed she was simply unable to control her drinking, had lost her license, and had been unable to stay out of trouble since. We thought we had it figured out. We're smart and caring, sensitive to the difficulties of substance abuse, and we were certainly not convened to judge her (the district court having had its way with her). On the other hand, our job was to help her better know how her actions imperiled the safety and security of our community. We just hoped to persuade her, as concerned community members, not to drive while under the influence and not to drive without a license. It all seemed so simple.

As soon as she began her story, however, things grew instantly more complex. When we asked her to tell us what led to her arrest, she began

From Wilson, J. (2001). Looking closer. *Hope, 27,* 64; reprinted by permission.

221

by describing how her teenage daughter had telephoned her for help because her boyfriend was hitting her. As any mother would, she drove off to rescue her daughter. The fact that she didn't have a license caused her no hesitation. After all, she told us, though she was almost forty, she had *never* had a license. But while rescuing her daughter, she was also assaulted, so when she returned home, she called the police. When she told them her story, they arrested *her*—for having driven without a license. She'd been stopped before, for the same offense. They felt they had no choice. One of their jobs is to keep unlicensed drivers off the road.

When we asked her why she had never gotten her license, she said she could not read very well, and she was terrified of the written exam. Worse, she was ashamed to admit that she still needed help reading. Even then, the solution seemed simple enough to us. We know that there are plenty of adults who cannot read but can get their licenses, and they can get help from organizations like Literacy Volunteers. And, while it's definitely inconvenient, they can also get rides from friends and family while they're preparing.

But then she told us she is also being treated for Anxiety Disorder—and one of her primary trigger situations is riding in cars with other drivers. If the driver drives too fast, talks too much, comes too close to tailgating, or passes another car (it's clear she could not ride with me), anxiety overpowers her, and she has to ask to be let out of the car, only to face the need for another anxiety-provoking ride home. And if she finds work in the opposite direction from her usually-but-not-always-understanding-and-patient husband, for example, getting to work can be next to impossible. That was when we realized that our operating assumptions were far from complete. And that is how it happened that a group of caring people established to help offenders understand their responsibility to their victims and the community learned a great lesson about a community's responsibility to its offenders.

Of course, we could have ignored this lesson, and just let something like this (or worse) happen again. But fortunately, a mentor arose from our ranks who can, just by caring about who the woman is, help her make permanent and positive changes in her life. As she did so, I suspect we all suddenly saw the power of what might be possible in that relationship. For myself, I marveled at the way things work out when we slow down enough to let them. It could have so easily have been—even if a caring one—just a community lecture. And as I think about how easy it is, even for those of intelligence and heart, to preconceive and presuppose based on the apparent rather than the true, I want to cry out to all of us—but mostly myself—to slow down; to look more closely and listen more carefully. For those of us in search of real possibilities in our encounters, we'll surely find them when we ditch our assumptions and listen with our hearts.

Photocopiable Materials

Assessment Cultural Linguistic Response Plan

Critical Incident Analysis Sheet

Cultural Consonance Profile

Cultural Data Table

Family Acculturation Screen

Funds of Knowledge Worksheet for Story Assessment

Guide to Identifying Cultural Data Related to Potential
    Culture Bumps

Home Language Usage Profile

Instructional Cultural Linguistic Response Plan

Relative Language Proficiency (RLP) Profile

Skilled Dialogue Self-Assessment

Strategies for Anchoring Understanding of Diversity

Strategies for Creating 3rd Space Options

Assessment Cultural Linguistic Response Plan

Child's name: _____ Date: _____ Completed by: _____

Specific Assessment Considerations

RE: *Language and communication*

RE: *Data-gathering procedures*

RE: *Assessment materials*

RE: *Reporting assessment results*

Underlying Process Reminders

	Anchored Understanding of Diversity	3rd Space
RESPECT	Acknowledge the range and validity of diverse perspectives.	Stay with the tension of differing perspectives.
RECIPROCITY	Establish interactions that allow equal voice for all participants.	Develop opportunities for equalizing power across interactions.
RESPONSIVENESS	Communicate respect and understanding of others' perspectives.	Create responses that integrate and provide access to the strengths of diverse perspectives.

Skilled Dialogue: Strategies for Responding to Cultural Diversity in Early Childhood
by Isaura Barrera and Robert M. Corso with Dianne Macpherson
© 2003 Paul H. Brookes Publishing Co., Inc.

Critical Incident Analysis Sheet

Child's name: _____ Date: _____ Completed by: _____

Incident description: _____

Quality	Anchored Understanding of Diversity	3rd Space
Respect	*Key Principle:* Acknowledge the range and validity of diverse perspectives.	*Key Principle:* Stay with the tension of differing perspectives.
Reciprocity	*Key Principle:* Establish interactions that allow equal voice for all participants.	*Key Principle:* Develop opportunities for equalizing power across interactions.
Responsiveness	*Key Principle:* Communicate respect and understanding of others' perspectives.	*Key Principle:* Create responses that integrate and provide access to the strengths of diverse perspectives.

Skilled Dialogue: Strategies for Responding to Cultural Diversity in Early Childhood by Isaura Barrera and Robert M. Corso with Dianne Macpherson © 2003 Paul H. Brookes Publishing Co., Inc.

Cultural Consonance Profile

Child's name: _____   Date: _____   Completed by: _____

	Highly similar to early childhood environment(s)/ practitioners' profiles ⟷			Highly dissimilar from early childhood environment(s)/ practitioners' profiles	

I. Communicative-Linguistic Area

Comments

Language(s) used in child's home	5	4	3	2	1 _____
Child's relative language proficiency	5	4	3	2	1 _____
Patterns of language usage	5	4	3	2	1 _____
Relative value placed on verbal/ nonverbal communication	5	4	3	2	1 _____
Relative status of language other than English and bilingualism	5	4	3	2	1 _____

II. Personal-Social Area

Family's degree of acculturation	5	4	3	2	1 _____
Sense of self/perception of identity/competence	5	4	3	2	1 _____
Parenting/child-rearing roles and rules	5	4	3	2	1 _____
Knowledge/experience regarding power and positioning	5	4	3	2	1 _____
Values and beliefs regarding support	5	4	3	2	1 _____

III. Sensory-Cognitive Area

Funds of knowledge/concept definition/structures	5	4	3	2	1 _____
Preferred learning strategies	5	4	3	2	1 _____
Preferred problem-solving/ decision-making strategies	5	4	3	2	1 _____
Worldview	5	4	3	2	1 _____

Degree of consonance with early childhood environment(s)/practitioners' profiles

Communicative-linguistic area	High	Moderate	Low	Minimal
Personal-social area	High	Moderate	Low	Minimal
Sensory-cognitive area	High	Moderate	Low	Minimal

Comments:

Skilled Dialogue: Strategies for Responding to Cultural Diversity in Early Childhood
by Isaura Barrera and Robert M. Corso with Dianne Macpherson
© 2003 Paul H. Brookes Publishing Co., Inc.

Cultural Data Table

Child's name: _____ Date completed: _____ Completed by: _____

Directions: Fill in responses to questions from the Guide to Identifying Cultural Data Related to Potential Culture Bumps.

Developmental/curricular area	Comments
Communicative-Linguistic	
Language(s) of child's primary caregiving environment(s)	
Child's relative language proficiency (proficiency in English and other language[s] used)	
Patterns of language usage in child's primary caregiving environment(s)	
Relative value placed on verbal and nonverbal communication	
Relative status associated with languages other than English and with bilingualism	

Skilled Dialogue: Strategies for Responding to Cultural Diversity in Early Childhood by Isaura Barrera and Robert M. Corso with Dianne Macpherson © 2003 Paul H. Brookes Publishing Co., Inc.

(continued)

Personal-Social						
Degree of acculturation into EuroAmerican Normative Culture (ENC)						
Degree of acculturation into U.S. early intervention/early childhood special education culture						
Sense of self (e.g., relative weight on independence, dependence, and interdependence)						
Perceptions of identity and competence						
Roles and rules associated with parenting and child rearing						
Knowledge and experience regarding power and social positioning						

Skilled Dialogue: Strategies for Responding to Cultural Diversity in Early Childhood by Isaura Barrera and Robert M. Corso with Dianne Macpherson © 2003 Paul H. Brookes Publishing Co., Inc.

(continued)

Values/beliefs/skills associated with instrumental and emotional support (e.g., gaining access to external resources and getting personal support)	
Sensory-Cognitive	
Funds of knowledge: what type of knowledge is valued; concept structures and definitions (e.g., how *family* is defined)	
Preferred strategies for acquiring new learning	
Preferred strategies for problem solving and decision making	
Worldview (i.e., assumptions about how the world works and about what is "right" and what is "wrong")	

Family Acculturation Screen

Child's name: _____ Date: _____ Completed by: _____

Degree of English spoken in child's home
(High = predominant; Low = minimal) High --➤ Low

Level of literacy reflected in child's
home (e.g., number of books, level High --➤ Low
of parent's vocabulary)

Degree of value placed on verbal skills as
compared with nonverbal communication High --➤ Low

Degree of familiarity with English idioms High --➤ Low

Parent's level of schooling in U.S. schools
(High = college; Low = none) High --➤ Low

Familiarity with classroom rules/expectations
(High = extensive; Low = minimal) High --➤ Low

Length of residence in United States
(High = more than 10 years; High --➤ Low
Low = less than 1 year)

Value placed on child's independence
and autonomy as defined within ENC High --➤ Low

Time spent with monolingual English speakers
(High = daily; Low = infrequently) High --➤ Low

Amount of time spent in environments
strongly reflective of EuroAmerican
Normative Culture (ENC) (e.g., schools,
libraries, offices of U.S. corporations)
(High = daily; Low = infrequently) High --➤ Low

Overall impression of degree of family's acculturation into ENC			
High	Moderate	Low	Minimal

Comments:

Skilled Dialogue: Strategies for Responding to Cultural Diversity in Early Childhood
by Isaura Barrera and Robert M. Corso with Dianne Macpherson
© 2003 Paul H. Brookes Publishing Co., Inc.

Funds of Knowledge Worksheet for Story Assessment

Story title: _____

Publisher/source: _____

Date: _____ Completed by: _____

Instructions: Select and read a children's story. Identify the reflected fund of knowledge (i.e., the knowledge that the reader needs for optimum comprehension and learning). Use the categories below as a guide to different aspects of the story's fund of knowledge.

Concepts necessary to understand the story	Experiences described in the story
Story grammar (e.g., event sequence, plot)	Social environment(s) in which the story takes place
Composition and organization of families/communities in the story	Problem-solving approaches used by characters in the story
Language(s) (e.g., actual language[s] used, vocabulary level, structure)	Other (e.g., values, beliefs, behaviors)

Skilled Dialogue: Strategies for Responding to Cultural Diversity in Early Childhood
by Isaura Barrera and Robert M. Corso with Dianne Macpherson
© 2003 Paul H. Brookes Publishing Co., Inc.

Guide to Identifying Cultural Data Related to Potential Culture Bumps

Child's name: _____ Date completed: _____ Completed by: _____

Note: The questions in the second column tend to arise frequently. There may be others that are not identified on this form. Feel free to add any other questions that need to be answered. Use this guide prior to completing the Cultural Data Table.

Developmental/curricular area	Questions to answer
Communicative-Linguistic Language(s) of child's primary caregiving environment(s)	1. What language(s) are spoken in the child's primary caregiving environment(s)? 2. Which caregivers speak which language(s) with the child?
Child's relative language proficiency (proficiency in English and other language[s] used)	1. How proficient is the child in understanding and using the language(s) other than English for communicating? 2. How proficient is the child in understanding and using English for communicating? 3. Would the child be considered monolingual? Partial bilingual (speaks and understands one language, only understands another)? Bilingual, dominant in one language (speaks and understands both languages but is significantly more proficient in one)? "Balanced" bilingual (similar levels of proficiency in both languages—may not be strong in either, or may be equally strong in both)?
Patterns of language usage in child's primary caregiving environment(s)	1. With what situations and topics does each language tend to be associated? 2. Which varieties of each language are spoken (e.g., if English is spoken, in which ways is it similar to or different from what is considered the "standard" variety of English)? 3. If two or more languages are used, what seems to govern which language is used when?

Skilled Dialogue: Strategies for Responding to Cultural Diversity in Early Childhood by Isaura Barrera and Robert M. Corso with Dianne Macpherson © 2003 Paul H. Brookes Publishing Co., Inc.

(continued)

Relative value placed on verbal and nonverbal communication	1. To what degree is communication in the home verbal? To what degree is it nonverbal?
	2. What is the relative value placed on nonverbal communication as compared with verbal communication? Is this true in all situations, or only in some?
Relative status associated languages other than English and with bilingualism	1. What is the social status accorded in the community to the language(s) other than English spoken in the child's home (e.g., is the accent associated with it considered a mark of distinction or of low education)?
	2. What is the social status accorded in the community to persons who are bilingual? Is being bilingual considered a desirable goal?
Personal-Social Degree of acculturation into EuroAmerican Normative Culture (ENC)	1. How familiar is the child/family with ENC?
	2. How much experience does the child/family have participating in this culture?
	3. How skilled is the child/family at negotiating within this culture (e.g., accomplishing desired activities/goals)?
Degree of acculturation into U.S. early intervention/early childhood special education culture	1. How familiar is the child/family with early intervention/early childhood special education culture (e.g., rules and expectations)?
	2. How much experience does the child/family have participating in this culture?
	3. How skilled is the child/family at negotiating within this culture (e.g., accomplishing desired activities/goals)?

Skilled Dialogue: Strategies for Responding to Cultural Diversity in Early Childhood by Isaura Barrera and Robert M. Corso with Dianne Macpherson © 2003 Paul H. Brookes Publishing Co., Inc.

(continued)

Sense of self (e.g., relative weight on independence, dependence, and interdependence)	1. How does the family define autonomy? To what degree is it valued? 2. To what degree is cooperation and group interaction/support valued? 3. What are the characteristics of persons with high credibility in the family's culture? Which characteristics/behaviors seem to be most highly valued?
Perceptions of identity and competence	1. How do family members define themselves; (e.g., by ethnic, professional, or other labels; by personal attributes)? 2. Which characteristics denote competence?
Roles and rules associated with parenting and child rearing	1. How would family members describe "good" parenting? 2. What skills/attributes do they consider desirable in a "well-brought-up" child? 3. What roles do different family members play in child rearing? Who is responsible for what?
Knowledge and experience regarding power and social positioning	1. What is the family's experience regarding social and personal power? In what situations, if any, would family members describe themselves as powerless or "at a disadvantage"? 2. Does the family belong to and identify with a group with "minority" status?

Skilled Dialogue: Strategies for Responding to Cultural Diversity in Early Childhood by Isaura Barrera and Robert M. Corso with Dianne Macpherson © 2003 Paul H. Brookes Publishing Co., Inc.

(continued)

Values/beliefs/skills associated with instrumental and emotional support (e.g., gaining access to external resources and getting personal support)	1. How does the family obtain support? What sources are valued? 2. When does the family believe that it is acceptable to seek instrumental support? Emotional support?
Sensory–Cognitive Funds of knowledge: what type of knowledge is valued; concept structures and definitions (e.g., how *family* is defined)	1. What areas of knowledge are valued and supported by the family? 2. About what are the family members very knowledgeable? 3. Are funds of knowledge primarily personal, communal, or institutionalized? 4. To what degree are funds of knowledge oral? To what degree are they written? 5. What role does the family's cultural identity (or identities) play in its funds of knowledge?
Preferred strategies for acquiring new learning	1. What are the child's/family's preferred strategies for learning (e.g., modeling, questioning)? 2. To what degree are the strategies explicit and direct? To what degree are they implicit and indirect? 3. To what degree are the strategies oral? To what degree are they nonverbal? 4. How do different family members teach the child something that they consider important?

Skilled Dialogue: Strategies for Responding to Cultural Diversity in Early Childhood by Isaura Barrera and Robert M. Corso with Dianne Macpherson © 2003 Paul H. Brookes Publishing Co., Inc.

(continued)

	5. Which of Gardner's (1993) seven intelligences tends to be favored?
Preferred strategies for problem solving and decision making	1. What are the child's/family's preferred strategies for problem solving and decision making? Do these differ according to certain characteristics of the problem or situation? If so, how?
	2. To what degree is problem solving or decision making independent? To what degree is problem solving or decision making a co-operative activity? If viewed as cooperative, who gets involved in the process?
	3. To what degree are the strategies linear? To what degree are they circular or global?
	4. To what degree is problem solving deductive? To what degree is it inductive?
Worldview (i.e., assumptions about how the world works and about what is "right" and what is "wrong")	1. How does the family tend to explain events such as their child's developmental challenges?
	2. What assumptions does the family hold about how the world works (e.g., mechanistic, organic-ecological)?
	3. What views do family members express about cultural and other differences? Do they favor the view that there is only one "right" way, or do they accept that multiple realities can exist?

Skilled Dialogue: Strategies for Responding to Cultural Diversity in Early Childhood by Isaura Barrera and Robert M. Corso with Dianne Macpherson © 2003 Paul H. Brookes Publishing Co., Inc.

Home Language Usage Profile

Child's name: _____ Date: _____ Completed by: _____

Person(s)	Languages used					
	Only L$_x$ Specify language other than English used in home: _____	Mostly L$_x$ (_____), some English	L$_x$ (_____) and English used equally	Some L$_x$ (_____), mostly English	Only English	Other language (specify) _____
Mother						
Father						
Siblings						
Maternal grandparents						
Paternal grandparents						
Caregiver (different from persons listed above)						
Neighborhood friends/peers						
Teacher(s)						
Social peers (e.g., at child care; at preschool)						

(*Key:* L$_x$ is the language other than English used in the home.)

Comments:

Skilled Dialogue: Strategies for Responding to Cultural Diversity in Early Childhood
by Isaura Barrera and Robert M. Corso with Dianne Macpherson
© 2003 Paul H. Brookes Publishing Co., Inc.
(*Source:* Williams & DeGaetano, 1985.)

Instructional Cultural Linguistic Response Plan

Child's name: _____ Date: _____ Completed by: _____

Specific Intervention and Instruction Considerations

RE: *Language and language differences*

RE: *Teaching and learning strategies*

RE: *Instruction content*

RE: *Teaching and learning materials*

Underlying Process Reminders

	Anchored Understanding of Diversity	3rd Space
RESPECT	Acknowledge the range and validity of diverse perspectives.	Stay with the tension of differing perspectives.
RECIPROCITY	Establish interactions that allow equal voice for all participants.	Develop opportunities for equalizing power across interactions.
RESPONSIVENESS	Communicate respect and understanding of others' perspectives.	Create responses that integrate and provide access to the strengths of diverse perspectives.

Skilled Dialogue: Strategies for Responding to Cultural Diversity in Early Childhood
by Isaura Barrera and Robert M. Corso with Dianne Macpherson
© 2003 Paul H. Brookes Publishing Co., Inc.

Relative Language Proficiency (RLP) Profile

Child's name: _____   Date: _____   Date of birth: _____

Chronological age: _____   Completed by: _____

Site: _____   Instrument: _____

Proficiency in Language Other than English (Specify language: _____)

Receptive:	5	4	3	2	1
	Good: No significant errors	Mildly limited: Some errors	Moderately limited: Consistent/ significant errors	Severely limited: Frequent and significant errors	Nonverbal and/or unintelligible
Expressive:	5	4	3	2	1

Comments:

English Proficiency

Receptive:	5	4	3	2	1
	Good: No significant errors	Mildly limited: Some errors	Moderately limited: Consistent/ significant errors	Severely limited: Frequent and significant errors	Nonverbal and/or unintelligible
Expressive:	5	4	3	2	1

Comments:

Relative Language Proficiency (Write language other than English in blanks below)

_____ Monolingual	Receptive Bilingual	Partial Bilingual	Bilingual	Partial Bilingual	Receptive Bilingual	English Monolingual
Has had minimal exposure to English	_____ dominant; understands some English	_____ dominant; limited English	_____ and English about the same	English dominant; limited	English dominant; understands some _____	Has had minimal exposure to _____

Comments:

Skilled Dialogue: Strategies for Responding to Cultural Diversity in Early Childhood
by Isaura Barrera and Robert M. Corso with Dianne Macpherson
© 2003 Paul H. Brookes Publishing Co., Inc.

Skilled Dialogue Self-Assessment

Practitioner's name: _____ Date: _____

	Anchored Understanding of Diversity	3rd Space
1 **Basic awareness**	☐ I understand and can define basic concepts (e.g., culture, culture bumps, reciprocity, Skilled Dialogue, paradox, funds of knowledge, 3rd Space).	
2 **Beginning applications**	☐ I can describe a range of diverse cultural perspectives, behaviors, values, practices, and belief systems (e.g., I can describe child-rearing practices associated with several different cultural groups).	☐ I demonstrate the ability to "stay with the tension" of contradictory perspectives without rushing to solutions/resolutions.
3 **Lower intermediate applications**	☐ I acknowledge the validity of diverse perspectives by listening mindfully and accurately identifying the meaning associated with both my own and others' perspectives.	☐ I equalize power across interactions by shifting the focus of the conversation and exploring complementary aspects of diverse perspectives.
4 **Upper intermediate applications**	☐ I identify and explore others' contributions and resources in relation to specific interactions and situations, independently and with fluency.	☐ I understand the process of reframing contradictions into complementary perspectives and can do so independently and with fluency.
5 **Advanced applications**	☐ I consistently communicate respect for and understanding of others' perspectives; families report feeling accepted and valued.	☐ I consistently create responses to children/families that integrate and provide access to the strengths of diverse perspectives; families report a sense of free choice rather than forced choice.

Comments:

Skilled Dialogue: Strategies for Responding to Cultural Diversity in Early Childhood
by Isaura Barrera and Robert M. Corso with Dianne Macpherson
© 2003 Paul H. Brookes Publishing Co., Inc.

Strategies for Anchoring Understanding of Diversity

Qualities that characterize Skilled Dialogue	Related strategies for developing Anchored Understanding of Diversity
1. Respect: Acknowledge the range and validity of diverse perspectives.	*Strategy 1.1:* Listen mindfully to others' comments/responses. 1. How much time am I allowing between perceiving and interpreting the content of others' messages? *Strategy 1.2:* Get information about others' perspectives. 1. Could you tell me more about X? 2. Could you describe for me what X means to you? 3. How would you describe what you want at this point? Could you give me a specific example? *Strategy 1.3:* Examine your own perspective. 1. What do I believe about persons who act in this fashion? 2. What meaning(s) am I attaching to the behavior(s)? 3. How are my assumptions affecting this interaction/communication?
2. Reciprocity: Establish interactions that allow equal voice for all perspectives (i.e., avoid privileging one perspective over another).	*Strategy 2.1:* Allow yourself to believe that others' contributions are of equal value to yours. *Strategy 2.2:* Clarify others' understanding of your perspective. 1. How do you see my actions? 2. What do you hear me saying/asking? 3. What are your thoughts when you see me do/say X? 4. What does responding to my request mean to you?

Skilled Dialogue: Strategies for Responding to Cultural Diversity in Early Childhood
by Isaura Barrera and Robert M. Corso with Dianne Macpherson
© 2003 Paul H. Brookes Publishing Co., Inc.

(continued)

	Strategy 2.3: Recognize the value of others' contributions. 1. What resources is X bringing to the interaction? 2. What can I learn from X? 3. What is positive about X's behavior?
3. Responsiveness: Communicate respect and understanding of others' perspectives.	*Strategy 3.1:* Remain mindful of and open to mystery (i.e., not knowing). 1. Am I overly focused on my goals, interpretations, and judgments? 2. What important information or alternative interpretations could I be missing? 3. To what degree am I willing to "trust the process" without knowing exactly what will happen? *Strategy 3.2:* Keep paying attention. 1. Listen and ask questions until you can credibly communicate respect and understanding. 2. Observe how other is responding to your words and behavior. *Strategy 3.3:* Reflect understanding of others' perspectives. 1. Let me see if I understand what you mean. Are you saying that . . . ? 2. Can I use an analogy to see if I really understand what you're saying? 3. Is this what you're talking about?

Skilled Dialogue: Strategies for Responding to Cultural Diversity in Early Childhood
by Isaura Barrera and Robert M. Corso with Dianne Macpherson
© 2003 Paul H. Brookes Publishing Co., Inc.

Strategies for Creating 3rd Space Options

Qualities that characterize Skilled Dialogue	Related strategies for creating 3rd Space options
1. Respect: Stay with the tension of differing perspectives.	*Strategy 1.1:* Release the natural inclination to focus on solutions/resolutions. 1. To what degree is my tendency to focus on solutions/resolutions interfering with my ability to express respect for perspectives or behavior diverse from my own? *Strategy 1.2:* Listen/observe without judgment. 1. Share verbal indicators of interest and curiosity (e.g., "I see," "That's interesting"). 2. Share nonverbal indicators of interest or curiosity. *Strategy 1.3:* Identify specific tension points. 1. How are we seeing this situation differently? 2. What aspects of others' behavior/perspective am I finding the most difficult or least agreeable? Why? What would happen if I did not contradict, oppose, or try to change that behavior/perspective? Listen to the answers.
2. Reciprocity: Develop opportunities for equalizing power across interactions.	*Strategy 2.1:* Recognize that there is no need to make one perspective wrong to justify another as right. *Strategy 2.2:* Shift the conversation's focus to "equalize" participation. 1. Share vulnerable statements such as "I'm not sure of where to go next." 2. Use an analogy/metaphor that is familiar to the other person or unfamiliar to both of you.

Skilled Dialogue: Strategies for Responding to Cultural Diversity in Early Childhood
by Isaura Barrera and Robert M. Corso with Dianne Macpherson
© 2003 Paul H. Brookes Publishing Co., Inc.

(continued)

	Strategy 2.3: Explore how contradictory behaviors/perspectives could be complementary. 1. How is one behavior/perspective balanced by the other?
	2. What if both are "right" and there is no need to choose between them?
3. Responsiveness: Create a response that integrates and provides access to the strengths of diverse perspectives.	*Strategy 3.1:* Trust the possibility of options that honor diversity.
	Strategy 3.2: Explore responses that integrate contradictions. 1. Use analogies (e.g., "half-full/half-empty" glass, musical chords).
	2. Reframe the "problem": tell different stories; use different lenses.
	3. Brainstorm 3rd (and 4th and 5th) choices other than those that are immediately obvious.
	4. Continue until finding a response that is agreeable to all concerned.

Skilled Dialogue: Strategies for Responding to Cultural Diversity in Early Childhood
by Isaura Barrera and Robert M. Corso with Dianne Macpherson
© 2003 Paul H. Brookes Publishing Co., Inc.

Guidelines for Using an Interpreter/ Translator During Test Administration

Appendix
D

Three basic steps should occur when using an interpreter/translator while administering tests: a meeting before the testing (Briefing), the testing itself (Interaction), and a meeting after the assessment (Debriefing). Some suggestions follow for each phase of the testing process.

1. BRIEFING

Prior to testing, practitioners and the interpreter/translator meet to

A. Review the general purpose of the testing session
B. Discuss which tests will be administered
C. Discuss test validity and reliability. Care should be taken to avoid unnecessary rephrasing or radically changing test items. Interpreters/ translators must also watch their use of gestures, voice patterns, and body language to avoid inadvertently providing cues
D. Share information on the child being assessed
E. Discuss the results of English language or other previous testing, if applicable
F. Remind the interpreter/translator to write down all of the child's behaviors (e.g., gestures, facial expressions, nonverbal responses to tasks)
G. Give the interpreter/translator time to organize the test materials, re-read test procedures, and ask for clarification on issues, if needed
H. Familiarize the interpreter/translator with terms and concepts that are specific to the test

---

Adapted from Medina, V. (1982). *Interpretation and translation in bilingual B.A.S.E.* San Diego: San Diego County Office of Education.

245

2. INTERACTION

During actual test situations, remember that

A. The practitioner is always present during the testing
B. The interpreter/translator *immediately* asks questions in their pre-scribed order
C. The practitioner writes down observations about the child during the testing
D. The practitioner observes the interpreter/translator for cues of poten-tial miscommunication or inappropriate translation:
    1. Body language
    2. Use of too many words or too many instructions (e.g., interpreter/translator speaks for 2 minutes after being asked to inquire about the child's place of birth)
    3. Overuse of reinforcement (type and frequency) (e.g., frequent head nods to confirm correct responses)
    4. Cues or prompts going beyond that required by assessment protocol
E. The practitioner observes the child for
    1. Use of two languages during a single task
    2. False starts
    3. Perseveration
    4. Attention span
    5. Appropriate turn taking
    6. Use of gestures
    7. Responses out of sequence (e.g., giving a response to a previous item or task)

3. DEBRIEFING

Following testing, the practitioner and the interpreter/translator meet for the following reasons:

A. They review the child's correct responses and errors. The interpreter/translator gives his or her impressions of the child but does not try to diagnose the child.
B. The interpreter/translator tells the practitioner what the child did and said in response to each question, including cultural or linguistic in-formation to clarify possible reasons for responses.
C. The practitioner carefully avoids professional jargon that the inter-preter/translator may not understand.

D. The interpreter/translator assists the practitioner in interpretation of scores, explaining which cultural or linguistic variables may have affected performance.

E. The practitioner and the interpreter/translator discuss any difficulties with the testing process.

F. The practitioner and the interpreter/translator discuss any difficulties with the interpretation/translation process.

Index

Page numbers followed by *f* indicate figures; those followed by *t* indicate tables.

Abuse, child, 201, 208–209, 211
  see also Trauma
Acculturation
  defined, 31
  examples, 102*f*, 104–105, 107*f*, 108,
    139*f*–140*f*
  Family Acculturation Screen, 98, 100*f*,
    107*f*
  and personal-social developmental/
    curricular area, 60*f*
  questions about, 60*f*, 64
Anchored Understanding of Diversity
  in assessment, 128
  in Critical Incident Analysis Sheet, 115*f*,
    116–117, 118*f*, 146*f*
  described, 42*f*, 50–51, 53–56, 187
  examples, 70–71, 72–74, 115*f*, 118*f*, 146*f*
  identifying cultural data, to develop,
    57–58, 59*f*–61*f*, 62–67, 99–100
  in Skilled Dialogue Self-Assessment,
    116, 117*f*
  strategies for, 67, 68*f*, 69–72, 241–242
Assessment
  and communicative-linguistic
    developmental/curricular area, 97,
    99–100, 100*f*, 101*f*, 104, 105*f*, 106*f*,
    139*f*, 141*f*
  cultural diversity and, 121–122
  dilemmas in, 122–136, 124*t*
  examples, 136–151, 147–150
  gathering information for, 128–130
  interpreting results of, 130–132
  during intervention, 172–173
  language and language differences,
    considerations for, 122–127, 124*t*
  and personal-social
    developmental/curricular area,
    104–105, 107*f*, 108
  reporting and using results, 132–136
  and sensory-cognitive developmental/
    curricular area, 108–109
  and standardized tests, 128–129
  translators, using during assessment/test
    administration, 245–247
  videotapes of, 127
Assessment Cultural Linguistic Response
    Plan
  blank form, 224
  described, 111–112
  examples, 113*f*, 143, 144*f*, 148
Autonomy, *see* Independence

Behavior
  behavior management example, 79–80
  positive emphasis of, 70, 71
Bilingual environments
  assessment dilemmas and, 122–127,
    124*t*, 130–132
  cultural data, identifying for, 58, 59*f*,
    62–63
  and culture bumps, 12*t*, 59*f*
  dominant language bilingual approach,
    158–159
  examples, 101*f*, 139*f*
  full bilingual approach, 158–159
  home language, 58, 62*t*, 63
  in Home Language Usage Profile, 58,
    100*f*, 104, 106*f*
  intervention and instruction, for
    children with, 156
  modified single language approach,
    159–160
  multicultural monolingual approach,
    160
  in Relative Language Proficiency (RLP)
    Profile, 62–63, 100, 100*f*, 104, 105*f*,
    135, 138, 141*f*
  see also Language
Biodiversity, relationship to cultural
    diversity, 9, 187–188
Blank forms, *see* Forms, photocopiable
Boundaries
  defined, 43–44
  3rd space perspective of, 77–79
Brainstorming, and developing 3rd space
    perspectives, 82*f*, 88
Breakthrough thinking, 88

Child abuse, *see* Abuse, child; Trauma
Child rearing
  examples, 102*f*, 108, 140*f*, 141, 143
  questions about, 60*f*, 65
Code switching, 132
Cognitive development, *see* Sensory-
    cognitive developmental/curricular
    area
Cognitive errors, as a result of trauma,
    211
Communicative-linguistic developmental/
    curricular area
  assessing, 97, 98–100, 101*f*, 104, 105*f*,
    106*f*, 139*f*, 141*f*

Communicative-linguistic developmental/
  curricular area—*continued*
  in Cultural Consonance Profile, 110*f*,
    142*f*
  cultural dimensions of, 11*t*, 13*t*
  and culture bumps, 12*t*, 59*f*
  dilemmas involving, 166
  examples, 97–98, 100, 101*f*, 104, 139*f*,
    178, 180
  and home language environment, 19,
    58, 59*f*, 62*t*, 101*f*, 139*f*
  in Home Language Usage Profile, 58,
    100*f*, 104, 106*f*
  identifying cultural data, regarding, 57,
    59*f*, 62–63
  and intervention and instruction, 156,
    157–165, 170
  language assessment decision matrix,
    124*t*
  manifestations of trauma, and, 205–206
  and materials, teaching and learning,
    173–174
  see also Cultural diversity; Language
Competence
  and culture bumps, 12*t*–13*t*
  examples, 102*f*, 108, 140*f*
  questions about, 60*f*, 64–65
Contradictions, *see* Paradoxes, Polarization
Copiable forms, *see* Forms, photocopiable
Critical Incident Analysis Sheet
  blank form, 225
  described, 114, 154
  examples, 115*f*, 116–117, 118*f*, 119,
    145, 146*f*
Cultural capital, 10
Cultural competency
  approaches to, 34–36, 42
  defined, 33–34
  importance of, 153
  influence of trauma on, 199–200
  problematic views of, 34–36
  as a process, 36, 91, 120
  Skilled Dialogue and, 36–37, 120
Cultural consonance
  in assessment, 121–122
  described, 109, 110*f*, 111
Cultural Consonance Profile
  blank form, 226
  described, 100*f*, 109
  examples, 109, 110*f*, 111, 138, 142*f*
Cultural data
  blank form for identifying, 232–236
  communicative-linguistic, 58, 59*f*, 62–63
  examples, 101*f*–103*f*, 139*f*–140*f*
  overview of, 57–58, 59*f*–61*f*, 232–236
  personal-social, 60*f*, 64–66
  sensory-cognitive, 61*f*, 66–67

Cultural Data Table
  blank form, 227–229
  described, 99–100, 100*f*
  examples, 101*f*–103*f*, 138, 139*f*–140*f*
Cultural diversity
  assessment and, 99–100, 100*f*,
    101*f*–103*f*, 104, 121–122, 139*f*–140*f*
  biodiversity and, 9
  challenges of, 4–5, 9–17
  and culture bumps, 12*t*–13*t*
  and curriculum issues, 11*t*, 12*t*–13*t*,
    19–21, 170–171
  defined, 3, 5–6
  distinguished from culture, 29–30
  ethnocentricity and, 4–5
  identity and, 8
  and information challenges, 10–11, 11*t*
  linguistic diversity, 97, 98–100, 101*f*,
    104, 105*f*, 106*f*, 139*f*, 141*f*
  personal-social diversity, 104–105, 107*f*,
    108
  relationship to ethnicity, 5, 7–8
  relative quality of, 6–7, 8, 41–42
  as a response to shifting demographics,
    17–18
  and sensory-cognitive developmental/
    curricular area, 108–109
Cultural Linguistic Response Plans
  (Assessment, Instructional)
  blank forms, 224, 238
  described, 111–112
  examples, 113*f*, 143, 144*f*, 148, 179*f*
Cultural melting, 21
Culture
  defined, 23, 27
  development and learning, relevance to,
    30–31
  distinguished from diversity, 29–30
  importance of understanding, 29–30, 42
  keys to understanding, 24–29
  layers of, 26*f*
  as a protective factor, 215–218
  similarities and differences spectrum for,
    24*f*
  trauma and, 28–29
Culture bumps
  in assessment, 122–136
  curriculum issues and, 11*t*, 12*t*–13*t*
  defined, 10
  identifying, 57–58, 59*f*–61*f*, 62–67
  in intervention and instruction, 154
  and misinterpretation of patterns and
    scripts, 13–14
Curriculum issues
  cultural diversity and, 19–21
  and culture bumps, 11*t*, 12*t*–13*t*
  dilemmas, 170–171

strategies and responses, 171–173
    see also Intervention and instruction

Decision making
    and culture bumps, 13*f*, 61*f*
    examples, 103*f*, 108, 140*f*
    questions about, 61*f*, 66
    and 3rd space perspective, 79
Demographics, responses to, 17–18
Development, culture and, 30–31
    see also Communicative-linguistic
        developmental/curricular area;
        Personal-social developmental/
        curricular area; Sensory-cognitive
        developmental/curricular area
Developmental/curricular area, *see*
    Communicative-linguistic
    developmental/curricular area;
    Personal-social developmental/
    curricular area; Sensory-cognitive
    developmental/curricular area
Dialogue, defined, 41
Dichotomies, *see* Paradoxes, Polarization
Discipline, differing perspectives on,
    208–209
Diversity, *see* Cultural diversity
Dualism, *see* Polarization

Early childhood practitioners, *see*
    Practitioners
Early childhood special education, family
    knowledge about
    assessing, 60*f*, 64
    examples, 102*f*, 108, 140*f*
Emotional development
    and manifestations of trauma, 205
    mirroring and, 18–19
Emotional support
    example, 103*f*
    for families, 60*f*, 65–66
Enculturation, compared with
    acculturation, 31
English
    English for Speakers of other Languages
        (ESOL), 130, 159, 160, 161
    use of, 8, 30, 63, 130, 157, 159–160, 169
Ethnicity, relationship to cultural diversity,
    5, 7–8
Ethnocentricity, of practitioners, 4–5
Evaluation, *see* Assessment
Exclusive polarization, 35
External support, *see* Instrumental support

Family, differing definitions of, 12*t*, 57

Family Acculturation Screen
    blank form, 230
    described, 98, 100*f*
    example, 107*f*
Forestructures
    defined, 34
    developing, 92*f*, 93–97
Forms, photocopiable
    Assessment Cultural Linguistic Response
        Plan, 224
    Critical Incident Analysis Sheet, 225
    Cultural Consonance Profile, 226
    Cultural Data Table, 227–229
    Family Acculturation Screen, 230
    Funds of Knowledge Worksheet for
        Story Assessment, 231
    Guide to Identifying Cultural Data,
        232–236
    Home Language Usage Profile, 237
    Instructional Cultural Linguistic
        Response Plan, 238
    Relative Language Proficiency (RLP)
        Profile, 239
    Skilled Dialogue Self-Assessment, 240
    Strategies for Anchoring Understanding
        of Diversity, 241–242
    Strategies for Creating 3rd Space
        Options, 243–244
Funds of knowledge, *see* Knowledge, funds
    of
Funds of Knowledge Worksheet for Story
    Assessment, 175, 231

Genetic diversity, *see* Biodiversity
Guide to Identifying Cultural Data
    blank form, 232–236
    sample version, 59*f*–61*f*
Guiding beliefs
    about cultural competency, 33, 36,
        41–42
    about cultural diversity, 3, 36, 41–42
    about culture, 23, 36, 41–42

Help-seeking behaviors, differences in,
    211–215
Home language
    assessment, influence on, 122–127, 124*t*
    curriculum considerations of, 171
    examples, 101*f*, 139*f*
    identity and, 16, 19, 30
    intervention and instruction, role in,
        158–165, 158*f*
    learning, influence on, 169
    in sample environments, 62*t*
    see also Language

Home Language Usage Profile
  blank form, 237
  described, 58, 100*f*
  example, 104, 106*f*

IDEA, *see* Individuals with Disabilities
      Education Act Amendments of 1997
      (PL 105-17)
Identity
  Anchored Understanding of Diversity
      and, 51
  compared with diversity, 8
  development of, 18–19
  examples, 102*f*, 108, 140*f*
  importance of, 187
  questions about, 60*f*, 64–65
  responsiveness and, 47–48
Immigration/relocation, trauma of,
      216–217
Independence
  example, 70–71, 72
  questions about, 60*f*, 64
Individuals with Disabilities Education Act
      Amendments of 1997 (PL 105-17),
      123–124
Information
  challenges of, 10–11, 11*t*, 12*t*–13*t*
  cultural competency, role in, 34–35
  gathering, for assessments, 128–130
  problematic nature of, 34–35, 53–56
  use in Skilled Dialogue, 94–95
  see also Knowledge, funds of
Instruction, *see* Intervention and
      instruction
Instructional Cultural Linguistic Response
      Plan
  blank form, 238
  described, 111–112, 114
  example, 179*f*
Instrumental support
  examples, 103*f*, 140*f*
  and personal-social developmental/
      curricular area, 60*f*, 65–66
Interpretation, *see* Judgment and
      interpretation
Interpreters
  children as, 203
  use of, during test administration,
      124–127, 245–247
Intervention and instruction
  curriculum strategies and responses,
      171–173
  dilemmas, 155–178
  examples, 178, 179*f*, 180–186
  and help-seeking behaviors, differences
      in, 211–215
  and language and language differences,
      155–165, 158*f*, 170

materials for, 173–178
  Skilled Dialogue as a curriculum for
      children, 173
  strategies for, 167–170

Judgment and interpretation
  challenges of, 13–14
  responsiveness and, 47–48, 72
  risks of, 221–222
  trauma, interaction with, 199–200

Knowledge, funds of
  as a cultural dimension, 10–11, 11*t*, 26*f*
  culture, influence on, 30–31
  and culture bumps, 13*t*, 61*f*
  examples, 103*f*, 108, 140*f*
  problematic nature of, 34–35, 53–56
  questions about, 61*f*, 66
  see also Anchored Understanding of
      Diversity

Labeling
  avoiding through responsiveness, 47–48
  relationship to cultural diversity, 5
Language
  assessment dilemmas and, 122–127,
      124*t*
  and cultural data, identifying, 59*f*
  cultural dimensions of, 11*t*
  and culture bumps, 12*t*, 59*f*
  delays of, 97–98, 129–130, 136
  dominant language bilingual approach,
      159
  English, 8, 30, 63, 130, 157, 159–160,
      169
  full bilingual approach, 158–159
  home language, use of, 19, 58, 59*f*, 62*t*,
      101*f*, 139*f*
  intervention and instruction, role in,
      155–165, 158*f*, 170
  language assessment decision matrix, 124*t*
  languages other than English, 59*f*, 63,
      101*f*, 122–127, 139*f*
  linguistic diversity, determining presence
      of, 98–99
  modified single language approach,
      159–160
  multicultural monolingual approach, 160
  patterns of usage, 59*f*, 63, 101*f*, 139*f*
  proficiency, 59*f*, 62–63, 101*f*, 123–124,
      127, 129, 139*f*, 161–162, 164–165
  verbal and nonverbal, 59*f*, 63, 101*f*, 139*f*
  see also Communicative-linguistic
      developmental/curricular area
Learning
  of cultural cues, 27

cultural diversity and, 19–21
culture, influence of, 30–31
and culture bumps, 61*f*
dilemmas, 165–170
examples, 103*f*, 108, 140*f*
mindful learning, 190
questions about learning strategies, 61*f*,
66
sideways learning, 190
situated learning, 54
Linguistic development, *see*
Communicative-linguistic
developmental/curricular area;
Language
Listening
importance of, 221–222
mindful listening, 67, 68*f*, 69
as a 3rd space skill, 82*f*, 83
in Skilled Dialogue, 41, 46

Maltreatment, of children, *see* Abuse, child;
Trauma
Mindful learning, 190
Minorities
connotations of the term, 15
overrepresentation in social services,
212
Mirroring, cultural responsivity in, 18–19
Modeling, as validation of cultural
diversity, 19
Multilingual environments
assessment dilemmas and, 122–127,
124*t*, 130–132
and home language(s), 58, 62*t*, 63
Home Language Usage Profile, 58, 100*f*,
104, 106*f*
and intervention and instruction,
156
one-person, one-language rule, 126
Relative Language Proficiency (RLP)
Profile, 62–63, 100, 100*f*, 104, 105*f*,
135, 138, 141*f*
see also Bilingual environments;
Language

Nonverbal communication
and culture bumps, 12*t*, 59*f*
examples, 101*f*, 139*f*
intervention and instruction, role in,
156
questions about, 59*f*, 63
3rd space perspective of, 82*f*, 83

Paradoxes, 35, 75
Parenting
examples, 102*f*, 108, 140*f*, 141, 143

participation of parent in assessment
and intervention, example, 43, 44–45,
46, 48–49, 73, 85
questions about, 60*f*, 65
Pedagogy, cultural diversity and, 20–21
Personal-social developmental/curricular
area
and acculturation, 60*f*, 64, 102*f*,
139*f*–140*f*
assessing, 102*f*–103*f*, 104–105, 107*f*,
108, 139*f*–140*f*
cultural dimensions of, 11*t*
and culture bumps, 12*t*–13*t*, 60*f*
dilemmas involving, 166–167
examples, 145, 146*f*, 147, 180
identifying cultural data, regarding, 60*f*,
64–66
and identity and competence, 60*f*,
64–65, 102*f*, 140*f*
and intervention and instruction, 157,
170–171
manifestations of trauma, and, 205
and materials, teaching and learning, 174
and parenting and child rearing, 60*f*, 65,
102*f*, 140*f*
power and social positioning,
relationship to 60*f*, 65, 102*f*, 140*f*
in sample Cultural Consonance Profile,
110*f*, 142*f*
and sense of self, 60*f*, 64, 102*f*, 140*f*
and support systems, 60*f*, 65–66, 103*f*,
140*f*
Photocopiable forms, *see* Forms,
photocopiable
Physical manifestations of trauma, 205
PL 105-17, *see* Individuals with Disabilities
Education Act Amendments of 1997
Plans, *see* Cultural Linguistic Response
Plans (Assessment, Instructional)
Polarization
avoiding, with 3rd Space skills, 51,
75–79, 83, 85
in development of cultural competency,
35–36
Post-Traumatic Stress Disorder (PTSD), 201
Power
examples, 102*f*, 108, 140*f*
imbalance of, 7
issues of in relationships, 14–17
perceptions of as a cultural dimension,
10–11, 11*t*, 26*f*
and personal-social
developmental/curricular area, 60*f*,
65, 102*f*, 140*f*
questions about, 60*f*, 65
reciprocity and, 45, 84
Practitioners
and approaches to cultural competency,
34–36

Practitioners—*continued*
  bilingual/multilingual skills of, 124–125
  and discussion of cultural dynamics with
    others, 95–96
  effects of trauma on, 210–211
  ethnocentric perspectives of, 4–5
  "as experts," example, 43, 44–45, 46,
    48–49, 73, 85
  as observers/recorders, 126–127
  and one-person, one-language rule, 126
  preparation of, 125
  working with interpreters, 124–126,
    245–247
Problem solving
  and culture bumps, 13f, 61f
  development of, 171
  examples, 103f, 108, 140f
  questions about, 61f, 66
  3rd space perspective of, 79
PTSD, *see* Post-Traumatic Stress Disorder
Punishment, differing perspectives on,
    208–209

Racial identity, relationship to cultural
    diversity, 5
Reciprocity
  in Anchored Understanding of Diversity,
    strategies for, 68f, 69–71, 241–242
  described, 42f, 45–46
  in development of 3rd space, strategies
    for, 82f, 84–85, 243–244
  in sample Critical Incident Analysis
    Sheet, 115f, 118f, 146f
Reframing problems, 3rd space perspective
    of, 82f, 86–87, 244
Relationship, challenges of, 14–17
Relative Language Proficiency (RLP)
    Profile
  blank form, 239
  described, 62–63, 100f, 135
  examples, 100, 104, 105f, 138, 141f
Relativity, as aspect of diversity, 6–7, 8
Respect
  in Anchored Understanding of Diversity,
    strategies for, 67, 68f, 69, 241
  described, 42f, 43–45
  in development of 3rd space, strategies
    for, 81, 82f, 83–84, 243
  in sample Critical Incident Analysis
    Sheet, 115f, 118f, 146f
Responsibility, compared with
    responsiveness, 49t
Responsiveness
  in Anchored Understanding of Diversity,
    strategies for, 68f, 71–72, 242
  compared with feeling responsible, 49t
  described, 42f, 46–50

  in development of 3rd space, strategies
    for, 82f, 86–88, 244
  in sample Critical Incident Analysis
    Sheet, 115f, 118f, 146f
RLP, *see* Relative Language Proficiency
    Profile

Scripts, role in cultural diversity, 13–14
Self, sense of
  as a cultural dimension, 10–11, 11t, 26f
  and culture bumps, 12t, 60f
  examples, 102f, 108, 140f
  and personal-social
    developmental/curricular area, 60f,
    64, 102f, 140f
  questions about, 60f, 64
Self-esteem
  developing, 170–171
  trauma, effects on, 206
Sensory-cognitive developmental/
    curricular area
  assessing, 103f, 108–109, 140f
  cultural dimensions of, 11t
  and culture bumps, 13t, 61f
  dilemmas involving, 167
  examples, 97–98, 180–181
  funds of knowledge, 61f, 103f, 108, 140f
  identifying cultural data, regarding, 61f,
    66–67
  and intervention and instruction, 157,
    171
  and learning strategies, 61f, 103f, 108,
    140f
  manifestations of trauma, and, 205
  and materials, teaching and learning,
    175
  mirroring in, 18–19
  and problem solving and decision
    making, 61f, 103f, 108, 140f
  in sample Cultural Consonance Profile,
    110f, 142f
  worldviews, 61f, 103f, 108–109, 140f
Services, *see* Support systems
Shared experiences, as an aspect of
    culture, 26, 26f
Sharing, as example of cultural diversity,
    23
Sideways learning, 190
Situated learning, 54
  see also Anchored Understanding of
    Diversity
Skilled Dialogue
  Anchored Understanding of Diversity, as
    a component of, 42f, 50–51
  conducting Skilled Dialogue, 92f,
    114–120
  as a curriculum for children, 173

and developing forestructures, 92*f*, 93–97
phases of, 92*f*
3rd space, as a component of, 42*f*, 51
reciprocity in, 42*f*, 45–46
respect in, 42*f*, 43–45
responsiveness in, 42*f*, 46–50
setting the stage for, 92*f*, 97–100,
    101*f*–103*f*, 104–114
Skilled Dialogue Self-Assessment
  blank form, 240
  described, 116
  example, 117*f*
Social development, *see* Personal-social
    developmental/curricular area
Social positioning
  examples, 102*f*, 108, 140*f*
  questions about, 60*f*, 65
  in relationships, 14–17
Special education, family knowledge about
  assessing, 60*f*, 64
  examples, 102*f*, 108, 140*f*
Standardized tests, 128–129, 135–136
Stereotypes
  created through knowledge, 54
  cultural diversity and, 21
  relationship to cultural diversity, 5
Stories
  exchange of, for Anchoring
    Understanding of Diversity, 72
  in Funds of Knowledge Worksheet for
    Story Assessment, 231
  as a protective mechanism, 216
  3rd space perspective of, 86–87
Strategies for Anchoring Understanding of
    Diversity, blank form, 241–242
Strategies for Creating 3rd Space Options,
    blank form, 243–244
Stress, *see* Trauma
Support systems
  determining cultural diversity in, 98–99
  examples, 103*f*, 140*f*
  questions about, 60*f*, 65–66
Symbols/symboling, role in culture, 23

Teachers, *see* Practitioners
Teaching formats
  cultural diversity and, 19–21
  dilemmas, 165–170
  and the value of uncertainty, 93
  see also Intervention and instruction

Testing, *see* Assessment
3rd space
  Critical Incident Analysis Sheet, 115*f*,
    116–117, 118*f*, 119, 146*f*
  described, 42*f*, 51, 75–79, 187, 188
  examples, 77, 79–81, 115*f*, 118*f*, 146*f*
  practicing 3rd Space options, 96–97
  in Skilled Dialogue Self-Assessment,
    116, 117*f*
  strategies for creating, 81–88, 82*f*,
    243–244
Translation issues
  children as translators, 203
  teaching materials, translation of, 174
  use of translators during test
    administration, 124–127, 245–247
Trauma
  and child maltreatment, 208–209
  cognitive errors and, 211
  and creating healing environments,
    218–219
  cross-cultural experiences of, 201–202
  cumulative nature of, 206–208
  defined, 200–201
  and help-seeking behaviors, 211–215
  interface with culture, 28–29, 199–200,
    203–204
  invalidation and, 202–203
  manifestations of in children, 205–206
  Post-Traumatic Stress Disorder (PTSD),
    201
  and protective nature of culture,
    215–218
  second-generation trauma, 209–211

Understanding, *see* Anchored
    Understanding of Diversity

Validation
  of cultural diversity, 18–19
  lack of, trauma and, 202–203
Videotaping of assessments, 127

Worldviews
  as an aspect of culture, 26, 26*f*
  and culture bumps, 13*f*, 61*f*
  examples, 103*f*, 108–109, 140*f*
  questions about, 61*f*, 66–67